LIFEWORLDS IN CRISIS

/ AFRICAN
/ ARGUMENTS

African Arguments is a series of short books about contemporary Africa and the critical issues and debates surrounding the continent. The books are scholarly and engaged, substantive and topical. They focus on questions of justice, rights and citizenship; politics, protests and revolutions; the environment, land, oil and other resources; health and disease; economy: growth, aid, taxation, debt and capital flight; and both Africa's international relations and country case studies.

Managing Editor, Stephanie Kitchen

Series editors

Adam Branch
Alex de Waal
Alcinda Honwana
Ebenezer Obadare
Carlos Oya
Nicholas Westcott

Additional longer monographs and edited volumes are published in association with the series, under the auspices of the International African Institute.

Associate editors

Eyob Gebremariam
Portia Roelofs
Jon Schubert

ANDREA BEHRENDS

Lifeworlds in Crisis

*Making Refugees in the
Chad–Sudan Borderlands*

HURST & COMPANY, LONDON

IAI International African Institute

Published in collaboration with the International African Institute.
First published in the United Kingdom in 2024 by
C. Hurst & Co. (Publishers) Ltd.,
New Wing, Somerset House, Strand, London WC2R 1LA
Copyright © Andrea Behrends, 2024
All rights reserved.

The right of Andrea Behrends to be identified as the author of this publication is asserted by her in accordance with the Copyright, Designs and Patents Act, 1988.

A Cataloguing-in-Publication data record for this book is available from the British Library.

ISBN: 9781911723226

www.hurstpublishers.com

CONTENTS

List of abbreviations — vii
List of names and places — ix
Acknowledgements — xv
Map of the region — xix

1. Tomorrow, there will be war! Living with crisis in the borderlands — 1

PART I
WAR COMES TO THE BORDERLANDS
DIFFERENCE AND BELONGING IN THE VILLAGES

2. We have to make a list: Representing lifeworlds in a crisis — 27
3. So, we went with them: Making sense of conflict and competition in the villages — 47
4. In general, they are comfortable: Opportunity and threat in a better-off town — 79

PART II
WARTIME IN THE BORDERLANDS
AID AND EMPLACEMENT AT THE CAMPS

5. Clearly, they are 'internally displaced persons': Aid agencies and the making of 'refugees' — 101

CONTENTS

6. Those are the only real refugees: Aid and competition in the camps and villages ... 117
7. The camps are very different: Negotiating security amidst uncertainty ... 141
8. They are our relatives now: Exiting aid, but exiting displacement? ... 165

PART III
THE AFTERMATH OF WAR
STATE AND DEVELOPMENT FROM THE CAPITAL TO THE BORDERLANDS

9. This is neither my first nor second time seeing war: Living through rebellion ... 199
10. Before oil, we were poor. Now, we're miserable: Oil's position at the margins of the state ... 213
11. This money belongs to the people of Chad: Oil, development, and imagining the state ... 229
12. Conclusion: Survival at the margins of the world ... 253

Epilogue: War, again ... 265

Notes ... 269
References ... 281
Index ... 299

LIST OF ABBREVIATIONS

CFA franc	Franc de la Communauté Financière Africaine / Franc of the African Financial Community
CNAR	Comité National d'Accueil et Enregistrement des Réfugiés / National Committee for the Accommodation and Registration of Refugees
CNARR	Commission Nationale d'Accueil et de Réinsertion des Réfugiés et des Rapatriés / National Commission for the Accommodation and Integration of Refugees and Repatriated Persons
CRASH	Centre de Recherches en Anthropologie et Sciences Humaines / Centre for Research in Anthropology and Human Sciences
DLA/M	Darfur Liberation Army/Movement
EUFOR	European Union Force
FAO	Food and Agriculture Organization
FROLINAT	Front de Libération Nationale du Tchad / National Liberation Front of Chad
GIZ	Gesellschaft für Internationale Zusammenarbeit / German Society for International Cooperation
GTZ	Gesellschaft für Technische Zusammenarbeit / German Society for Technical Cooperation
ICRC	International Committee of the Red Cross

LIST OF ABBREVIATIONS

IDP	Internally Displaced Person
JEM	Justice and Equality Movement
MINURCAT	Mission des Nations Unies en République Centrafricaine et au Tchad/United Nations Mission in the Central African Republic and Chad
MSF	Médecins Sans Frontières/Doctors Without Borders
NGO	Non-governmental organisation
OCHA	United Nations Office for the Coordination of Humanitarian Affairs
ONDR	Organisation Nationale du Développement Rural/National Office of Rural Development
RSF	Rapid Support Forces
SAF	Sudanese Armed Forces
SECADEV	Secours Catholique du Développement
UNDP	United Nations Development Programme
UNHCR	The Office of the United Nations High Commissioner for Refugees
UNICEF	United Nations International Children's Emergency Fund, and since 1953 the United Nations Children's Fund
WFP	World Food Programme

LIST OF NAMES AND PLACES

Interview partners and (historical) actors in the borderlands

Abdallah	Former chief of refugees in Farchana camp in 2010.
Abdoulaye Hafadine	Prefect in the border town of Adré in 2001.
Abdullahi el-Tom	Senior lecturer at Maynooth University and spokesperson for the Sudanese JEM rebel group.
Ahmed Moussa	Senegalese Head of Africare in 2001, based in Abéché.
Ashta Ibrahim	Deceased mother of four and daughter of Ibrahim Bakhit Mahamat, called Daldoum and Hawaye, who came with her old parents from Tabari in Sudan to Hachaba.
Ashta Touboudja	My deceased host in Hachaba, former wife of Dahab.
Baldal Oyamta	Head of the *Ligue Tchadienne des Droits de l'Homme*, the Chadian League for Human Rights.

LIST OF NAMES AND PLACES

Barka Yakhoub Mahamat	Grand marabout from Kourgnon Mallan who moved to Abéché. Father of Zombo.
Beral	Opposition politician and musician.
Brahim Mahamat Ali	My friend, translator and research partner, father of seven, husband of Sureiya in Hadjer Hadid.
Dahab	Former husband of Ashta Touboudja and *firshe*, representative of the *Chef de Canton*.
Djamal Ahmat Senoussi	Uncle of Brahim Mahamat Ali and Khassim Mahamat Assed.
Djiti Dahab	Youngest daughter of Ashta Touboudja and Dahab, sister of Halime and Naima.
Ekhlas	NGO activist in Abéché and wife of Peter Abdoullai.
Fadoul	Young Chadian aid worker employed by SEDADEV in 2001.
Fatime	Sister of Brahim Mahamat Ali, working for the UNHCR in Farchana.
Goni	Young man from the Arab village of Tiléha.
Hamdan Aboubakar	*Chef de faction* of the Arab family of the Mahariye in Tiléha.
Haoua Abdullai	Mayor's secretary in Abéché.
Hassan Brahim	Translator sent to me by the prefect as 'protection' during the time before the war, today *Chef de Canton* in Guergné.
Hawaye	Farmer, wife of Daldoum.

LIST OF NAMES AND PLACES

Henri Marcel	UNHCR representative in Abéché in 2000 and 2001.
Ibrahim Bakhit Mahamat, called Daldoum	*Chef de réfugiés* in Hachaba, husband of Hawaye.
Idriss Saley Adjidey	Head of SECADEV in Adré during my visits in 2010 and 2011.
Izze	Mother of Brahim Mahamat Ali.
J-P	Cameroonian chef at an Abéché restaurant.
Khalil Alio	Deceased former director of CRASH, colleague and research partner.
Khassim Mahamat Assed	Deceased contractor in Abéché, my first contact in eastern Chad and good friend, husband of Suleikha and Zenaba.
Kodjinar Touloum	*Directeur de Cabinet* of the governor of Wadai.
Latifa	First daughter of Zenaba and Khassim.
Mahamat Ismael	Sudanese newcomer in Hachaba and activist in various development-oriented activities.
Mahamat Khassim Mahamat	Oldest son of Khassim Mahamat Assed.
Mahamat Saleh Ahmat Adam	Mayor-elect of Abéché in 2011.
Moussa Mahamat Saleh Youssif, called Moussa or Cheikh Moussa	Head of the Wandalou group and later president of 'refugees' in the UNHCR's Farchana camp.
Nanyalta	Former staff of SECADEV in Adré, later employed by UNICEF in Abéché and now N'Djamena.

LIST OF NAMES AND PLACES

Perikles	Greek senior UNHCR programme officer in Farchana in 2011.
Peter Abdoullai	Anaesthesiology assistant in Abéche, husband of Ekhlas.
Senoussi Barka	Son of Barka Yakhoub Mahamat and founder of Quartier Zombo in Adré together with his brother Zombo, who became a grand marabout in Adré centre.
Suleikha	First wife of Khassim in Abéché and mother of ten.
Sureiya	Brahim Mahamat Ali's wife and mother of their seven sons.
Yaya Ahmad	Interpreter in Adré in 2007.
Younous	Large-scale fruit and vegetable gardener who lived in villages on both sides of the Chad–Sudan border.
Zenaba	Midwife and mother of six, second wife of Khassim in Adré.
Zombo Barka	Son of Barka Yakhoub Mahamat, founder of Quartier Zombo in Adré together with his brother Senoussi.

Places

Abéché	Capital of Wadai in eastern Chad.
Adré	Border town in the Chad–Sudan borderlands and former French garrison town.

<u>Adré's Quartiers:</u>

Hille Borno, later Quartier Hayachati (Quarter close to the lake)

LIST OF NAMES AND PLACES

Hille Djidíde (New Town where the people from Hachaba and other villages south of Adré have moved to during the Darfur War that began in 2003)

Hille Fog (town on a hill, where people infected with leprosy used to live)

Koukaie (named after a particular tree)

Quartier Amdjarras (referring to President Idriss Déby's home village and quarter of the richer Zaghawa newcomers to Adré)

Quartier BET (with people from the Chadian regions Biltine, Ennedi, Tibesti)

Quartier Kanembu, later called Quartier Claire (because of the clear light in the quarter)

Quartier Masalit, later Quartier Maharadjan (close to the central square)

Quartier Zombo, later Quartier Souhour (Quarter of the Flowers)

Shig al-Fakhara (Quartier with a dividing line between the jurisdictions of two marabouts)

Amkharouba	Village near Adré.
Ardébé	Village near Adré.
Bredjine	UNHCR refugee camp.
Darfur	Region in western Sudan.
Dar Masalit	Region in western Sudan and eastern Chad.
Dar Tama	Region in western Sudan and eastern Chad.
Dar Zaghawa	Region in western Sudan and eastern Chad.
El Geneina	Capital of West Darfur, Sudan.
Farchana	Village in Chad and UNHCR refugee camp.

LIST OF NAMES AND PLACES

Gedarif	Region in Sudan where many Masalit live and work.
Guilane	Neighbouring village to Hachaba.
Gulu	Garrison town in Darfur, first rebel attack in February 2003.
Hachaba	Village near Adré.
Hadjer Hadid	Village near Abéché and UNHCR refugee camp.
N'Djamena	Capital of Chad.
Wadai	Eastern region of Chad.
Wadi Asoungha	Department in Wadai.

ACKNOWLEDGEMENTS

This book, like many written in turbulent times, has taken a long time to see the light of day. I started my postdoctoral research in Chad with generous funding from the Max Planck Institute for Social Anthropology in Halle/Saale, where Günther Schlee, as head of the Department of Integration and Conflict, had hired me in 2000. In 2006, I started to work with Richard Rottenburg at the Institute for Social and Cultural Anthropology at Halle University on the project 'Travelling Models in Conflict Management', which was funded by the Volkswagen Foundation. In 2011 I became principal investigator on another cooperative research project, 'Oil and Social Change in Niger and Chad', which was funded by the German Research Foundation (DFG). I am grateful to all these institutions.

My main interlocutors in Chad will appear throughout the book. Above all, Brahim Mahamat Ali has been an invaluable research partner and dear friend. Brahim's uncle Djamal; my deceased friend Khassim, his two wives Suleikha and Zenaba and his eldest son Mahamat; my dear host Ashta Touboudja, her daughter Djiti; and of course my very dear colleagues and friends in N'Djamena, Remadji Hoinathy, Oumar Abdelbanat, Allah-Kauis Neneck, Djimet Seli and the late Khalil Alio are just a few who have made clear to me that my life has become entangled with yours.

The next part is in French for my friends and research partners in Chad. Chers collègues et amis au Tchad ! Je vous remercie de tout cœur pour votre générosité, votre hospitalité, votre gentillesse,

ACKNOWLEDGEMENTS

votre curiosité et votre patience pendant mes séjours chez vous. Je ne saurais exprimer toute ma reconnaissance envers vous. Ce livre n'aurait pas pu être réalisé sans votre aide. J'espère que le résultat vous satisfera. Tout d'abord, je remercie mon ami, mon frère, mon assistant et mon co-auteur Brahim Mahamat Ali qui m'a consacré son temps chaque fois j'étais au Tchad—et au-delà. Il m'a renseignée et accompagnée pendant tous mes entreprises et voyages. Sans lui, rien ne se serait arrangé. Et comme nous le disons depuis notre première rencontre à Adré en 2001: on garde le contact ! Le grand cœur de mon frère, Khassim Mahamat Assed, ne sera jamais oublié. C'est avec Khassim que ma recherche à l'est du Tchad a commencé. Il n'est malheureusement plus là pour voir naître ce livre. Il m'a présentée à de nombreux interlocuteurs, m'a accueillie très généreusement dans ses maisons à Adré et à Abéché. Il m'a acceptée comme sa sœur et m'a présentée à (presque) toute sa famille. Il me manque toujours. À Adré, je remercie la famille de Khassim : surtout Djamal Ahmat Senoussi, Zenaba et ses filles et fils, et toute la famille de Brahim Mahamat Ali, sa femme Sureiya et leurs fils, sa mère Izze, et ses sœurs, particulièrement Fatime avec sa famille. Mon hôtesse à Hachaba, Ashta Touboudja était une femme extraordinaire que je n'oublierai jamais. Je suis reconnaissante de l'amitié et l'hospitalité de Ashta et ses filles, surtout Djiti, Naima et Halime ainsi que Sureiya, la fille de Djiti. Je voudrais exprimer encore des remerciements à Dahab, le père de Djiti, pour son expertise en ce qui concerne les questions du droit traditionnel au Dar Masalit. Je remercie les gens de Hachaba, et aussi les gens de Tiléha, surtout Cheikh Hamdan et sa famille. À Abéché, je remercie Sureiya et son fils Mahamat Khassim. De plus, je voudrais remercier Peter Abdoullai et Ekhlas pour leur hospitalité et leur amitié depuis tant d'années. Je remercie Moussa Mahamat Saleh Youssif de Farchana pour tout le temps qu'il m'a accordé et pour nos discussions. À N'Djamena je remercie mes amis et collègues du Centre de Recherches et Sciences Humaines (CRASH), surtout Remadji Hoinathy, Khalil Alio, Djimet Séli, Allah-Kauis Neneck, Lewa Eli Doksala, Oumar Abdelbanat, et Laguerre Djerandi. Je remercie Nanyalta pour ses idées qui m'ont aidée à comprendre la situation des 'réfugiés' dans la région d'Adré et dans les camps du

ACKNOWLEDGEMENTS

UNHCR. Et pour finir, je crois qu'il est convenable de compter parmi ces remerciés Stephen Reyna, car s'il ne vient pas lui-même du Tchad, il y a longtemps vécu et y est très attaché. On continue à partager cette fascination et notre amitié.

After so many years of research, of writing and of travel to and from Chad, I have many people to thank for their inspirations, comments, criticism and encouragement. I therefore beg forgiveness if I name only a few whose impact has been especially significant for bringing this book together. I want to thank the following people in Halle or connected to the Max Planck Institute and the Martin Luther University of Halle-Wittenberg for inspiration, support and discussions: Nina Glick Schiller, Richard Rottenburg, Günther Schlee, Sung-Joon Park, Katharina Schramm, Ralph Buchenhorst, Stephanie Bognitz, Fazil Moradi, Sandra Calkins, Daniele Cantini, Ronn Müller, Norman Schräpel, Jim Thompson, Pamila Gupta and many of the other members of Richard's LOST group. My thanks also go to Conny Heimann and Manuela Schmittke and my colleagues at both the Max Planck Institute for Social Anthropology and the Institute for Social and Cultural Anthropology of Halle University.

I have presented this work at workshops and conferences where colleagues and friends from throughout the world have given their valuable comments and have contributed to this project in many different ways. I want to thank Musa Adam Abdul-Jalil, Mahaman Tidjani Alou, Kurt Beck, Uli Beisel, Thomas Bierschenk, Michael Bollig, Mirjam de Bruijn, Inge Butter, Veronica Davidoff, Julia Eckert, Joël Glasman, Amanda Hammar, Babett Jàsnzky, Carola Lentz, Géraud Magrin, Ismaël Maazaz, Jean-Pierre Olivier de Sardan, Julia Pauli, Janet Roitman, Nikolaus Schareika, Barbara Schmenk, Jannik Schritt, Tatjana Thelen, and Saulesh Yessenova.

The writing processes is never easy, but for me it became much easier with the help of my friend and coach, Katja Günther. Through her and her ingenious interventions, I found not only the time but the desire to write and to continue writing, up to the point of these acknowledgements. Thank you for your creativity, friendship and support! Without Daniel Flaumenhaft and Gita Rajan this text would not be what it has become. For your constant

ACKNOWLEDGEMENTS

commitment and positive ways of commenting and correcting I am most grateful! At times, writing has become a collective affair. For this experience I thank Carolin Leutloff-Grandits for our good times in the library, and Gisa Weszkalnys, Ulrike Boskamp, Nora Geißler and Tomoko Mamine for a long series of two-hour sessions and, of course, the breaks.

The last word goes to my family and loved ones. I thank you all for your love, patience and support, and most of all Hannah and Leo for sharing your mother with so many other people and places. This book is for you.

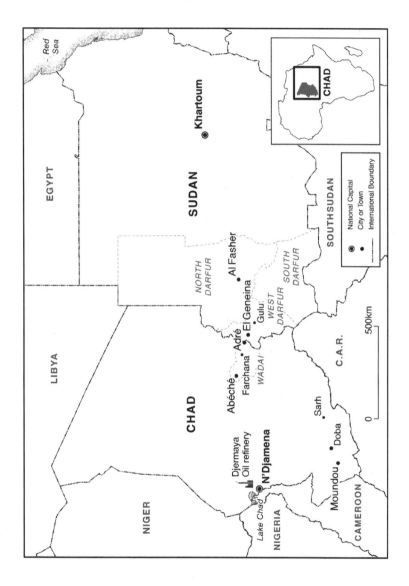

1

TOMORROW, THERE WILL BE WAR!

LIVING WITH CRISIS IN THE BORDERLANDS

'Tomorrow, no one should go to the market: there will be war.'

This message from the council of elders of the Chadian village of Hachaba, less than a kilometre from the border with Sudan, reached me one evening in 2001 as I was returning from an interview. The village was dark at night—there was no electricity—and after the harvest the lush green millet that had previously blocked the view had been replaced by dry, sandy tranquillity. Only minutes before, I had been sitting around a fire with Hachaba's *chef de réfugiés*, Ibrahim Bakhit Mahamat, whom everyone called Daldoum, as well as his wife Hawaye and Brahim Mahamat Ali, who remains my research associate more than 20 years later. Daldoum had struggled to express how and why he had come to the village as Brahim translated from the local dialect of Chadian Arabic and described teaching the Quran to some of the village children. Then, the four of us had shared a meal of millet and chicken that Hawaye had prepared. As my hosts were only vaguely aware of what lay beyond the Red Sea and Malta, the first European destination of those who took on the journey from Chad, I had drawn maps in the sand to explain where I came from: 'beyond Malta, further north'.

Although Daldoum had described being tortured by government agents in Darfur (because he was his village's chief, they had accused him of having hidden weapons in the bush and leading attacks on villagers over the course of three years), the situation now still seemed incongruously peaceful. Indeed, it seemed so peaceful that I was inclined to dismiss that late-night message about a war that would start tomorrow. How could the elders know? What signs indicated a war? Who had alerted them? I had not yet become aware of the suddenness of attacks, of how people read the evidence of everyday occurrences, of how abruptly fighting broke out and of how one constantly had to know where to find refuge. I had imagined that such news would come from the media—radio, television or newspapers—but none of these existed in the village at the time. (There was radio reception, but the broadcasts paid little attention to what happened in this remote area straddling the border between Chad and Sudan.)

In February 2017, Brahim and I again discussed this incident. 'How did they know war was imminent?', I asked, and he replied that rebels and others planning to attack a place would often warn some of its residents. 'They don't want any family members living in that place to be affected,' he added, but sometimes the information might not be real, or the rebels' plans might change. 'They often choose to attack on a market day to have a larger impact. But often the people are told, and even the military.'

Brahim had once been a teacher in another village and had frequently crossed the international border to go to a market in Sudan. He recalled an attack that had happened in 1998, around eleven in the morning on Monday, a market day. This time, no one had been informed.

> When the Janjaweed attacked, it was abrupt. It was so abrupt that the people left all their belongings and bags and ran. About ten people died that day; twenty were injured. Before the attack, the Janjaweed waited outside the town, hiding with their horses in the bush, and no one saw them. They sent some of their people to the market like normal visitors to scout out the situation. Then, suddenly, you were only aware of a noise—the sound the Arabs are known to make when they attack—'wohohohoho!' But even

then, the Masalit militias were nearby, not far from the market, and they repelled the Janjaweed when they arrived. And we civilians, we just ran! I didn't even have a chance to untie my horse—I just cut the rope with my knife. In that situation, you can only see what's right in front of you, and that's how you act.

Origins of the crisis

When I started my research in the borderlands in 2001, I had no idea that there would be a war there only two years later. The prefect of Adré at the time, Abdoulaye Hafadine, was a self-identified 'Masalit' (a term I discuss below) and interested in having someone document the difficulties faced by his extremely poor and marginal region. He advised me to move to the village of Hachaba and to stay with Ashta Touboudja, whose father had founded the village and whose family still owned most of the land. Ashta was in her fifties then and had lived all over Chad: her former husband, Dahab, had been a soldier and with their four daughters they had moved from one garrison to another. When I first met her in 2001, she was divorced and had moved back to the village, where she was both respected for her knowledge and feared for her quick tongue and sternness. Her compound, where I stayed with her, her youngest daughter Djiti, and her granddaughter, Sureiya, during three extended periods of fieldwork in 2000 and 2001, included four houses and an enclosed yard with a dog, two donkeys and a large flock of chickens. During my last stay with Ashta at the end of 2001, she complained about pain in her chest, against which the doctors gave her aspirin. She died shortly after my departure.

Hachaba is located in the somewhat hilly, very sandy, and sometimes quite barren-looking land called Dar Masalit (the homeland of the 'Masalit'). 'Masalit' and other similar labels (in Europe just as much as in Africa) have a constructed character, and group boundaries are more fluid than the idea of 'ethnicity' usually implies. Indeed, much of this book concerns how people continuously cross such boundaries to survive during times of uncertainty, war and displacement. However, it is impossible to describe the last twenty years of events in the borderlands without sometimes referring to terms people used to describe themselves and others. When pointing to the constructed character of a group ascription, I will sometimes use single quotes to indicate that this categorisation is not as fixed or exclusive as it may sound. Most of this region, including the current seat of the Masalit sultan in El Geneina, now lies in Sudan: only a few Masalit were cut off when the British and French empires established the current border in 1924 (Behrends 2007; Harir 1994: 150; Kapteijns 1985; Meier 1995; O'Fahey 2007).[1] Today's ethnic ascriptions—as well as who is classified as 'native' to the land— were consolidated under colonial rule, which in Chad officially lasted until 1960 (see Harir 1994; Mamdani 2009, 2012; Prunier 2005). But even within Dar Masalit, the borderlands are home to a complex mixture of people who originate from migrations from different places and at different times. Some settlers fled droughts, wars or, in the past, slave raids; some were pilgrims on the way to or from Mecca; and some were nomads who settled near existing villages.

Crises have a specific meaning in the borderlands and recur regularly. Natural phenomena threaten agriculture and herding, political tensions often involve transborder (im)mobilities, and many inequalities are prevalent that can quickly and situationally lead to extreme violence. This book is based on my interlocutors' personal experiences of some of these crises, but it also shows how their homeland is both marginal and central to understanding wider issues of access to land and resources, of control and regulation, and of how personal motives or grievances are closely entangled with regional, national and international aspirations for dominance and control. Two successful coups have been launched from the region and all subsequent Chadian and Sudanese heads of state have remained aware of its volatility. And while the population on each side of the international border situationally clearly identifies as Chadian or Sudanese (or something else), such regional denominations as Dar Masalit, Darfur, Dar Tama and Dar Zaghawa signify additional ethno-spatial affiliations—'Masalit', 'Fur', 'Tama', or 'Zaghawa'—that date back to the precolonial sultanates and have found new political meanings since the area was divided between British (in Sudan) and French (in Chad) colonial rule.

The powerful precolonial sultanates of Wadai and Dar Fur—and especially their overlapping zones of influence—provided space into which to retreat when one came into conflict with local authorities or fellow subjects. What is now the borderlands was historically divided among several smaller and much weaker sultanates and kingdoms that owed allegiance to one of the big two and often copied or retained their social and political structures (Kapteijns 1985; Kapteijns and Spaulding 1988; O'Fahey and Spaulding 1974; O'Fahey 1980). Such areas, as Kopytoff (1987) shows, were often perceived as buffer zones. On the one hand, they were dangerous for travellers under the protection of one of the rival powers, whose power declined in the transitional zone. On the other, subjects of smaller kingdoms could resist their rulers by aligning with their rivals. Wadai and Dar Fur, especially, defined their territorial claims by their ability to conduct slave raids, access trade routes, establish settlements, and recruit soldiers.[2] While some of these patterns of allegiance and opposition continue today, new actors and global entanglements have complicated the situation in the borderlands. Civilian and military representatives of national governments; international agencies and military forces; and rebels, traders, and kin groups now contribute to a large range of local and national hierarchies.

People in the village spoke of the *harb* (war) or *machákil* (problems) when they referred to what the world media would later (in 2003) describe as the 'first genocide of the twenty-first century'. The level of violence and intensity of this conflict began to rise by 1995 (Flint and de Waal 2005) and roughly followed the lasting entanglements of colonial rule; local, national and international political interests; conflicting regulations on landholding and use; and a system of governance that privileges certain ethnically defined populations, among other factors. All of these contributed to the political marginalisation of the people who regard that area as their 'home' (Abdul-Jalil 2006, 2008, 2016). As I write this in the spring of 2023, the war has again reached this region, this time with two generals fighting over governmental power. Again, people are fleeing into Chad, and many are killed during the fighting.

The world took notice of the Darfur War in February 2003 after a rebel attack on the Sudanese garrison town of Gulu. Several academic publications sought to understand this apparently sudden outbreak of violence, with most seeking to explain the causes and trajectory of the conflict and the actors involved in it based on what the authors already knew about the region (see for example Beck 2004; de Waal 2005; Flint and de Waal 2005, 2008). At first, I participated in this endeavour and tried to explain this dramatic increase in violence in terms of a recurring historical pattern of rebel groups breaking up and realigning, as described in Kapteijns' (1985) history of the Masalit Sultanate. I saw the latest unrest as representing historical continuity under changing— and increasingly globalised—circumstances that caused repeated outbreaks of violence (Behrends 2007; Behrends and Schlee 2008).

In their analysis of the Darfur War, both Sudanese and other authors have concentrated on the Sudanese government's fierce intervention in local affairs that unleashed militias along regional lines of conflict (Marchal 2006). Hassan and Ray (2009) speak more generally of a 'crisis of governance', relating regional conflict to the national failure to peacefully regulate the situation, while Prunier (2005) and Mamdani (2007) focused on the impact of this governmental intervention on the Darfur War's progression, categorising it as 'genocide', 'civil war' or 'insurgency'. After the conflict had become world news, several authors turned to the question of who was fighting whom and why. In the following years, publications proliferated, with their authors becoming known for articles on governments' use of 'cheap' counter-insurgency (de Waal 2004) as a strategy to contain regional conflicts and prevent rebels from becoming a national threat. These studies included an analysis of the complex and fast-changing structures of rebel movements and the reasons for movements' frequent divisions and realignments, particularly at the height of the fighting (Marchal 2004; Tubiana 2008; Hansen 2011).

Sudanese analyses of the situation in Darfur, in contrast to this emphasis on national and international involvement in open military intervention and the clandestine arms trade, trace the conflict's roots to the region's colonial legacy. In 'The Short-Cut to Decay', an analysis of the political situation in Darfur in the late 1980s and early 1990s, Harir and Tvedt (1994) attribute local grievances and the outbreak of war to a long-term desire to regain the partial autonomy Darfur had enjoyed under colonial law and opposition to the Sudanese government's increasing replacement of local Fur and Masalit administrators with northern Arabs and a government technique of counter-insurgency that armed the neighbours of warring groups to contain the conflict at a regional level and far from the capital, Khartoum. El-Battahani (2004) and El-Tom (2006) relate the conflict in Darfur to the government's unwillingness to regulate a combination of long-term local conflict factors: inter-communal rivalries originating in colonial-era land administration, organisational changes in administrative institutions, and the question of access to land and land rights as modes of belonging and citizenship. However, Abdul-Jalil (2006) emphasises that although land may be one cause of conflict in Darfur, cooperation and friendly relations have prevailed much of the time. Competition over land would not cause war on its own, he argues. It must be considered one 'part of wider factors', such as 'underdevelopment, lack of democracy, competition over political office, armed robbery, ethnic politics, restructuring of the native administration, population increase (both people and animals), the Libyan-Chadian conflict, the Chadian civil war and the spread of modern firearms' (Abdul-Jalil 2006: 22).

Lifeworlds during a crisis

Understanding how suddenly attacks threatened and what kind of news called for what kind of reaction informs the lives of the people in this book. The title *Lifeworlds in Crisis* refers to the ways they live through ongoing tensions that range from smouldering mutual suspicion and ill will to sudden bursts of brutal violence. For generations, people's lives in this region have alternated between periods of calm and moments of the highest uncertainty about both the immediate and long-term prospects for one's life and family. The term crisis also describes the continual interventions of international organisations, military and non-governmental organisations (NGOs) that have contributed to the constant reordering of the borderland's social landscapes. By looking at people's lives during extended periods of emergency, this study goes beyond the concept of 'bare life' (Agamben 2005) and its exclusion of modalities of continued everyday living and the maintenance of community relations (Ticktin 2006) to focus on practices of manoeuvring through conflicts by gathering situationally relevant knowledge and negotiating sameness and difference with others who are also living through intense times. Greg Beckett's (2019) writings on how people perceive and live through crisis in Haiti share this anthropological 'concern to dwell in the lived experience of others as they encounter the world, to pay attention to "the indeterminate and ambiguous character of everyday life" and to give priority "to embodied, intersubjective, temporally informed engagements in the world"' (Beckett 2019: 10, quoting Jackson 1996: 2).

The concept of lifeworld (*Lebenswelt*) was introduced in the phenomenological philosophy of Edmund Husserl (1913), which understands knowledge as originating in the immediate phenomena surrounding a person and, thus, as embodied and experience based. Hans Blumenberg (2018) extends Husserl's concept of the lifeworld as a sphere of thinking beyond the individual to describe an intersubjective sphere of shared experiences (see Schmitz and Stiegler 2015). The concept is also the basis of Harold Garfinkel's (1967) ethnomethodological approach, which focuses on revealing the unspoken and seemingly self-evident knowledge that underlies how people act in everyday social situations. The ethnographic approach of bracketing such knowledge means reconstructing events based on how people experience their everyday lives, past and present, and omitting what lies outside that experience. It means anthropological researchers must immerse themselves in these lifeworlds to understand 'other ways of living *on their own terms*' as far as possible (Beckett 2019: 11). In anthropology, Michael Jackson's work on 'existential anthropology' (e.g. 1996, 2013, 2017) has most prominently taken up Husserl's concept.

In explicitly contrasting the concepts of lifeworld and society, he follows 'Husserl's claim that we live in a world of intersubjective relationships "directly conscious" and "plainly certain" of this experience' in 'open, complex and never self-contained' lifeworlds that the anthropologist enters 'as a participant as well as an observer' (2017: 2). His followers have investigated such topics as embodiment and (inter)subjectivity (Dejarlais and Throop 2011), flight and emplacement in Europe's margins (Lucht 2011), situated knowledge systems regarding, for instance, natural phenomena (Schnegg 2019, 2021), or the ways in which daily routines lead to an economy of opportunity among precariously employed NGO staff in West Africa (Kalfelis 2020, 2021). In all such circumstances, lifeworlds comprehend fluid practices informed by situational and sometimes contradictory knowledge that is related to life in uncertainty under fast-changing conditions. Crisis thus seems a likely association, but debates on this subject have taken a different turn, becoming less focused on interior experiences and often externally defined by internationally operating actors.

I have adopted a phenomenological approach to my findings in order to enable incremental research and data collection and receptivity to any unexpected juxtapositions of incommensurable and disparate elements and to the production of personal rather than official narratives. This research is based on stories that I heard—or that I was told directly and that were perhaps elicited by my presence and questions—about people's experiences in the Chad–Sudan borderlands and beyond. Through active listening, discussion, and reflection on these narratives, I focus on how people co-create their personal circumstances through situative ascriptions of the self and the other. I show how different perspectives on the question of the borderlands play out in practice, including those of villagers who had to flee their homes, residents of refugee camps, local officials like chiefs and imams, national and international aid personnel, rebels and former rebels, soldiers and government employees. These research partners have shaped this study—and their own circumstances—through this information, which they have readily and self-reflectively shared with me. Although my approach is descriptive, it is also meant to engage my readers in making sense of how people presented their situations—whether on their own initiative, in response to a sudden new development, or in response to my questions—and allow them to accompany me to the sites that have helped make the borderlands, and where people have lived through war and displacement.

One could argue that the term crisis is now overused and 'attests more to a diffuse manner of speaking than it contributes to the diagnosis of our situation' (Koselleck 2002: 236). Derived from a Greek word for 'a definitive, irrevocable decision', medical use has lent it a 'temporal dimension' (ibid.: 237): a medical crisis has a clear beginning, a phase of acceleration, and an end, and once it is acknowledged action becomes imperative to preserve life. But who is to define when a crisis begins? And moreover, what happens when one is declared? Roitman's book on anti-crisis (2014) also points to the consequences of 'declaring a crisis' and the tangible effects of making this official; to this, I would add the questions of who claims what regarding a crisis and with which effects. As I mention above, the people of the borderlands spoke of problems (*machákil*) that repeatedly interrupted daily life without completely stopping it. Meanwhile, the foreign aid workers I met were in full crisis mode and followed strict rules about leaving home, maintaining radio contact, travelling only in convoys escorted by security, and so on.

People continue to live their lives throughout turbulent times: they maintain their lifeworlds during a crisis. This book is about the everydayness that persists through what others call an emergency. It reflects on how governments, international agencies or others declare a situation to be a crisis, resulting in measures that may cause very abrupt changes in people's access to basic needs or government services. We can observe lifeworlds in people's narratives of life in the volatile borderlands, experiencing uncertainty and being caught in between, and in their accounts of waiting outside government or aid agency offices to which they are almost never admitted. While studies of crises often focus on events and their immediate contexts, this book's temporal frame extends both before and after the internationally declared crisis and encompasses a period whose beginning and end are often left out, especially in accounts of the Chad–Sudan region. This regional situation's marginal centrality becomes prominent in many ways—temporal, social, political and geographic—as actors had to react not only to what happened in national and international power centres, but also at the sites of violence, displacement and everyday insecurity.

Entangled lifeworlds: Categorising people during a crisis

Against this background of different and highly entangled lifeworlds, I foreground all actors' mutual and changing practices of categorising. Categories and their definitions structure connections between places, knowledges and concepts. Looking at intertwined categorisations does not enclose or isolate the situation but rather shows how they interfere with how people see or imagine themselves, their histories, and their experiences under changing circumstances as well as (internationally applied) norms and regulations. This premise is why I focus, among all those whom violence and economic desperation has driven to cross borders, on people who have stayed on the African continent and sought safety as 'refugees'[3] somewhere new but still close to their home country in hopes that this move will eventually offer them a better chance of social mobility, integration and productivity. But my observations concerning policy and practice suggest that social mobility, integration and productivity are only possible insofar as the categories used to identify human subjects can be rendered both mutable and multiple to accurately represent their practices and undertakings. For example, Chadian Arabic refers to people remaining close to their home as 'refugees who remain in place' (*ladjiin al-sakinin*), but international aid agencies classify these people as 'internally displaced people (IDPs)', 'returnees' or 'integrated refugees', depending on the circumstances. The category of 'integrated refugees' reflects their recent efforts to integrate people into the 'host population' (another humanitarian aid-related category) before their missions end or lose their funding. Such 'refugees' may not comply fully with the international regulations that define them: many leave the camps from time to time or move back and forth between different camps, their former homes and other places to seek greener pastures and other opportunities. The category also includes some people who (unlike internationally defined 'refugees') hope to continue their temporary status indefinitely. They do not expect to return home or resettle elsewhere but try to create alternative lifeworlds where they are.

This manipulation of flexible categories outside the purview of international aid agencies may be especially characteristic of strife-ridden contexts in which borders remain somewhat fluid, as Abdul-Jalil's (1984) above-quoted analysis also shows. In such settings, individual neighbourliness is sometimes a small step, but of course limitations and problems also abound at various levels. Instead of emphasising marginalisation and violence in such places, my study recognises that cooperation exists alongside conflict and acknowledges demands for both human dignity and personal/ professional redefinition and growth.

Belonging is relational and co-constituted, particularly in highly uncertain situations like war, displacement and large-scale humanitarian and development aid, and it is connected to the diverse knowledge and situational practices of actors. In studying people and how they narrate lifeworlds, relationships and the conditions in the borderlands, I seek to understand the mechanisms adopted by those who have chosen to remain near their homes and communities but thus also to live with high uncertainty and among old and new conflicts. I present the perspectives of the borderlands' population and of policymakers and development brokers—but also (former) rebels and international humanitarian personnel— as a theoretical contribution to an anthropology of belonging and emplacement under circumstances of exacerbated uncertainty and insecurity that one could call a crisis as well as old and new forms of violence, humanitarian aid and military intervention.

Knowing to which categories one might belong is critical for survival in the face of constant danger (Massumi 2010). Following Stefan Hirschauer's analysis (2014, Dizdar et al. 2021), categories are both partly institutionalised and partly contingent and can be revealed or rendered invisible during everyday interactions.

Foregrounding and backgrounding—'doing' and 'undoing' categorisations, as Hirschauer (2014) puts it—mean knowing where one can belong, individually or as a community.

Knowing where one cannot belong particularly characterises a form of entanglement that denies people essential services. This translates into inequality between those who have the means to define and impose categories and those who must resort to creatively manipulating them. Throughout the book, I will focus on such manipulations, repeatedly pointing to situations where the definition of categories depends on the circumstances and the actors present, who constantly redefine apparently stringent regulations to fit their own demands. This approach is suggested by Stengers's (2005: 194) reference to 'diplomacy': discussing exchanges between diplomats who must each represent their respective parties, she maintains that

> what is true is what succeeds in producing a communication between diverging parties, without anything in common being discovered or advanced. Each party will indeed keep its own version of the agreement, just as in the famous example given by Deleuze of a *'noce contre nature'* (unnatural coupling) of the wasp and the orchid, we get no wasp-orchid unity. Wasps and orchids give each quite other meanings to the relation which was produced between them.

With the help of the narratives and the cases in this book, I will move beyond this explanation to show that some of the parties involved might gradually adapt and eventually change what Stengers calls different 'versions of the agreement'—for instance, the categorisation as 'refugees'. Importantly, this process can be initiated by either party to the exchange: an international agency or villagers in the borderlands.

Flexible belonging: Responses to categorisation

In volatile circumstances where situations can easily become violent, it is important to know the implications of all the religious denominations, national or ethnic ascriptions, territories, age groups, insurgent groups or other groups to which one belongs. Thus, people can account for changing social environments caused by new actors in humanitarian or development aid, new governmental regimes, and the impact of natural or man-made disasters on livelihoods. This flexibility is related to changes in occupations, personal or kin relations, and connections across (international) borders and restricted by governmental change, restrictive categories used by aid programmes, and the lingering effects of past conflicts and alliances.

In fact, this flexibility of belonging made the Chad–Sudan borderlands one of anthropology's most prominent sites after the introduction of Fredrik Barth's (1969) analysis of 'ethnic boundaries' introduced a new standard of looking at how social boundaries are created in interactions instead of at ethnic groups as bounded entities. In this perspective, ethnic belonging was simultaneously flexible and persistent and individuals able to cross ethnic boundaries in many ways, such as with a change in occupation. In making this point, Barth invoked Gunnar Haaland's (1968) observation that in this region (unlike others he had investigated), changing one's ethnic affiliation was unproblematic and, indeed, frequently caused by occupational changes: when farmers became herders, they became part of another ethnically defined community and vice versa. Barth also asked what role ethnic boundaries even played, if individual and whole communities could cross them. He answered this question with economics: people might change their ethnic belonging to better invest their wealth (such as in animals rather than in land) but the values attached to specific forms of ethnic belonging continued to be defined differently in different groups.

For example, my research partner Brahim told me stories about how members of his family had experienced such changes in belonging several times during their lives. The colonial administration declared his paternal grandfather 'chief' of the people he settled among after he had worked for years as a translator for French officials. Meanwhile, his mother's father had migrated to Sudan to work in a British agricultural project and later invested his savings in cattle. Although he originally came from a farming community, he brought up his children in an Arab herding community and for a time changed his affiliation to become 'Arab'. Thus, Brahim felt comfortable among people of various backgrounds, moving freely, speaking their languages and dialects, and referring to his parents and grandparents in situations of doubt about his belonging.[4]

Changing modes of individual belonging also appear in Abdul-Jalil's (1984) authoritative anthropological study of what he calls the 'ethnically mixed' village of Dor in Northern Darfur, Sudan, in the 1970s. Extending Barth's focus on the fluidity of ethnic boundaries, Abdul-Jalil considers 'ethnic identification' to be dynamic, concluding that 'the nature of this dynamism lies in the fact that both the criteria for the identification of ethnic groups and the way in which individual members express their allegiances to them change over time and with respect to the circumstances under which such processes take place' (1984: 56). His thoughtful contribution interprets events such as buying and selling in the market, marriage transactions, and participation in disputes as displaying 'situational ethnic identity' (1984: 62). He explicitly refutes Haaland and Barth's 'simplistic view' that defines ethnic belonging exclusively through the economic lens of occupations.

> While the economy is an important factor in ethnic dynamics, it is by no means the only one. However, ethnic groups may be defined in terms of occupation only in a situation where this criterion is relevant. Other criteria, or a combination of them, may be more relevant in other situations, in which case they should not be ignored for the sake of the first one. (1984: 66)

Throughout, Abdul-Jalil explicates conditions of conviviality and flexible identification using two proverbs: 'Blood is compelling, but co-living is achieved by co-operation' and 'Conflict reveals origins' (1984: 71). The latter addresses the mobilisation of ethnically based group membership in conflict situations where the contradiction between the two proverbs is resolved by allowing people to choose membership in communities or kin 'according to the nature of the interaction' (1984: 73). He concludes that 'actors manipulate ... criteria to identify with groups according to their interests and situations of interaction'. Four of these are most important for ethnic belonging: 'territory, occupation, language and genealogy' (1984: 82). While many marriages cross ethnic lines, ancestry is most important when paying blood money after violent conflict and when arranging marriages. Language, for instance, was the most important criterion for belonging in the marketplace, while one's place of residence (or the homeland one claimed to belong to) affected taxes and water rights. Abdul-Jalil describes the possibility of referencing a different aspect of one's belonging (and also mentions changes in ethnic affiliation) when shifting one's livelihood from farming to herding or vice versa.

While I generally follow Abdul-Jalil's analysis, I consider two points most important to my own approach. First, ownership of and access to land are vital to people's survival in both war and peacetime and become pivotal when deciding whether to move to a camp for 'refugees' or to stay in the conflict zone. During times of the utmost uncertainty and under threat of violence, they also constitute a basis for negotiation between those who define themselves as newcomers and those who consider themselves locals. The second point concerns people's general readiness to cooperate and relate to each other. And while much has been written about the *making* of difference and othering, it is also important to understand the role the *unmaking* of difference plays in relations in the borderlands at any given time.

Making and unmaking difference: Emplacement and displacement

In understanding the *making* and *unmaking* of differences, the concept of 'emplacement' is more revealing than focusing on 'difference' itself. Emplacement occurs when certain differences are rendered unimportant and is less concerned with disconnecting or disruptive factors like war than with the creation of alternative alliances in new situations. Here, I follow the formulation of Glick Schiller and Çağlar (2015: 7), who define displacement and emplacement in urban situations in relation to 'social processes through which a dispossessed individual builds or rebuilds networks of connection within the constraints and opportunities of a specific city'. Their spatial analysis 'see[s] emplacement as a processual concept that links together space, place, and power' to define new ways of belonging. This builds on their earlier work (Glick Schiller and Çağlar 2015) examining 'domains of commonality' that lead to various emplacements and focusing on the common creation of 'sociabilities'. This harkens back to Simmel's ([1910] 1949) definition of sociabilities as relationships in which 'one "acts" as though all were equal' (Simmel [1910] 1949: 257 quoted in Glick Schiller and Çağlar 2015: 3). This is not a naïve concept that minimises the hardships of war and the precarity that results from them in cases like that of the Chad–Sudan borderlands, but instead aims to show how frequently cooperation in the face of difference occurs.

Bjarnesen and Vigh (2016, see also Hammar 2014) similarly define the dialectics of displacement and emplacement as referring not to physical locations but relational concepts. Displacement, framed thus, may be a state of being for people who have had to move away from the place where they lived before, whether or not this was by force. However, people may also feel displaced when they take in others who have been displaced from elsewhere: although they have remained in one place, they still find themselves in a new and possibly precarious situation. Quoting Doreen Massey (1993: 62, in Bjarnesen and Vigh 2016: 14), Bjarnesen and Vigh understand displacement and emplacement as 'enabling an empirical understanding of "the politics of mobility and access"'. In understanding how mobility restructures contexts, I follow their suggestion of viewing mobility as voluntary as well as involuntary. Despite their convincing conceptual move 'away from place as a location toward place as a process of socio-affective attachment', the issue of place persists.

As Bjarnesen and Vigh underline, focusing on both displacement and emplacement requires 'a view from within the actual social fields and formations in question, necessitating a commitment to a type of fieldwork that most researchers are, understandably, unwilling to undertake' (2016: 9). In other words, remaining within a field for a longer term generates perspectives on spectacular events, but also on quite unspectacular everyday happenings that show that generosity and cooperation in times of war can be just as important as violence and fear.

Temporalities of research: Getting situated

I began my research in Chad in 2000 as a postdoctoral researcher in the Department of Integration and Conflict at the Max Planck Institute for Social Anthropology. I had originally planned to study how Sudanese people who fled to Chadian villages interacted with the villagers hosting them. I conducted interviews, visited houses, and lived with people in various villages which were mainly inhabited by people who identified as 'Masalit' or members of various 'Arab' family groups (Braukämper 1993). What I found during this phase of research contrasts with the ruptures and changes that happened later, when full-blown war broke out in 2003. Once that had become an undeniable reality for the people in the region, I did not immediately return; the data I had collected suddenly seemed irrelevant: dated, and no longer useful. There had been no camps before, but since then hundreds of thousands of people had moved to them. To remain close to my original site and topic, I changed my focus to the effects of oil production. In Chad, this had begun around the same time as the Darfur War and was directly related to it in at least one way: the war and a directly related Chadian rebellion that started with military defections from the Chadian army in 2004, directed against President Déby and his politics in relation to the Darfur War,[5] offered a perfect justification for diverting oil revenues, previously allocated for development, to the military (Behrends 2008; Reyna 2010; Debos 2011, 2016).

Although I returned to the borderlands in 2007, I could not do much fieldwork. It was the height of the war and Sudanese rebels—whom the Chadian regime supported, just as the Sudanese regime supported Chadian rebels—roamed freely throughout the borderlands. I visited the people, from various places of origin, whom I had known most closely during previous stays. Some had abandoned their villages for the border town of Adré, others had remained, and still others had decided to move to the refugee camps. It was obvious that the different modes of belonging and not belonging that I had observed before the war had led to very different reactions to it. The most pressing question for me was why these ways of surviving war and dealing with the highest level of uncertainty differed so much when all the people seemed to have a very similar background, to have a common language and religion, and—most importantly—even to often know one another quite well. Then, from 2007 until 2019, I travelled to Chad for a couple of weeks almost every year and visited colleagues and friends in N'Djamena and in the eastern part of the country in and around Abéché and Adré. The empirical findings I present in this book are based on these journeys and the interviews, journals and fieldnotes I kept. For better readability, I decided to refrain from indicating the exact diary, page and date of the situations I refer to.

Temporalities of research: Periodisation

My analysis is divided into three phases that I define both temporally (in relation to the war) and spatially (following people's displacement over a wider area and the involvement of more distant actors in the situation). These phases parallel my fieldwork, which began before the war and continues today. The three analytical phases correspond to the three parts of this book.

The phase *before the war* extended from 2000 to 2003. I visited Chad three times in 2000 and 2001 and stayed for three months each time. I mainly lived in Hachaba, a village less than a kilometre from the border with Sudan along the Wadi Asoungha and about 8 kilometres south of Adré, the largest Chadian border town. On these visits, I mainly gathered information about how new arrivals from Sudan integrated into existing villages along the border and about the help a small number of aid organisations offered them. In those days, there were no camps and the United Nations Refugee Agency's (UNHCR) single representative in eastern Chad was based in Abéché, about 140 kilometres west of the border. I found that '*réfugiés*' did not always identify themselves as such and that the ways in which they accessed aid and were welcomed in the villages also differed quite widely and often depended on the access they had to national institutions and international organisations. My spatial focus remained very close to the border during this period, so my analysis here looks at the relations between villages; between those categorised (or categorising themselves) as 'townspeople', 'NGOs' and 'villagers'; and between people as they defined their belonging based on ethnic terms, including 'Masalit', 'Arab', and 'Maba'. These experiences during this period before the war are the ones that most influenced how people later defined their situation and characterised conflict and belonging, as well as how difference and privilege became visible through crisis, mobility, and aid.

The second phase—*during the war*—extended from 2003 to 2010. When Sudanese rebels from what was then called the Darfur Liberation Army/Movement (DLA/M) captured the Sudanese town of Gulu in February 2003, this prompted the first severe government attacks on the population of Darfur: bombing villages in the borderlands and inciting the Janjaweed militias against them (Beck 2004; de Waal 2004; Flint and de Waal 2005, 2008; Reyna 2010). In 2005, and related to the unrest in Darfur, a rebellion against Déby started, making the situation even more volatile. While, at the time, Chadian rebels were supported by the Sudanese government, Chad's president started to openly support rebel groups, the so-called Toroboro in Sudan (see also Chapter 10). Several years of increasing turbulence, uncertainty and mobility followed, during which it was mainly people from Sudan who looked for safety in nearby Chad; however, national and international military and global aid organisations also sent troops and local and international staff to the Chadian border region of Wadai. Most of the Sudanese people who had been forced to leave their homes were villagers and moved less than 50 kilometres away. Beginning in 2004, Chadian villagers also began to flee their villages and fields and move either to one of the newly opened United Nations refugee camps or to the nearest large town, usually Adré.

During this phase, I visited the country significantly less frequently. In 2007, I made one trip to Adré and an almost deserted Hachaba. After 2007, I returned to the border area between Chad and Sudan once or twice a year, but only for a couple of weeks at a time. My research by then had come to revolve around the increased mobility brought about by the war and looked at how the greatly increased number of agencies in the region structured aid and how their presence led to new ways of redefining categories of belonging. This focus on social settings and how they were reordered and reorganised also included how people alternately attempted to avoid or creatively access humanitarian and development aid. For this phase, my spatial focus in this book expands from the immediate border region to include the UN camps (50 to 100 kilometres away) and the Chadian capital of N'Djamena, the aid agencies' headquarters during the war.

I consider this second phase to have ended with the 2010 peace accord between Chad and Sudan, which also ended the rebellion in Chad, even though this did not bring full 'peace' to either side of the international border. In February 2008, Chadian rebels had again attacked the capital of N'Djamena, their last and most severe assault so far, and even though the government's army was able to defeat the rebels (this time with the help of French troops) its approach to the war changed. In 2010, President Idriss Déby signed a peace accord with his Sudanese counterpart, Omar al-Bashir, that established joint military operations along the entire border and resulted in Chad's unilateral termination of two years of international peacekeeping missions.[6]

Although I describe the third phase beginning in 2010 as *the war's aftermath*, I agree with Marielle Debos' refusal to refer to that period as 'peace'. She proposes opposing the term 'inter-war' to 'war' because 'in countries such as Chad, there is no such thing as the "normalcy" of the pre-conflict' (Debos 2016: 8). Violence continues to affect the population in Chad through marginalisation, a distinct lack of care for the concerns of the people, aggressive rejection of any public opposition, and ongoing severe insecurity concerning food, health, education or future ambition. None of these issues have been addressed by the government: in fact, its actions have exacerbated them. In considering this phase, I focus on the longer-term effects of the 2008 rebellion, looking beyond the immediate border region to the regional capital of Abéché and at how the end of the war once again changed national politics. I focus on two aspects in particular: how oil production since 2003 has affected the war (and wider contexts) and how notions of development are related to each other on a regional, national and international level.

The sequence of the book's three parts follows a particular spatial and temporal pattern. Part I offers an intimate perspective on villagers who live within sight of the international border. In Part II, I turn to the nearby camps managed by the United Nations High Commissioner for Refugees (UNHCR). In Part III, I shift the focus first to Chad's national capital, N'Djamena, and then back to the eastern region's capital, Abéché. I thus proceed from the marginal borderlands, the locus of the various states of (perceived and real) emergency, to the national administrative centre, which has not been paralysed by the crisis (except when directly attacked, and then only partially) and remains the seat of planning, management and control. Each part of the book will cover all three phases, before, during, and after the war in the particular spatial situations it refers to. I start each part with a personal take on the situation *during* the war. A discussion on how these different sites relate is vital. In the same way, a discussion about perceptions of Chad's emergence as an oil producer demands a multi-scalar analysis as there have been insurgencies almost throughout the country's periphery. Ironically, this puts the margins at centre stage—at least politically, if not in the eyes of the capital's residents.

After crisis?

My opening story about the urgent warning from the elders of Hachaba exemplifies everyday life in an area where war is a constant menace. The Chad–Sudan borderlands are among many such areas (see, for instance, Nordstrom 2004; Finnstrøm 2008; Stepputat and Sørensen 2014). The people I met there had experienced multiple kinds of war in their lifetimes and remembered their parents' and grandparents' stories of how they had also experienced war in various ways.

TOMORROW, THERE WILL BE WAR!

In this part of the world, war comes fast, an ambush with little advance warning. Young men ride or drive through town, shouting and shooting, and most people run or hide—if, that is, they do not decide to stay and cheer their presumptive new rulers. Only once the attack ends will the town's imam announce over the mosque's megaphone that it is now safe to go out and look for relatives. Any wounded people must be taken to the border town's hospital and the dead must be buried. Then life will go on. This kind of war passes through the town like a storm and usually does not last long. With luck, one can stay inside and not be affected. In a village a few miles away, one might hear only gunfire or the sounds of many cars and trucks. However, the approach of war can also lead to a more sustained situation of vigilance as rebels roam the area, looking for food and shelter but not attacking the villagers and town dwellers directly. In this kind of war, young people may be attracted to join the rebels who display their manliness by carrying weapons openly and showing off their wild hairstyles around people who can only react to their presence. But the worst kind of war is directed against civilians. This kind would come to the Chad–Sudan borderlands eventually, but not when the elders warned against going to the market during my stay in Hachaba in 2001. And all-out war would only come a few years later, after the rebel attack in Gulu, Sudan, in February 2003, escalating when the government of Sudan unleashed the Janjaweed militias.

In a situation where current events are only known through rumour and how people act, my hosts' calm and cheerful manner gave me no sign that danger was near. It was only when war broke out so violently, just two years after I left the village, that I realised that the elders' warning had indeed indicated rising tensions. Rumour and being aware of one's surroundings are crucial in highly uncertain or insecure situations. Decisions about survival must be made instantly. The growing turbulence often invoked in declaring a crisis does not seem to make sense when a collapse in living standards constantly looms and conditions might temporarily worsen or improve. Where neither the national government, nor significant remittances from family members abroad, nor other kinds of opportunity and support seem to improve the situation, a particular kind of lifeworld emerges that constantly grapples with the lack, loss and uncertainty experienced in places at the low end of the global capitalist hierarchy. I call such conditions 'lifeworlds in crisis'.

PART I

WAR COMES TO THE BORDERLANDS

DIFFERENCE AND BELONGING IN THE VILLAGES

2

WE HAVE TO MAKE A LIST

REPRESENTING LIFEWORLDS IN A CRISIS

'We're happy to see you back here,' said Mahamat Ismael when I returned to the borderlands in 2007 for the first time after the war began. 'But is bringing us sugar, tea and these photographs really all you can do?' This friendly but frank reaction made me feel just how inadequate these gifts—usually much appreciated in more peaceful times—had become. In the six years I had been away, the war had started and the vast majority of people from Hachaba and many other villages had fled their homes and moved closer to Adré, the regional capital. A few were staying with relatives in town, but most had built makeshift shelters in an area on the outskirts that they optimistically called Hille Djidíde (New Town). When I arrived there, I was greeted with a flood of tears. One woman after another ran up and threw her arms around me, sobbing. I was at a loss: were they weeping with joy to see me despite the difficult circumstances? However, I think it is more likely that they were mourning those who had died in my absence and that I had especially reminded them of my friend and host Ashta, who had succumbed to cancer shortly after my last departure in late 2001. The men also came out to greet me. They did not cry, but their serious faces and emaciated bodies testified to the dire situation.

Mahamat's question about how a visitor from a more prosperous part of the world could help left me feeling lost. I had known these people before as farmers who lived in houses and had animals, a few belongings and a livelihood that had sustained them for decades. Now, they could no longer work their farms and lived in makeshift shacks. Many of the younger children were ill and not in school, while some older boys, who lacked other avenues for self-expression and were eager for a chance to demonstrate their courage and get the reputation of being tough, were said to have been drawn into the rebellion themselves.

I assumed that the main need was money to buy food and other necessities at the market since in the village they had mostly lived from subsistence agriculture and produced only a small surplus to sell or exchange for necessities like soap, sugar, tea or clothes. But the women in Hille Djidíde told me their most immediate concerns were better housing and healthcare: 'Our children are sick, and the houses won't last through the next rainy season.' Mahamat, however, had a more sustainable long-term plan in mind. 'What we need,' he explained, 'are seeds'. 'We want to farm the land that we found to the west of Adré. When the situation is calmer, we'll return to the villages to work on our former fields, but the war has destroyed our harvests and the seed that we always keep for the next farming season has been stolen or burnt.' Last year, he said, the United Nations Food and Agriculture Organization (FAO) had distributed seeds, and they had been able to live off the harvest. But this year, they had only received food that had lasted, he emphasised, 'only fifteen days'. To my great surprise, however, the former villagers turned out to know exactly what to do. 'We have to make a list,' Mahamat Ibrahim declared in the most matter-of-fact way, 'a list of all the people who have fled the villages, all the people of Hille Djidíde who now need help.'

Fleeing the war

By the summer of 2007, the people of the borderlands were living through a cruel and protracted civil war in two countries. The governments of Chad and Sudan both simultaneously fought insurgents within their own borders and supported the rebels on the other side. At the same time, each continually orchestrated attacks against their own civilians. The members of the rebel groups and the government-backed militias and the civilians all came from the borderlands. Whether they claimed to belong to 'the Masalit', 'the Zaghawa', 'the Tama', 'the Fur' or various 'Arab' families (and these are only some of the most prominent ethnic affiliations), all were Muslim, spoke Arabic as their first or second language, and shared a common experience of physical and environmental trauma. But now, some were in favour with one of the governments and some with the other.

In 2007, the rebellion against President Idriss Déby's government in Chad was in full swing and the Darfur War that had begun in 2003 still raged across the border and was the focus of large amounts of aid. People fleeing violence and fighting in Sudan circulated in eastern Chad, while Chadian rebels moved freely across the border in Sudan. As I travelled to the borderlands, I saw them sitting and eating in small roadside restaurants on the mats next to me and my travelling companions and driving along the dirt roads in Toyota pickup trucks outfitted as war vehicles.[1] Both the Chadian and the Sudanese state feared a coup d'état enough to have launched pre-emptive attacks on the rebels in the borderlands, where they most commonly appeared, and surrounded the people there with unpredictable fighting.

The rebels mainly recruited young men, who joined for various reasons. As Marielle Debos (2011, 2016) explains, 'living by the gun' has become one of the most reliable occupations in countries torn by wars and rebellions, where there is always a demand for police, customs and security officers, and (of course) soldiers. At the same time, the conflicts severely affected civilians in the borderlands: since their own governments accepted high civilian casualties as the price of staying in power, they became targets of both counter-insurgency operations and of the rebels.

When the war first broke out—in 2003 in Darfur and two years later on the Chadian side of the border—the crisis manifested in various ways: a shortage of food, arbitrary attacks and both potential and actual violence, and a complete lack of governmental measures to counter food insecurity and provide civil protection. Those affected had already been leading precarious lives as farmers or herders and had run out of ways to provide their families with food or medical care. Once the violence became pervasive, many left the villages and moved to Adré, which hosted an army garrison and was considered safer than other border towns; some also moved to twelve newly established camps that the UNHCR had installed about 50 kilometres from the border (in case sudden attacks shifted the front lines). Those who went to the camps were predominantly Masalit and Fur from the east of Sudan's Darfur region who did not have close relatives near the border. Unlike many others who had fled across the border, they were now at least several days' walk away from their homes. Some Masalit elders had remained in their villages but had fully switched to crisis mode and subsisted on wild fruits and berries and the food their adult children brought them from Adré. Nearby 'Arab' communities (which had settled in the borderlands at least five decades before) also remained in their villages and did not move to the New Town at Adré or the international camps. During my 2007 visit, the women from these villages had gone to stay temporarily with relatives in Sudan. The cattle, on the other hand, remained deeper in Chad and the men had stayed: they felt unwelcome in the New Town and refused to live in the camps. They were also less worried about the Sudanese Janjaweed fighters—who they thought would not attack fellow Arabs—than about their Masalit neighbours, some of whom also took part in the rebellion and roamed freely in Chad under the protection of the country's president and who, according to the older Arab men, attacked regularly. They even showed me some evidence: an impressively large piece of a shell that had been launched from Adré towards their village, where it destroyed a house and killed three people and three camels. No one could find out exactly who the attackers had been.

The borderlands' inhabitants at the time included 'Masalit' who owned the land they cultivated, other people who had recently moved to Masalit villages from Sudan, 'Arabs' living in villages who had leased land from its Masalit owners, and people who had moved to the UNHCR's camps but continued to periodically return to their villages. There was also an established urban population in Adré, which could afford solidly built houses, had the resources to start and develop businesses, and were able to send their children to regular schools. These families had come from Abéché and beyond to work as translators, traders and administrative staff when the town was founded by the colonial army in the 1920s. Many profited from the war due to lucrative jobs at aid agencies, in the service sector, or on construction projects funded by the international community, but they were still not safe once it began. By 2004, everyone who had not moved to the newly installed UNHCR refugee camps was on their own in the war zone, with almost no access to food, other material aid, or military protection. Rumours became the main source of information, and people relied on past experiences to interpret those subtle signals and decide if it was safe to go to a market for food. Meanwhile, the markets had shrunk and moved to safer areas inside the town. Many struggled to get by, with menial jobs and meagre earnings that were barely enough to buy food and water for themselves and their families. And even the livelihoods of the more affluent townspeople were jeopardised when rebels passed through town or encountered government troops or militias nearby.

Compiling the list

Once Mahamat Ismael and the others understood that I was willing to help, things moved very quickly. I consulted Djamal, a respected elder from the established Maba community in Adré[2] who had been one of my first contacts there and was the town's representative for the National Office of Rural Development (ONDR). (Although the ONDR is notoriously underfunded and barely operational, international aid organisations needed to partner with a national agency in order to work in the area.) Djamal offered to help me gather basic data and make calculations based on it, so I quickly bought a paper notebook and a ballpoint pen at the market. The next day, we sat down on mats under a large tree and some of the men prepared and served us tea which they brewed on small fireplaces. Djamal and I watched Yaya Ahmat, our interpreter and a former employee of the ONDR, begin to write a list and Mahamat Ismail helped him. There was no need for preliminary discussion: the two seemed to know exactly where to start. I did not fully understand what they were doing at the time, but it was very clear that their main argument would be quantitative. Yaya Ahmat, who would continue writing incessantly for the next two days, confidently divided the page into five columns, one for a serial number and the others for the household head's names and patronymics, the number of persons in the family, their genders, and other comments. To make the list intelligible to the international community for whom it was intended, Yaya Ahmat wrote in French and not in the regional common language, Arabic. They started with inhabitants of the village of Hachaba and the serial number 001, and I expected hundreds of entries to follow, maybe even a thousand. The first person on the list was Ali Daldoum, the village chief. He had a family of six and an 'M' for *masculin* indicated a male head of the household. Mahamat was second, with a family of ten.

They did not distinguish between people formerly considered as refugees and those considered as hosts. When I was in Hachaba for the first time, I had aimed to study the integration of people who had fled from the other side of the border to Chad in tens of thousands since 1995, even before the war had fully broken out. Back then, differentiating 'refugees' from 'villagers' seemed very important, but now it was no longer significant: Mahamat Ismail, the leader of the *groupements des réfugiés* and the most active spokesperson of the cross-border newcomers' community in Hachaba and Guilane, was listed as belonging to the village of Hachaba. The list did not even mention the word refugee. I thus came to understand that the 'refugee' category that I had encountered during my previous stay in the village had been situational and relational: it had allowed people to come together to secure aid from those who were most likely to provide it and was only important so long as aid agencies were assisting 'refugees' in the villages. Now that refugee camps had opened, those who had decided not to move to them had no further use for this designation. The difference—at least at this point—had been undone.

WE HAVE TO MAKE A LIST

When we started making the list, only a couple of people were involved. These included Mahamat, who dictated the names and numbers; Yaya Ahmat, who wrote; and myself, watching. As the list grew, more and more people gathered to watch what we were doing. More bystanders started to comment, adding more and more names, not only those of their own families but also those of their neighbours, relatives and friends. The crowd encircling us grew further, and many shouted and pushed forward in order to get heard and have their names and family sizes written down. Some of their comments indicated their knowledge of aid agency criteria. They wondered, for instance, if a section dedicated to the 'most vulnerable' should be added. When a blind old man asked for a special list for the disabled, people loudly protested. 'No, no! Everybody must remain on the same list. We'll distribute the seeds among everybody.' Some pointed out that the list named children who did not live in Hille Djidíde with their parents but had remained back in the villages with elderly relatives. I later understood that everyone wanted the total number to be high but also worried that others might claim more than their share. Even though the goal was to count as many members of each household as possible, at certain points bystanders corrected people who blatantly exaggerated their family size.

After a while, about twenty of us adjourned to an enclosed, hot, and stuffy room where many bags of grain were stored. Mahamat quickly explained that the bags belonged to individuals from various villages and that he was keeping them safe here, away from the envious gaze of neighbours and relatives. A couple of younger men in the room took it upon themselves to push people away from the door and to guard it from the crowd waiting to enter. They shouted out names as Yaya Ahmat wrote them down, filling pages with the details. As I look at the list years later, I notice that male-headed households dominate the beginning of the list and female-headed ones are relegated to its end. Family size ranges from three to twelve members: no household has only one person. In the fifth column on the page, the one for 'comments', Yaya Ahmat made one entry in French—*vieille* (elderly woman)—in a short-lived attempt to add another criterion.

We were exhausted after completing the list of people in Hachaba—from the stuffy air inside the storage room, by the shouting, and even by the physical effort of writing the list or at least the strain of watching Yaya Ahmat write it—but we still had to listen to the chiefs of the other villages. They demanded that we count not just the single village that had hosted me but also their own villages: they too had been displaced and were living in Hille Djidíde in the same destitute situation with no means of support and no seeds to start farming again. However, by that point it was obvious that listing and counting all the inhabitants of every village would take much too long and Yaya Ahmat suggested a new procedure: each village chief would produce a list with the relevant details for each of his village's residents, from which he could copy only the totals into my notebook. In other words, while the first list was (at least in principle) a direct record of the detailed information the villagers of Hachaba had shouted out to us, the other villages' chiefs would only supply the totals. Thus, I have an itemised list for Hachaba with detailed information about the villagers and their households and genders but only an abstraction of that model for the other villages. The sheet of paper on which the list was written was vital. Former villagers were aware of the possibilities of accessing aid and all the village chiefs (who had often been hard to find during my first trips to the area) were present, acknowledging the list's importance in gaining access to outside help. I also realised that this desire was situational. They could have produced a list earlier, taken it to the aid agencies, and demanded that they, too, become eligible. That they had only decided to do so when I arrived suggests that even though they were well versed in the power of written evidence and adapting to the circumstances of international aid, they had seen me as an effective mediator with closer or more direct access to aid providers. These circumstances had been known at least since the 1980s, when the UNHCR had first opened refugee camps in the borderlands, in Darfur. I knew that many of the people now seeking a safer haven in Hille Djidíde had moved to Sudan to look for help during an earlier war and drought in the 1980s.

WE HAVE TO MAKE A LIST

In fact, the experience of famine in UNHCR camps in the 1980s (de Waal 1988) might have been a reason that people chose not to move to the new camps in 2007. Lists might also have been known since that time, but this sort of list-making has an even longer history. The British and French colonisers made lists for tax purposes that had the opposite result: large villages only reported a few households in order to minimise what they had to pay the colonial administration and their local representatives, the new *chefs de canton*. People's attitudes towards lists and their contents reflect their purposes. We listed 152 households containing 844 persons in 2007, a total we had no time to verify but which was much higher than that of a survey of the households of Hachaba that I had conducted six years earlier, which identified 87 households with 376 inhabitants living in 134 separate houses. I assume that in 2007 the prospect of attracting more aid outweighed the fear of higher taxes, one reason they might have underreported the population in 2001.

The list for Guilane, Hachaba's neighbouring village, was ready at 8 am the next morning. Again, we sat under a tree waiting for the results from the various villages as Yaya Ahmat started to translate the full list from Arabic into French. Along with some villagers from Hachaba, we waited for more lists. As Yaya Ahmat was finishing the list for Guilane, the older men who served as village chiefs in the canton's remaining border villages arrived and introduced themselves. They brought lists of displaced people from south of Adré, either newly written or based on a survey they had conducted the previous year. Ahmat complained that transcribing all the lists was making his hand 'fall off', so everybody agreed to our proposal that for the nine remaining villages (Cheikhata, Siegnon, Mahamatta, Baratta, Yadarta, South Ardebe, Aboussogo, Wandalou and Wewerita) he would record only the village name and the actual number of households. Everybody stayed seated and we ate peanuts and drank tea. The village elders shelled peanuts to plant as seeds and a couple of teenage boys sat in an open-sided shed a little way off, watching us and joking. After a while, I approached them to ask how they were and what they did in their respective villages. Instead of a direct response, though, I received another demand: 'We want a school.' They explained that they could not afford the fees the school in Adré charged. Then, they told me that they had seen the Janjaweed burn their village down and had been too young to stop them from stealing their cattle and abducting girls. I did not wonder then why they had changed the subject: not going to school somehow seemed connected to their traumatic experience of flight. At a loss for words, I just listened and nodded. Posing like rebels, with longish hair and challenging gazes, they asked me to photograph them (almost everybody did this, knowing that I would bring them the pictures when I returned) and I wondered how close they actually were to the men who had crossed the border to join rebel movements in the bush and fight their respective governments' troops.

I had been staying at Zenaba and Khassim's house in Adré. Before I returned there in the evening, I was invited to another house for tea and sweet vermicelli, and was asked to add some more households to the list. I had been placed in a position of influence and felt like an actor in a play when Yaya Ahmat asked me if it would still be possible to take further requests and, going along, I solemnly agreed. We added another seventeen household heads and 90 more people to the list, which now included 170 households and 934 members in Adré, with those from Hachaba heavily represented. Mahamat drove back another way and stopped at the house of people from the neighbouring village of Guilane, where his second wife had lived. Here, we were offered grilled chicken and savoury vermicelli and added five more families to the list. I don't know whether these invitations were to thank us for our help or because we could add names without the formal approval of the other villagers and chiefs. The people controlling the list-making—here, the chiefs—probably thought about the list in terms of a later distribution of aid, so it would be advantageous to be on the main list if one had been left off of the chiefs'. I also thought that adding names after a private invitation could be considered bribery, but I did not want to haphazardly add another instance of control without knowing more about the actual procedures. Having completed the first step, I decided to observe, let things take their course, and accept any role I might be accorded in the next step of the process.

Lists as 'boundary objects'

Richard Rottenburg (2009) discusses the role lists might play in a hypothetical international water management project and how they might contribute to controlling the ratio of water usage to payment in the community. He shows that lists are aggregate representations of reality directed towards a particular goal, so that there can be no 'true' list: what they include and what they leave out is underpinned by a strategic decision that influences the indicators and the numbers—even though they represent a supposed reality (Rottenburg et al. 2015)—and obscures the list makers' intentions and the narratives from which they have derived their numbers. How a list is generated reflects the region's history and circumstances and the modes of interaction specific to this particular effort of institutionalisation. In the case of the list of displaced people in Hille Djidíde, its anchoring in history can be seen against a backdrop of earlier procedures through which they gained international humanitarian and development intervention and aid. Thus, the modality of the list might still be rooted in the tax or development procedures of the national government or in living memories of lists produced by the colonial powers before 1960.

A list can also function as what Bowker and Star (1999) call a 'boundary object', which translates information about the people's circumstances in a manner that balances different categories and meanings deemed valid in different communities of practice[3] (Star and Griesemer 1989).

> Boundary objects are those objects that both inhabit several communities of practice and satisfy the informational requirements of each of them. Boundary objects are thus both plastic enough to adapt to local needs and constraints of the several parties employing them, and yet robust enough to maintain a common identity across sites. They are weakly structured in common use and become strongly structured in individual-site use. These objects may be abstract or concrete (…) Such

objects have different meanings in different social worlds, but their structure is common enough to more than one world to make them recognizable, a means of translation. The creation and management of boundary objects is a key process in developing and maintaining coherence across intersecting communities. (Bowker and Star 1999: 297)

As a boundary object, the list could impose (colonial) standards on local practices and demand compliance with form, but it could also be creatively transformed to better represent local concerns and circumstances to the aid agencies. It represented an accepted institutional practice that not only standardises but also demands diverse understandings of how to deal with crises. Its makers intended not only to reflect people's knowledge about the history of their communities but also to adapt this to meet the requirements of the readers, who would interpret it and make a decision. As a bridging concept, the list addressed something lacking in the approach adopted by aid institutions. As Boltanski (2010) has described in another context, it actively sought to engage with and alter an established practice of international institutions in response to the realities of the borderland's villagers during the war in 2007. The people I met that year were clearly enthusiastic about the chance of gaining aid that so far had been beyond their reach unless they decided to move to the refugee camps. But although interlocutors in the field recognise the importance of interviews, they are not always satisfied with just being asked questions: they also demand what Scheper-Hughes has called engaged anthropology (1992: 17–18). The mediatory boundary objects that help to navigate different modes of knowing in diverse communities of practice have effects in real life. They create affective relations through the 'names we give to patterns and indicators. If someone is comfortable with the things and language used by a group of others, we say that he or she is a member of that group. In this sense, categories—our own and those of others—come from action and in turn from relationships' (Bowker and Star 1999: 285).

Rottenburg (2009: 139f.) distinguishes between three stages of list-making: (1) collecting elementary facts and figures that correspond to some countable reality; (2) elementary procedures involved in aggregating facts and figures, whether logically true or false; and (3) strategic procedures for defining a specific reality. He maintains that while, normally, a list would proceed from step one to step three, the causal logic also works the other way around: a list could also represent an intended reality, with the aggregate facts and figures later verified by producing an elementary list that assesses 'the truth' of the recorded numbers. In the case I had observed in Adré, tracking the procedural sequence in the reverse order—from intention and representation to list-making—was more productive. The list of the residents of Hille Djidíde was made with a clear goal in mind—to produce evidence of need—and it was immediately obvious that including more people would make it more effective. Thus, measures were taken to ensure the collection of not only many names but also many household members. In other words, procedures for defining a specific reality were not a part of this process. From the beginning, the entries represented an aggregation—no one could confirm the numbers related to some countable reality. I could not even verify the identity of the names or whether each person really belonged to the same household as those they were listed with. And while I witnessed the making of the first list, with people calling out their names and those of their friends and neighbours, I had no way to verify the lists the village chiefs brought on the second day—and only later noticed the hierarchical order that placed male-headed households at the top and female households at the bottom, a feature of ordering that Grätz (1995) and others explicitly characterise as an essential part of list-making.

Susan Leigh Star proposes an 'indirect reading' of 'the dramas inherent in system design creating' (1999: 377f.) of 'boring things' like 'lists of numbers and technical specifications'. In Star's terminology, former differences between families in Hille Djidíde had been 'made other' or 'unnamed' by disregarding details such as displacement and suffering, number of children, and disability and ill health. Star (1999: 388) calls this kind of analysis 'discovering the status of the indicator'. She warns, however, that this discovery is 'complex', partly due to 'our elisions as researchers, and partly due to sleights of hand of those creating them'. Looking at the list at a later stage, I understood it as a 'boundary object' that explained the practice of one community, the former villagers now living in Hille Djidíde, to another, the aid agencies. When they made the list, I learned that my agreement to bring their numerical evidence to the agencies' offices in Abéché and N'Djamena had restored their hopes of receiving some aid. Viewed through the lens of Stengers' (2005) ecology approach, their knowledge about dealing with crisis had led the people of Hachaba to remain close to their land so that they would be able to return once it was safe, even though not moving to the camps meant forgoing the chance of aid. That awareness now had to be updated to adapt to international aid agencies' definitions of eligibility—to demonstrate need, you need numbers. Then came the next stage of the list-making: after we had collected lists and numbers from every village, these had to be translated into aid measurements.

Translating the list

After the list was finished, I took it back to Djamal. We sat down in his courtyard, and he started to interpret it. Together, we calculated the average amount of seed to be distributed. According to Djamal, each hectare required one kilogram of millet seeds, at 150 CFA francs (about 0.20 euros), or of seed peanuts, at 240 CFA francs (about 0.40 euros). He allocated 10 kilograms of millet and 50 of peanuts per family. When we added up the numbers from the village chiefs, we found there were 1,719 families who would need 4,000 euros worth of millet and 31,000 euros worth of peanuts. 'The FAO will not fund that,' Djamal emphasised. In his experience, their maximum was 600,000 CFA francs (less than 1,000 euros), so we needed to support only 250 families and to concentrate on peanuts instead of millet, which was apparently a less profitable crop. According to him, the people would understand and would share what they were given with the most needy or eligible. Then, he suggested that the people from the villages where I had stayed—Hachaba and the neighbouring village of Guilane—should profit from whatever help I succeeded in getting. The others would most likely accept this: after all, I was 'Hachaba's foreigner'.

But what if no one was willing to help? At this point, the politics of numbers and the significance of the list as a boundary object entered the game. According to Djamal, it was important to create visibility—to communicate the need to the FAO in a way that would enable them to plan ahead: that is, to include the people of Adré in their budget for the *following* year. Those who could not immediately plant their own fields could work elsewhere in the meantime: some people in Adré had more land than they could cultivate themselves. This issue mainly concerned women, who would receive a *koro* (a small bowl, the local unit of measurement) of millet towards feeding their families daily and could supplement this with income from gathering firewood to sell at the market or transporting unfired bricks from the wadi, where they had been made from local clay, to the kilns.[4] (Many houses were being built then, mainly by better-off townspeople.) Men who had left their villages, according to Djamal, preferred to migrate to places like Libya—'in search of money nowhere to be found', as he put it—while their children worked carrying goods for customers at the markets. That way, all could contribute something to support the family. At this point, Djamal was translating the hopes of those who had fought to have their households on the list. By trying to adapt to the aid agencies' procedural requirements, he hoped to influence policies for the next year in the absence of sufficient immediate relief. Better housing and healthcare for children—most people's original requests—would be left out of the application for now. 'But without seeds this year,' he confirmed, 'they won't have seeds next year either.' With most of them making only 1.50 euros a day, they would lose any chance of rebuilding their lives, so the prospect of help in the coming year was already of considerable worth.

With Djamal's calculations, the list was now taking on a new form. It was an aggregate, an interpretation, and an adaptation to the eligibility categories used by aid agencies—with some additions of my own. Providing seed peanuts but no millet seed and reducing the number of people to 250 would cost 5,600,000

CFA francs (about 8,500 euros), but the 600,000 CFA francs (less than 1,000 euros) that Djamal thought could be expected from the FAO would not fully support even one village. Hachaba alone would need 1,000 euros and Guilane (if everybody planted millet and peanuts) 8,000 more. Djamal's calculation also assumed that every family would receive the same quantity of seed, despite differences in family size. Thus, the actual numbers of people on the list and the amount of aid anticipated already differed greatly and according to Djamal's adaptive calculations only a miniscule segment of the population could be provided for. Still, the higher numbers on the 'translated' list that I was to bring to the aid agencies in Abéché were intended to leave them feeling that they were only scratching the surface of actual need and thus serve both as an appeal and an adaptation to the realities of aid. In Boltanski's (2010) pragmatic sociology of critique, this 'adapted appeal' is a way of formulating critique and aimed at changing institutional practice. And to make this appeal, informed actors would have to link the knowledge of both communities of practice, the former villagers and the aid agencies. A small amount of money or aid was still better than nothing at all, according to Djamal. The story of the list continues in Chapter 5, with my experiences at the aid agencies in Abéché and N'Djamena. I will then explain their systems of classification, their regulations, restrictions and their opportunities of providing aid, as well as their reaction to my evidence.

The implications of 'crisis'

Making the list exemplified one aspect of what I call lifeworlds in crisis in the borderlands: seizing opportunities by readjusting and adapting classificatory boundaries. Although crisis might be said to be chronic in a volatile place like the Chad–Sudan borderlands with frequent droughts, and a general neglect from both countries' governments, the main crisis I refer to here is the Darfur War and its aftermath. My analysis follows my own process of coming to understand people's practices and especially how these varied during the crisis. As I have explained, this process had three sequential phases: 'before' the war, when they still lived in their villages and I stayed with them there; 'during' the war, when I tried to learn what future they anticipated, and how they made their decisions and changed their practices in response to it; and 'after' the war, when life nonetheless remained complicated and precarious.

By asking which pre-existing institutions, laws, experiences and morals have most influenced the situation, the temporal element suggests a historical perspective, but it is also interwoven with a spatial element. Where did the people of the borderlands move to? How did they recreate belonging and ownership? Why did some choose to remain near their villages while others chose to move to the camps? This has a bearing on the specific or even individual lessons people from Hachaba (and later Hille Djidíde) drew from the experience of uncertainty. Sandra Calkins (2016) argues that processing uncertainty involves combining what is already known with creative innovation, an argument which closely resembles both Dewey's (1929) ideas on the normality of uncertainty and Boltanski's (2010) later ones in the pragmatic sociology of critique, where a generalised uncertainty is characteristic of reality's fragility.

When the former villagers of Hachaba put together the list, they also expressed their unwillingness to move to areas where international humanitarian aid was available. During my visit in 2007, the people now living in the border town of Adré proposed the list as their last chance for aid. Their knowledge of what was required to be eligible helped us gauge possibilities for challenging the boundaries of the aid agencies' categories and to aim to be included in one that would qualify them for aid in wartime. Having decided to stay near their land in hopes of a better future if they survived the crisis, they also needed to state their specific lack: seeds. The list enabled them to transcend and expose the pettiness of the aid agencies' categories, which they knew limited their access to aid, but also mobilised them to engage proactively in social action. It created a unified language based on collective need and a readiness to transcend the politics underlying the war situation while remaining cognisant of it.

In the following chapters, I will continue to look at categories of difference and of belonging that I saw evolve during the crisis. Differences were not only reinforced within the communities but also constantly undone when the situation called for boundary- and category-crossing practices. I hold that moves and countermoves to define belonging and eligibility by erasing and redrawing boundaries are more pronounced and more frequent in wartime and war zones. Different people in the borderlands responded to the violence by choosing different options. These choices were based in its recent history, as perceived by local people who had lived through decades of war, drought, migration and various phases and methods of internationally organised and orchestrated aid (see de Waal 1988, 1989; Ruiz 1987). The remainder of Part I focuses on people in the borderlands—mainly from Masalit and Arab communities—who had refrained from moving to the internationally managed camps for 'refugees' (which will figure centrally in the second part of the book) and instead decided to remain in the war zone and in the vicinity of their (former) communities, homes and property.

Given the scope for cooperation, contestation and movement, the situation I have described in this chapter should be seen not just as a perpetual state of emergency but as a mode of knowledge about recurrent crises and a way of building on past experiences through collective memory (Argenti and Schramm 2010; Palmberger 2016). I argue that people who do not expect the conflict to be solved in either the short or long term choose to create a life amidst conflict—a lifeworld in crisis—and, understanding the importance of maintaining the spaces and modes of normalcy, make the best of the current circumstances. Vigh's (2008, 2010) paradoxical 'chronicity' of crisis supports this view and along with it highlights the ability to navigate uncertainty. Similarly, Roitman (2014) insists on reflecting on what range of analyses a 'crisis' enables, instead of simply proclaiming one and allowing that concept to guide one's thinking. For the people in the borderlands, this means interpreting their circumstances for themselves in a manner that international aid agencies might eventually take notice of and effectively incorporate into formal policies. Translating their situation into a numerical and tabular form—a list—was the result of a deeper process through which they took their fates into their own hands at a moment when the national regime had seemed conspicuously deaf to their concerns.

3

SO, WE WENT WITH THEM

MAKING SENSE OF CONFLICT AND COMPETITION IN THE VILLAGES

I soon learned that just one question would not elicit a long story from people who had fled in fear of their lives. They answered my questions about their experiences of displacement tersely, sometimes with a single sentence. Ibrahim Bakhit Mahamat, (Daldoum) told me a short story in 2001—about three years after he had arrived on the Chadian side of the border—that was more than many had told me before. It is important to know that his experiences had taken place two years before the war escalated in 2003, and they convey the atmosphere of rising tension and fear. Daldoum's words were short and clear, but they carried a great weight of ambivalence and loss.

> I was the chief of the village of Tabari and the sultan's representative *(firshé)*. Arab fighters had attacked our village in Sudan twice already. They had burnt our houses and taken our livestock. We were left with nothing. My brother had been a rich man, but the Arabs wounded him and took all he had. All he could give me was the money for his funeral. In his former house, you could only find the burnt black ashes of our former stock of grain. After the first attack, most of the villagers had left. That

included our daughter Ashta and her children. But my wife and I, we stayed, along with one other woman. She said, she would do whatever I did, and if it meant staying in the ruined village, she would also stay. I could not leave my grandfather's land. After the second attack, the villagers from Hachaba came. They said: 'If you stay here any longer you will die. The next time the Arabs will kill you.' So, we went with them.

In 2001, the violence that had begun in Darfur during the mid-1990s had diminished somewhat. People from Sudan seemed to be integrating into the Chadian borderland villages with the help of international aid agencies, but no camps had been set up so far. In fact, the situation at that time seemed to be improving so much that the agencies had begun to plan their exit from the region, enabling the newcomers from Sudan to settle more securely in the border villages. When I interviewed Daldoum in October of 2001, I found him among the most knowledgeable villagers. He had reflected on his life experience and concluded that once he left his village it would not be easy to return. His daughter, Ashta Ibrahim, had moved to Hachaba before her parents and took them in. They had other relatives in that village: an uncle, Ibrahim Barra, came from the family that owned most of the land around the village and gave them land on which to build their houses, land to farm, and land in the wadi for a vegetable garden. Daldoum later became the *chef de réfugiés* in Hachaba. Starting in 1998, the UNHCR and World Food Programme (WFP) provided food and other items to people settling in the villages and he became responsible for distributing and accounting for this aid. All that had happened during the two years before I first visited Chad and about five years before war had broken out full scale in Darfur in 2003. 'What caused the violence to erupt?', I asked repeatedly, but no one answered. Daldoum told me only that he had been imprisoned when he was still living in Tabari. He recalled that 'a woman' had 'told lies about him' and that he and six other men were subsequently arrested while leaving the mosque and sent to a prison in El Geneina, the capital of West Darfur. As the only one to resist capture, he had been interrogated, asked where their weapons were hidden and tortured by having cold water poured over him when he insisted that they had none.

Sharif Harir (1994) traces the origins of the conflict that led to the 2003 war within elite political circles in Khartoum and in Darfur's towns and cities. Like others (among them Beck 2004; de Waal 2004; Prunier 2005; Reyna 2010), he understands the war as a consequence of a complicated situation that had emerged in Darfur during the 1980s. International involvement in a Chadian civil war, along with drought, famine and the Chadian and Sudanese governments' arming of communities against South Sudanese rebels, led to a situation that turned out to be impossible for local politicians in Darfur to solve. In 1980, the former Sudanese president Jafaar Nimeiry decided to appoint an ethnic Fur, Ahmad Ibrahim Diraige, as governor. As descendants of the dominant group in the formerly powerful Dar Fur Sultanate, Fur owned most of the region's land. On the national level, however, they had limited representation in political circles and when decisions were made, even about their home region. Harir argues that while this move to give the region more autonomy and honour its communities was desired by many, it ended up being counterproductive. Introducing an ethnic element into local politics did not calm tensions. In fact, it only escalated them, despite the integrity of individual politicians (Harir 1994: 161; see also Behrends 2007, 2015; Marchal 2004: 51; Prunier 2005: 50). The ethnicisation of government positions in Darfur backfired after 1989 with a violent change in the central government in Sudan. With Omar al-Bashir as the new Sudanese leader in 1995—he would hold this position for 30 years until he was removed during the popular uprising in 2019—the central Sudanese government instituted the first reforms to Darfur's 'Native Administration' (Tubiana, Tanner and Abdul-Jalil 2012: 14). Bashir started to turn over positions formerly held by local chiefs and elders to Arab allies of the government, who had not previously held any offices in the area. Ultimately, this move reduced the authority of the leaders in the three largest landowning groups—Zaghawa, Fur and Masalit—and rendered them mere 'tribal chiefs'.[1] Despite this move happening during a phase of relative calm, it allegedly led these communities in Darfur, who felt ignored by the state, to begin to ally against the central government—their common opponent in the late 1990s—and put forward their claims to land ownership and political authority.

The people whom I met in the villages had only been generally aware of rising tensions. They might have known that a resistance front had started to recruit fighters for the first major attack, but they did not know what exactly was causing this aggression. 'We, the people of the villages, are not informed,' Daldoum's wife Hawaye quickly replied when I repeated my question about what had caused the violence. Maybe she wanted to keep Daldoum from saying something that could get him into further trouble. It seemed clear to me that they got their information from different sources. One method, of course, was to interpret what they saw. Thus, Daldoum offered a simple explanation: 'The Arabs want to kill all Masalit.' Lacking information from official statements or further literature, all I learned from Daldoum and others at that point was that a vaguely defined group of 'Arabs' had attacked their villages with Kalashnikov rifles. While such weapons were ubiquitous, it was particularly the area's Masalit population along the Sudanese border to Chad who would have been punished for carrying such weapons or even hiding them in the bush. Daldoum said that because of this threat of punishment, all they had were their so-called *armes blanches* (white weapons): locally made knives and spears that every man carried openly or covertly. In contrast, the rough division between 'Arabs' and 'Masalit' in Chad was at that time less explicit and conflict-laden than across the border in Sudan, at least according to the people who had fled (Behrends and Schlee 2008). In fact, there was an 'Arab' village only 2 kilometres from Hachaba.

When I walked through a small grove of wild acacia trees to this Arab settlement called Tiléha, I could see that it was not only the Masalit communities that had begun to leave their villages in Sudan during the pre-war phase in 2003. In Tiléha, however, recent newcomers from Sudan were not referred to as 'refugees'. It turned out that many had come from the same village as Daldoum and his family, which they called 'Tabari Arab'. How could the 'refugees' in Hachaba live alongside those whom they accused of having burnt their villages only shortly before? And how could the 'Arabs' constantly live with the threat of retaliation for crimes they denied having committed? I will next discuss how belonging is constantly and situationally altered by how people make and unmake differences between 'Arabs' and 'Masalit' in the borderlands.

Telling stories of belonging and difference

The children gathered on a large straw mat, our place to sit after sunset in Ashta Touboudja's house. The mild evening breeze cooled the skin, but the sand was still warm from the day's dry heat. Two-metre-high millet plants towered around the house, ready to be harvested.[2] People told scary stories. One was about the 'millet man', who looked like a millet stalk and wandered the fields silently with a scythe and cut off the heads of those he encountered. This made me uncomfortable, as I detest horror stories, especially at night. However, the children laughed and shrieked in delight as Ashta added sound effects and made such vivid faces that the children looked around to make sure the millet man was not about to attack our cosy gathering. They wanted to hear more! So Ashta told them another story about a man from a Masalit village south of Guilane who used to have very close relations with the Arabs and bought grain from his Masalit neighbours to trade with them. In return, they gave him other goods that—the others added— they had taken from Masalit in Sudan whom they had killed and robbed. Despite warnings from his people to stop, the man had continued his trading until the chief (I was not sure if this was the village's chief or some higher-level chief like the *chef de canton*) finally ordered that the man be killed, as well as another family that also maintained close trade relations with its Arab neighbours. The gruesome details of the story left the listeners aghast, their mouths gaping, interrupting the silence with only an occasional 'ts, ts, ts' and hanging on every word that fell from Ashta's lips, probably because of the realism and topicality of the story.

This story about the situation on the Sudanese side of the border might seem to suggest a violent animosity between the different communities on the Chadian side, but when I asked directly people always denied that it had been their neighbours from Tabari Arab or other nearby Arab settlements who had burnt their village and stolen their possession. Shaking their heads, they would say: 'It wasn't them, even if they hosted the perpetrators. But they were from among their people.' Evidently, there was a difference between stories and how relations were formulated on the ground. I had set out to understand how the different communities dealt with old conflicts on an everyday basis by focusing on their relations with each other and under what terms they lived together during the very tense period before the war. How people referred to different authorities was especially revealing about their past experiences, which served as points of reference in local knowledge and a basis for dealing with war and crisis. Categorising people according to belonging thus also characterised the everyday practice of politics, which influenced not only conflict resolution but also land ownership and access to communal services and support.

During my time in the village, I found as many explanations for conflict as I found modes of resolving it. Asha's grim story about the Masalit villager who traded with the enemy had been chosen to scare the listeners but also contained a typical warning: do not fraternise with 'the others', particularly not in such times as these. And although this was by no means the only story of death that I heard, it was the only one that directly referred to killing people because they maintained relations with 'the others'. In many other cases, confrontational situations like animals destroying crops and quarrelling children or practical suggestions to ease tensions were more in evidence than the attempts to ossify differences in stories like Ashta's. I did, however, hear stories about people who had been attacked, and in many cases killed, on the way to or from the market, during nightly village raids for cattle or camels, or in direct confrontations over access to land and water. Such stories often included accusations that reflected relations of belonging: belonging to a place, as well as possessions like land and livestock. These increased awareness of the possibility of conflict and the general feeling of uncertainty about the present and the future and provoked discussions about how people might make a living under such circumstances.

SO, WE WENT WITH THEM

Everyday uncertainties: Managing conflict as tensions rise

Sandra Calkins (2016) uses the example of the Rashaida of northern Sudan to define uncertainty as an overall mood and disposition in which the usual practices of everyday survival only work partially. If tried and true methods of coping with the help of neighbours, kin, or local administrative institutions cease to function, new 'forms' must be invented, often by combining different past practices or allowing new forms to evolve from them. Calkins draws on Dewey (1929), who argues that while uncertainty underpins every daily experience it is not this uncertainty itself 'which men dislike, but the fact that uncertainty involves us in perils of evil' (1929: 12). Similarly, practical confrontations with uncertainty might mean taking drastic measures (such as the ones people in the borderlands have developed during the crises they have seen come and go throughout their lives). According to Dewey, developing better responses to crises involves learning from previous ones and using all known ways to evade the 'perils of evil' that take a grasp on one's life or one's family.

Many factors increase not only everyday uncertainty but also the need for reciprocity and conviviality. They include natural incidents like failed harvests, which cause severe crises when the prices of staple foods rise and people must find other ways to feed their families. In less severe cases when the bad harvest does not affect everyone to the same extent (for instance, a particular farmer might be more vulnerable due to illness), people look to their neighbours and kin for help. Borrowing and lending staples is a general practice and inviting others to join meals is another common practice in many places and may be among those most widespread. When a meal is organised in public, it is considered obligatory to invite a visitor or even a mere passerby. People in Hachaba certainly had differing levels of success in their harvest depending on factors such as how much help they could call on, how much land they cultivated, whether they had a garden in the fertile wadi, and so on. Halime, a neighbour of my host Ashta whose legs had been paralysed by polio and who moved by dragging herself across the ground with her arms, relied on people's gifts and her teenage sons' wages from working other people's fields. Although she was very poor, she managed to survive and always offered visitors tea with sugar, a bowl of *madide* (a sweet soup made of rice, sugar, ginger and peanuts) or even some vermicelli that she had sent someone to the market to buy. On the other hand, she visited us almost every day, often at mealtimes. One day, as Ashta's daughter Djiti and I sat inside the house eating salad from the wadi garden, we heard a neighbour shout '*Kurnanga!*' outside. This Masalit greeting is normally shouted regardless of whether the neighbour can see you. The usual response is to shout back '*Afi de kurnanga!*' (I am fine!), but this time Djiti only smiled at me and began to chew conspicuously but silently. When the neighbour had gone, she returned to chewing normally. If she had responded, politeness would have meant inviting the neighbour to join us and she did not want to be rude. Here, not responding to the greeting was in order to not have to share and thus be able to have lunch in private. I realised that practices like this also might be used in times of scarcity when even finding enough food to feed the family was uncertain.

Even worse than scarcity due to failed harvests, poverty or physical disabilities were incidents of intentional or unintentional violence and destruction. In 2001, minor conflicts between Arab and Masalit neighbours were frequent in the Hachaba and Tiléha area: cattle destroyed part of a millet field or children stole fruit and vegetables from the wadi gardens when their owners were in the villages. There were also frequent skirmishes at the water wells, especially when several Arab children who were herding goats and sheep all wanted water at the same time. In these situations, the families involved tried to find solutions amongst themselves or asked the village chiefs to help. These conflicts were the order of the day, especially between the Arab and Masalit communities. In order not to have to go to the subprefect in Adré (the official responsible for such cases) every time a cow trampled someone's field, the villagers had developed their own practices and institutions. Cattle seen damaging a field were caught and taken to an enclosure formed by thorny hedges whose French name, *fruiel,* may point to colonial practices for regulating exactly this

SO, WE WENT WITH THEM

kind of tension. Now, I was told, every village has at least one *chef de fruiels* to guard such animals and release them to their owners when they pay for the damage. This payment is split between the owner of the field, the *chef de fruiel*, and other officials from the *chef de village* up to the *chef de canton* and the subprefect. Despite being complicated and involving several levels of administration, this system made problems easier for the Masalit to solve. However, the Arab villagers from neighbouring Tiléha complained that their stray cattle were caught and brought to the *fruiel* for the payments, even if they had not damaged any crops. Thus, even institutions and practices that could resolve conflicts could prove expensive and subject to manipulation for gain.

One case in which individuals situationally referred to different modes of belonging to escalate or de-escalate conflict involved my host Ashta and Goni, a man from Tiléha. One day, I returned after having been out all afternoon and learned that Ashta's guard dog Tout Passe ('all things pass [but life continues]', a common name for animals) had been killed 'by the Arabs of Tiléha'. I learned that this dog had run towards Tiléha—where there was a dog in heat—and a child had screamed; someone had then yelled 'the dog killed my child'. Goni, a young man, had immediately mounted a horse and chased and killed the dog. As we sat outside on our mats in the evening, Ashta again told the story: after she had heard about the dog's death, she immediately walked over to Tiléha to look for the dead child but returned when she saw that no child had died or even been hurt. Goni ran after her, making excuses and claiming that it was not as if the dog was a person and there was no need 'to get excited', but Ashta did not respond. Early the next morning, he came to Hachaba with his older brother, who I thought had come to mediate, and Ashta stayed polite and understanding until they left. I am not sure now if the visit—despite seeming amicable—had also carried a threat of escalation that Ashta, unlike me, was well aware of. Maybe the presence of a stranger also encouraged everyone to behave more peacefully. But Ashta had already acted responsibly the day before by inquiring about the injured child, and a dog's life certainly does not mean very much in Chad.

However, there was another story behind this one. Ashta remembered that soon after their arrival many years before Goni's family had gone to the subprefect in Adré, the region's highest ranking state official. He had granted them (under national law) the land on which they now lived, which had previously belonged to Ashta's father, Touboudja. Ashta recalled that they had not paid any compensation to them then, 'not even the seeds we had used to sow'. But she also remembered that relations between Masalit and Arab neighbours had been much better then: they had given each other gifts of clothes and millet. Later, I heard another story about Goni from Ashta's younger sister Mariam, who also lived in Hachaba. She told me that, some time before, Goni had intentionally taken his cattle to graze in her field. Seeing this, she had bravely told him he would have to kill her if he wanted his cow to get past her. In a fit of rage, Goni had raised his hand, as if to hit her, but his mother had run out to stop him, shouting: 'Don't you know who this is? This is the daughter of Touboudja, the man who gave us his land. She is your mother!' He stopped immediately and apologised. 'I did not know that,' he said, and never again sent his cattle into her field. In retrospect, one might see Goni's killing of the dog and grazing his cattle in the neighbouring village's fields as a desperate demonstration of power. In both instances, he resorted to friendly behaviour when he learned about the status of his opponents. Living together under differing notions of belonging and with variable property rights seems to imply a constant need to navigate between escalation and de-escalation of conflict. While Ashta remained magnanimous about the dog, her sister Mariam firmly resisted Goni's aggression against her crops, which were vital for her family's survival. These events show ways of processing uncertainties and conflict in contested arenas where both escalation and attempts at preserving peaceful relations happen in a matter of seconds.

Friendly behaviour among neighbours, however, could not disguise a deep-seated mutual distrust. Abderahman, an elderly man from Hachaba, once invited Brahim and me to his melon field near the wadi. The melons were ripe and sweet and promised a good income for weeks to come. The field was protected with a fence made from thorny branches, and Abderahman came there every day to maintain it and guard his melons. As we enjoyed one, he told us that each day he would wait until sunset, when the 'Arab kids' passed by with their goats and sheep. When the 'kids' came by on the day of our visit, they stood at the fence laughing and waving. Abderahman slowly stood up and cut up a melon for them to eat on the spot, which they obviously enjoyed. Laws concerning, for instance, protection of property, did not seem to be much of a deterrent, so people like Abderahman felt the need to take matters of security into their own hands. On the other hand, their existence prevented the escalation of daily conflicts. Measures were required to minimise and defend against uncertainties caused by the actions of other people or by their animals: putting up fences, keeping weapons, or participating in community forces like the *groupements de chevaux*, an association of men with horses who pursue thieves to recapture stolen goods, especially cattle. Abdallah was a young man from Hachaba who had previously migrated to Sudan for seasonal work. Asked what he did to stay safe when walking at night, he said that he trusted in his weapons. He had five spears and reported that most of his friends had only four. Immediately after their ritual circumcisions at the age of 12 or 13, young men would start to collect spears and other weapons to defend themselves against thieves and other threats to their security. I also observed that no one walked around without weapons, most often daggers, knives, spears or javelins. Abdallah was also part of the horse association and had recently been in a posse chasing cattle thieves deep into Sudanese territory. If thieves were caught, the outcome depended on the situation: if the posse was big enough, the cattle could be recaptured, but if it was outnumbered, it would have to back off or the young men would risk being killed. And sometimes the thieves would have already sold or slaughtered the cattle; in this case, justice could be sought from the state, or the issue could be solved by mutual agreement: normally, once again, by paying compensation.

LIFEWORLDS IN CRISIS

From crisis to war: Everyday understandings no longer hold

Alongside this local and everyday tension, during my first visits to the Chad–Sudan borderlands I observed an upward trend in general tensions that suggested a broader uncertainty. This was connected to the ethnic definition of Idriss Déby, then the president of Chad, as a Zaghawa, a group who live only a little to the north of the borderlands around Adré. Many served in the police and army or worked for the regional administration, something generally considered pernicious because of their lack of accountability:[3] they were not bound by the usual legal processes or bent them to their own ends. 'The Zaghawa soldiers came into a village and asked the farmers if they had weapons,' Ashta told me one day. If they said no, they were beaten. If they eventually gave in and confessed to stop the beatings, they were penalised and had to pay high fines. Later, the same soldiers sent thieves to steal the farmer's cows. One young man summed up the many reports I had heard about different levels of cruelty: the only category of people who currently enjoyed impunity were Déby's 'Zaghawa relatives'. The recent killing of a road construction worker from southern Chad was a case in point: when they returned home from the construction site, he and his co-workers were threatened by hooded men with guns. The workers had nothing to steal, but one resisted, was shot, and later died in hospital. Were these the infamous *coupeurs de route*, the highway robbers everyone had warned me about? The young man sighed with resignation: 'There's only one group of people who can dare to commit this kind of crime and go unpunished. If you kill him—that is, someone from that group—they'll tell you he was military. If he kills you, they say he was a *coupeur de route*.' Such experiences of one side's legal and cultural impunity led to general uncertainty. In other words, I understood, no one would help you if you experienced injustice.

For members of a specific community to enjoy impunity was no great novelty for people in the borderlands: their recent history is dominated by a pattern of impunity for the ruling group and powerlessness of the rest that leads to enduring and predictable aggressions and submissions. Before Idriss Déby took power in

SO, WE WENT WITH THEM

1990, the Goran of northern Chad had been the dominant ethnic community. The Arab communities in the borderlands had also ruled for a number of years with support from the regimes of Muammar Ghaddafi in Libya and Jaafar Nimeiry in Sudan. Each of these episodes had resulted in repression, unpunished crimes, and increased uncertainty. As I have mentioned, Abdoulaye Hafadine, the first Masalit to have been appointed prefect of the region, had welcomed me on my arrival in Adré and suggested Ashta's home as my research base. (He had met her when her former husband had been stationed in Adré and recommended her because he knew that she had seen many places in the country.) Having set himself the Herculean task of uplifting the region, he was clearly interested in having someone write about this remote and marginal region and its lack of good schools or about possibilities for development. Unfortunately, when I returned after six months he had been transferred after trying to resolve a conflict between a Masalit and a Zaghawa who had claimed his field. This Zaghawa was said to live in Adré, while the field was to the west in Ligné Disang. The man from Adré asked the farmer to leave immediately so that he could use the field himself, but he refused. The next time he saw him, he struck at him with his whip; the farmer then drew his knife and killed him; then took the body to the police station in Adré, turned himself in and was imprisoned. A group of Zaghawa men retaliated by raiding four villages close to Ligné Disang and I was told they did not leave 'even a single tea leaf' behind. Two more Masalit men were killed at first and a third later. The subprefect, *chef de canton* and *firshé* (my host Ashta's former husband Dahab) were still struggling to solve the case, but people said that Hafadine had been sent a thousand kilometres away to a post on the other side of the country. When I saw him twelve years later in N'Djamena, he still held to the belief that young people from the social and geographical margins of the state had no educational opportunities and thus could not take up their region's government.

Daily uncertainties differed significantly across the international border. In Chad, the Zaghawa ability to attack with impunity continued to impose a general sense of insecurity on Masalit, the Arabs and even the better-off Maba and other people in larger towns like Adré and Abéché. Each community coped with this situation differently, but the root cause remained the same. Differential access to state authorities affected relations between the Masalit and the Arab villagers, while the impunity accorded to the president's community resulted in problems that usually involved the most senior officials in the region and often were never 'resolved'. Just across the border in Sudan, meanwhile, these same Zaghawa were among the marginalised peoples of the borderlands: there, government-sponsored Arab supremacy was the main cause of trouble.[4]

When it came to open conflict, the fundamentalist Islamic government of Sudan of President Omar al-Bashir backed Arab communities in Sudan, whom it considered 'real Muslims' despite long-term complaints of marginalisation from Fur intellectuals. Thus, the national regimes on both sides of the border backed certain communities and granted them impunity. In both cases, these were heavily armed even though members of other communities faced severe punishment if they were caught armed. Certainly, the categories of 'armed Sudanese-backed non-landowning Arabs' and 'Chadian-supported Zaghawa who can do whatever they want with impunity' also clearly indicate internal differences within this crude categorisation in terms of the social status individuals enjoyed. Nonetheless, their presence in people's narratives and the fast-spreading rumours stoked fears that affected the reality about them as it was perceived by the borderland population. This underlying knowledge about finding and interpreting signals against the background of war was of immense importance in everyday decisions and exchanges. It was obvious that even mere scraps of information could move people to act in a certain way. And if people in the villages and in Adré had no direct information, they observed the actions of those who were thought to have more. 'If the Zaghawa don't come to the market in the morning, we all wait for two or three hours before going there ourselves,' Brahim told me one day during the height of the war. As Zaghawa from Chad had been fighting alongside their kin in Sudan, they were thought to know about attacks sooner and people observed their actions carefully as indicators.

SO, WE WENT WITH THEM

The different ways in which rising tensions manifested themselves exposed the divergent positions of borderland communities towards the state concerning the mounting crisis. Masalit villagers had the least governmental support on both sides of the border, but cross-border differences between Zaghawa and Arabs were particularly visible in the two bordering countries. While everyone else felt threatened when crossing into Sudan to go to the market, check on the land they left behind, or attend social events, residents of Arab borderland communities like Tiléha moved freely across the border: the young women even made some profit buying goods at the El Geneina market to sell them in Chad. The Sudanese Arab population, while supported by the ruling regime, was also the one who lacked land titles.[5] This goes back to British colonial rule and the way the British perceived Arab populations as 'nomadic'. Killing or displacing whole villages was thus a frequent crime of war in Sudan. And while there was also violence on the Chadian side, including theft and homicide, the atrocities observed in Sudan, where villages were burnt, women raped, and men, women and children indiscriminately killed, did not happen in Chad on a similar scale. On the Sudanese side, however, violence has escalated up to the point where, according to some reports, chemical weapons were used against civilians.[6]

There had been several warnings about rising tensions throughout the time I spent in the village in 2001, two years before the war began, but people did not yet feel threatened enough to start planning to leave. Still, mounting tensions were palpable and there was open mistrust, particularly between the Arab and Masalit communities along the border. In addition, the arrival of around 10,000 people from Sudan had rendered food supplies unreliable. As in the 1980s, the threat of famine caused by drought and war interfered with ordinary conflict-solving practices. Escalation was in the air. Attacks became more lethal, and people feared losing not only their land and belongings but also their lives. Small skirmishes could spark larger conflicts. An increasing number of young men (and a few women) who sought to cross the border and join the rebels assembling in Sudan further complicated the question of security. Meanwhile, the national military presences along the border surged but no institutions offered adequate security to residents. When my host Ashta's brother-in-law visited from Sudan in late 2001, he explained that he had harvested a lot of tomatoes in his wadi garden but taking them to the best market, in El Geneina, had become too risky. Once, he and his neighbours could travel there with more than 20 loaded donkeys, but now 'there [were] too many *coupeurs de route*' who would steal their goods, their money and their donkeys. Instead, they went to smaller markets nearby, even though that meant more trips, lower prices and fewer customers. These broader effects of insecurity affected entire communities. Thus, while young Arab women from Tiléha 'did not encounter obstacles in going to El Geneina', most Masalit refrained from going there. This established new linkages or even new spatial and economic practices.[7]

Individual adaptations: Prospering through the crisis

Even though most people acted similarly in this situation, some individuals were able to maintain a greater scope of mobility and cross-border movement. One such case is Younous. During my first stay in Hachaba, I had already heard about his 'fantastic' orchard in the wadi, where he grew not only the usual vegetables but also fruit, spices and trees. As he had chosen a site further from the village than most others, he had been able to claim a large piece of land. He used a motorised pump to irrigate it from a large well that other people from the village used for bathing and as a place to relax in the early afternoon heat. I first saw the orchard when Younous asked me if a particular plant was coffee: he had bought the seeds from a man in El Geneina but had never seen coffee growing before. The colourful plant, which had yellow flowers and strange parallel leaves, did not seem like coffee to me either, but the orchard was by far the most impressive planting I had seen anywhere in the borderlands. Younous told me that he had crossed the border with people from Tabari and particularly mentioned Daldoum, the former *firshé* and current *chef de réfugiés* in Hachaba. He told me that he had been born nearby, had moved to Sudan as a young man, because he 'liked it better there', and had returned

SO, WE WENT WITH THEM

to Chad in 1990 when 'Idriss' (Déby) came to power and brought in what he considered a more peaceful era. Back in Hachaba, he found a second wife, but when the 'troubles with the Arabs' began, he was still mainly living in a village across the border. He recalled that, before he came to Chad, 'Arabs gathered in a place before they came into our villages on horseback, equipped with guns'. He fled when they set the village on fire and he saw many running away being killed, even children and old people. 'Those who were not fast enough were killed.' He was only repeating something I had already heard from many others: 'They came to take away our land.' In 2001, his first wife was still in Sudan, and he intended to build a third house, closer to the orchard in the wadi by the border and thus between the two villages.

His two wives made it easier for Younous to maintain a presence on both sides of the border because they gave him more than one place to take refuge. He took advantage of my presence to ask for money for fuel and spare parts for his water pump, thus investing in his equipment and future fruit and vegetables for the market. I gave it to him and tried to ease his discomfort about the situation by affirming the reciprocity of this gesture: 'Many villagers have made good use of the water and we ate so much fruit from your orchard.' When it was time to harvest his fruit, he hired people from the villages and paid them by the day. I visited him then and noticed two Arab children filling their water bottles at his well. Younous said that he generally did not let the Arabs draw water from his well to take with them but only to drink as they passed by. However, that time he also gave them two melons to eat. I asked him why I did not see more orchards like his. How had he gotten the idea? He said that he had seen orchards like this in Libya and in other parts of Sudan. And that he was motivated![8] But could motivation preserve him from the destruction of war? I will return to his story below.

Grounded practice: Remembering past crises

The 2003 Darfur War created a situation in which the established modes of subsistence in the borderlands no longer held. Between

1995 and 2003, villages in Chad remained relatively calm despite the increasing violence in Sudan. Although there were signs of rising tensions in 2001, people continued to farm, herd, garden and trade. Meanwhile, only a few kilometres to the east many of their relatives already felt an urgent need to escape the volatile situation across the border. It was only later that I realised that this was why Hafadine, the prefect of Adré, had sent Hassan Brahim to keep me safe during my stay in the village. With the slightly pompous manner of an elder statesman,[9] Hassan was well connected and seemed better informed about borderland events and histories than the villagers. According to my fieldnotes, he told me on our first day in Hachaba that 'the story of the Masalit and the Arabs still has to be written'. He explained that conflicts, which often arose from accusations of 'theft', escalated easily. His frequent tales of people being 'hanged, their bodies slit open, and their intestines eaten by their enemies' gave me the impression that all sides were equally brutal in conflict situations. Even in the still-peaceful situation of 2001, he was convinced that the conflict would 'continue', that 'Arab' troops were gathering north of Adré and that 'Masalit' fighters were assembling to the south.[10] This kind of assessment of the situation mirrored people's perception of the rising tensions in their home region. Should they invest, as Younous had invested in his vegetable and fruit garden? And if so, how would they be able to protect their investments? Or should they remain on guard about how things would develop and be ready to leave at any point in time, as they had repeatedly done in the past?

Faced with deteriorating security, different communities made different decisions. Among the people I met in 2001, the Masalit of Hachaba, Guilane and the surrounding villages—both those who had lived in the village for decades and those who had recently moved there or returned from Sudan—sought safety and protection near the larger and better-protected town of Adré. The Arab families who lived in Tiléha remained in the village, but during the most intense period of the war (roughly from 2004 to 2008) the men relied on their ability to defend their homes while sending their families and cattle to stay with relatives in Sudan where they would be safer.

SO, WE WENT WITH THEM

By late 2003, the UNHCR had opened refugee camps about 50 kilometres to the west of the border, but people from Hachaba or Tiléha refused to go there, most likely based on their experiences during the drought and war of the early 1980s, when many had moved to Sudan. The normal practice in times of drought had been to move temporarily but maintain a small base of cultivated land to return to. However, in 1984 a proxy war in the borderlands between the governments of Chad, Libya and Sudan and various rebel factions, particularly on the Chadian side (Burr and Collins 1999), prevented this. As Alex de Waal (1988) mentions, two factors caused famine in the aftermath of these movements. First, the war prevented Chadians who had moved into the UNHCR camps from returning to their land and thus from preparing for their return by 'preserving a productive base for the post-famine years' (1988: 130). Second, aid agencies misinterpreted the situation as people 'fleeing the drought' rather than 'fleeing the war'. Thus, they underestimated how long they would be trapped in the camps and provided insufficient supplies, causing a famine while people who had not moved to the camps were no longer suffering from hunger (1988: 131). De Waal notes that during a previous food crisis in 1973 about 200,000 people briefly moved from Chad to Sudan to escape drought and then returned to their land. 'But in 1985, because they were war refugees, they stayed. And it was the fact that they had stayed, and that even more had come, that created the second crisis' (ibid.: 132). In other words, while drought and hunger had originally caused people to flee, war had forced them to extend their stay, along with those who had followed them into the camps. Drought refugees had unexpectedly become war refugees, making the famine worse.

Not being able to return—or rather not wanting to (Ruiz 1987)—also impacted village hierarchies in Hachaba during the time I spent there. As I would learn, leaving also meant relinquishing or at least significantly weakening certain rights—such as to land or public office—even when someone could still theoretically claim them. I learned this through a situation that was slightly unpleasant for all parties concerned. In 2001, after attempting to interview Hachaba's *chef de village* several times, I finally sat down with him in his yard, where he had agreed to let me record the interview and allowed me to install my equipment. Hassan Brahim, the 'protector' I had been assigned by the prefect, was there to translate. Everything had been set up, but we first had to wait for the *chef* to eat. After he had finished, he remained silent for a long time; then mumbled something to Hassan, who glanced at me uncomfortably and said, 'he refuses': he did not want to talk about his position. Although confused, I still thanked him and we quickly packed up and left his house. When we got back, Ashta told us the backstory. When the old *chef de village* had left the village and moved to Sudan in 1984, he had temporarily transferred the position to another man 'until his return'. But he did not return. After many years, the son of the chief who had left for Sudan came to Hachaba and demanded to be made the *chef de village*, as the position is hereditary. Meanwhile, the son-in-law of the man who had taken his place also expected to become the chief. This matter went all the way to the *chef de canton*, who appointed the village's imam as the acting *chef*, even though he was unwilling. Although the former chief's son claimed to be supported by more people, this matter was disputed. His father had left the village under duress and new demands had emerged in his absence. The man who had refused to talk to me was the imam, who occupied a temporary position. Most likely, he did not want to jeopardise his relationship with whoever finally took office by talking to a stranger, especially one who wanted to record his words and might let anyone listen to them later.

I then talked to Ali, the former chief's son, who had travelled to Libya and to other places in Sudan and who had returned to Hachaba during the recent attacks on Masalit villages. He traced his right to the position back to his father and grandfather, who had both served in more than one village at a time. He also wanted to end the current system of tax collection, which he considered 'corrupt', and 'return to the old system of collecting millet for tax' that his father had practised. He regretted that so many people had left the village during the 1980s and remembered the villages being much larger in his childhood. The former *chef de village*, I learned, owned a lot of land that had been (temporarily) taken over by other people for use, but would have to be returned to him upon his return to the village. Ownership claims seemed to be honoured when people remembered who owned which land, but ownership and belonging did not only depend on who could justify their claims and prove their property rights: they were also granted on a first-come-first-served basis that has been called 'firstcomer/latecomer' logic (see Kopytoff 1987; Lentz 2000, 2003, 2006, 2013). The Arab groups, unlike the former *chef's* son, with his 'legitimate' claims, were 'latecomers' in all respects. Their land never had belonged to them: it had always been transferred to them only intermittently for subsistence purposes, either by the Masalit villagers or (as with Goni the dog-killer) by the state administration in Adré. And although the Arab settlers' intermittent land titles had now been in place for 50 or 60 years, the different ways in which they had taken possession of land significantly affected how people reacted after war broke out in Chad.

Surviving in a 'war zone'

In many ways, the decision to remain near Hachaba and only move to the nearest larger town was a reaction to having experienced the famine in the UNHCR's camps in 1984 that de Waal (1988) analysed. Even once the Darfur War had started to massively affect the Chadian borderlands in 2004, the people of Hachaba still refused to move to the camps and preferred to suffer in the makeshift shelters of Hille Djidíde on the outskirts of Adré. By that time, Janjaweed militia had begun to cross the international border regularly, entering Chadian villages at dawn and threatening to kill the people and destroy their villages when they returned. And when the villagers moved to town, they were hit hard by the need to pay cash for food and water instead of exchanging millet for them, as was typical in villages. Thus, they had to work at menial jobs—as carriers in the markets, brick-makers, or agricultural workers for townspeople—rather than as subsistence farmers to support themselves.

Daldoum, once the *firshé* of Tabari in Sudan and later the *chef de réfugiés* of Hachaba, had stubbornly remained on his forefathers' land in his village in 1995. Now, he did not want to leave or relinquish the land that the villagers of Hachaba had given to him. He and his wife remained there, and when I saw them in 2007, during the war, I barely recognised the active, thoughtful and friendly man with whom I had stayed up late talking and drinking sweetened milk by the fire in 2001. Now, Daldoum was bone-thin, and his clothes were dirty rags. His daughter, another Ashta, had moved to Adré but regularly walked back to Hachaba to bring her parents food and farm the land around their house—just what she had been doing in their Sudanese village, Tabari, when we first met in 2001. Preserving a productive base in order to eventually return, as Alex de Waal has called it, was the villagers' first choice, even if that disqualified them from receiving aid from any of the more than 100 agencies present in Abéché and around the refugee camps during the years of the crisis. While no one in Hachaba told me explicitly that the reason they had not moved to the camps was the 1984 aid-induced famine that de Waal describes, I suspect their knowledge of it was one reason for this decision.

During the war years, the Arab population of Tiléha made different decisions. None of them moved to Adré. And none of the men left the village: instead, they moved their cattle further from the border and sent their wives and children to stay with relatives in Sudan. 'The war in Darfur does not affect us in any way,' Hamdan Aboubakar, the local leader of the Mahariye, an Arab family in Tiléha, explained to me. But although they felt safe from the Janjaweed, they faced other menaces: 'All this started two years ago,' he whispered, 'when thieves colluded with the Chadian government's forces to take our cattle and shoot at us.' Then, they had no more meat. 'Now we can't leave the village. The Sudanese rebels hide along the 2-kilometre circle, and they shoot at us whenever we go further than that.' They could not get to any markets other than those in Adré and El Geneina, or get further south than Guilane. 'But we're Chadians. We're not part of this war, and we want to live in peace!' Hamdan was very upset. He continued that an 80-year-old Arab man had been beaten up two months earlier and badly hurt. He had been invited to take part in a peace dialogue with a group of Masalit, but the 'Toroboro', as the

SO, WE WENT WITH THEM

Sudanese rebels were generally called in an allusion to Al Qaida's mountain hideout called Tora Bora in Afghanistan, had blocked the road to the meeting point and killed three respected elders. Their relations with the Masalit were not actually bad, Hamdan insisted: it was the Chadian army and the Sudanese rebels—who at the time were allied against the Chadian rebels against the government in N'Djamena—on whom he blamed their calamities. 'Right now, we have no one to fight for our rights,' he lamented. Again, I felt helpless, with nothing to offer him except for photographs of our former encounters.

Joining the rebel groups and finding weapons were among the easiest things to do in wartime. While they did not pay their fighters salaries, they equipped them with guns or cars that they stole from the army bases they attacked. 'If you need a weapon, where do you look?' I asked a driver I met in Abéché. 'Everywhere,' he answered. 'You only have to ask an acquaintance: give him money and he'll bring you the gun.' The people of Hachaba considered the Arabs of Tiléha Janjaweed, the infamous 'devils on horseback' whom the Sudanese government supported against the landowning Fur, Masalit and Zaghawa in Darfur, and blamed them for chasing them away from their land. 'Even Sheikh Hamdan of Tiléha?' I asked the people in Hachaba, thinking of the sad-looking man I had talked to the other day. 'Even him,' they answered. 'No, not him,' insisted Djiti, who seemed to know more than others, 'but the Awlad Zed.[11] They are the real Janjaweed.'

Observing crisis as an outsider

The truth, as should have become evident, lies in the eyes of the beholder, and I will certainly refrain from making it a category to judge from outside or, even worse, from above. The narratives and the attempts to create evidence described in this part of the book (like the opening story of the list) all indicate how perceptions of reality are constructed in relation to particular incentives—like eligibility—and, of course, the people involved in producing the evidence. It became clear to me that the Arab communities on both sides of the international border, like those living in Tiléha or

Tabari Arab, did not have the same access to state agencies as my Masalit hosts in the village, but also that they reacted differently to offers of aid as well as to my presence.

I always remained an outsider, despite living for months in Hachaba and regularly visiting Tiléha. People slept, ate, socialised, danced and worked, and I shared their lives. But the ways in which all these activities transpired or were orchestrated were new to me. Farm work was gruelling in that arid climate, especially when the thermometer rose as high as 50°C. To get water, you had to dig as much as 2 metres into the sand of the wadi with a calabash made from half a dried gourd. (Calabashes were also used to cook *esh*, a staple food whose shape gave it its French name, 'la boule'—the ball.) The water was cloudy but safe to drink as it had been filtered by the sand when the wells refilled at night. Girls and women would typically carry it up to 2 kilometres, in open containers on their heads or else on the back of donkeys. I thought that I might eventually learn to do some of these tasks, but others seemed out of the question. I could brush my teeth with sticks from the 'toothbrush tree' or eat with my hands without difficulty. I could shower using a bucket under the starry sky with only the privacy of a thin screen of millet stems. I could share a house with so-called stinking mice and a variety of large insects and sleep on the floor. But my teeth could not chew the meat like those of the other women and girls. My eyes did not see as far as theirs, though by European standards my eyesight was perfect then. At night, a border guard might suddenly appear right in front of me although Brahim had already seen him from afar. Nor could my ears hear a far-off car moving over the sand, or the hoofs of an approaching horse, or people chatting in the next yard. Much to everyone's amusement, I simply could not ride a donkey and fell off as soon as the animal started to move.

But I had already begun to learn some things. At first, I found it hard to tell 'Arab' and 'Masalit' people apart, but the local criteria for differentiation became more obvious to me. I learned which kinds of grass to avoid walking through after spending hours removing burrs from my trousers and socks. I developed an appreciation for certain new foods and sometimes tried what was put before me even though I did not enjoy its taste (though sometimes I could not bring myself to eat, as when, for example, I was assured that a heap of grilled locusts was a delicacy). But I never experienced the kind of hunger that people around me knew only too well. Although I sometimes went to bed on an empty stomach because there had not been enough food to feed everyone that particular day, I still was not forced to starve[12] and could afford chicken, fish or millet when so many others around me could not. I also had a large bag full of medicine: antiseptics for wounds, antibiotics in case of prolonged problems. But what created the greatest gulf was simply that I could leave if conditions became intolerable and fly back to a safe place in Germany. And although my experience of village life was as privileged as it could be, living in Hachaba was one of the strangest experiences of my whole life.

Only a few have returned: Internal competition and social differentiation after crisis

One would think that the village's land would have become safe to return to in the years after 2008, as the rebellion receded, its leaders fled, were killed, or, alternately, were co-opted into the government, and the regimes in Chad and Sudan became new allies in a peace agreement that established a mixed force of Chadian and Sudanese soldiers with rotating leadership. But the residents of the new town of Hille Djidíde did not return. Some worked their fields in the village, but most preferred to organise their lives in this new, more urban neighbourhood. Some young people found new occupations driving horse-drawn carts or motorbike taxis and some continued to work making and laying bricks, as they had done at the height of the war when farming was too dangerous.

'The war has destroyed everything that people had built up before,' Djamal explained. 'Before the war, people invested in their fields and their gardens, everyone went to the markets.' But during the war, 'bandits put down roots, had helpers everywhere and took everything away. Even people who never did things like that became thieves.' It was only after the Chad–Sudan peace agreement when the *troupes mixtes* (joint forces) arrived that the theft and harassment slowed down a little. Some of the bandits were arrested and the prospect of a good harvest brought hope that the situation would stabilise. 'People are rebuilding their lives, piece by piece. Some have bought a horse or cart or have improved their houses. In small things you can feel that we are progressing again so maybe the region can regenerate.'

Djamal, the wise elder who had helped me calculate how many seeds the villagers would need based on the list, was a thoughtful observer of the borderland situation. His account of the former villagers' situation sounded like a process of class formation. I realised that living in town was key to eventually leading a better life in a village. The latter seemed to many to be a last resort because it meant hard physical work that rarely yielded enough to save anything beyond what was required to invest in the next season. Physical health and a strong neighbourly exchange network were essential to survival in 'village mode'. As my host Ashta Touboudja's brother-in-law once told me, living in a village was like always having to decide between losing 'an arm or a leg'—both are equally essential and you can't afford to lose either. However, Djamal also observed that by 2010 many people from Hille Djidíde had returned to their villages to sow and work on the fields. But they were not alone: former camp residents, mainly from the UNHCR camp in Farchana, were also settling in villages and farming fields that the villagers no longer worked. Their crops did not only supply their own families and the local markets: much of what they produced was also transported across the border and sold to herding communities on the Sudanese side where according to Djamal millet had 'become scarce'. Although the prefect had banned its export, people were trading it across the border at night because, as Djiti had observed, 'they simply do not have enough farmers in Darfur anymore' (ibid.).

As I have tried to show, people found different ways to return to their pre-war lives when the war was over. After my host Ashta died, her sister Mariam returned to the village with her husband and all her children. They moved into Ashta's former compound and took over all her fields to cultivate and make a living as farmers. Although Ashta's daughters complained, their aunt only returned a few fields to her nieces and kept the rest to develop for larger-scale commercial farming rather than subsistence. Thus, she resumed the life she had led before the war. She struck me as among the most serious about her investment in farming. Many former villagers preferred life in town and after cultivating a small field for a while returned to brick-making and other odd jobs to make money in town. Daldoum's daughter Ashta Ibrahim, who had been among the *réfugiées* in Hachaba and later came to Hille Djidíde with the rest of the villagers, came to visit after she 'had looked everywhere for us'. (We had gone to her house in the morning but had not seen her as she was working in the field.) She looked emaciated. Her son lived with her and took care of her and his younger sister, and her older daughter had married a farmer from near Adré. But the harvest had been bad this year and there was only enough millet for her own family, at least for now. She said she would go and get a chicken to cook for me, but I told her to stay with us and eat the chicken with her children instead. Brahim, who knew how poor she was, said later that she would probably not eat it: she only ate chicken 'once or twice a year' and felt that she might as well 'not eat it at all'. Although it was hard for me to understand this logic, I suppose that it meant not wanting to feel that one had to forgo something unaffordable but preferring to not eat it at all in case of beginning to desire it. When Zenaba offered us lunch, Ashta first rejected it. 'She will eat it in the end,' Brahim explained. He was right, and eventually she ate the soup and salad too—but only very slowly.

Ashta Ibrahim told us that even after the war many people worked the fields in the villages but continued to live in Hille Djidíde. The situation was 'far from safe' and there were still raids, thefts and other problems. With some women from Hille Djidíde, she had formed a farming collective, a so-called *groupement*,[13] and applied for financial support from a larger FAO initiative called PADL (Programme d'Appui au Développement Local/Local Development Support Programme), an EU fund for agricultural development. I was surprised to hear that she had not applied with the other women from Hachaba, but she explained that they were considered 'autochthones' and she was a 'former refugee'. The reappearance of this differentiation between the very early 'refugees' from before 2000 and the villagers that had been neglected during the war surprised me. There were also tensions within these groupings. She explained that she could not apply for funding with Mahamat Ismael, who had asked me to help prepare the list, although he had been very active with the aid agencies before the villagers' displacement. After all the trouble they had taken to compile the list together four years earlier, when they had never mentioned any differences among the 'people of Hille Djidíde', this surprised me. I would have thought that displacement and settlement in Hille Djidíde would have wiped out some of these finely tuned differentiations, but they obviously had not.

Some people had also managed to protect their investments throughout the years of war and afterwards. For example, Younous had been able to hold on to the 'Libyan-style' orchard that I had admired throughout the years of turbulence. I had often wondered what had happened to him since I first heard about the devastating attacks and killings in Darfur. As his orchard was located on the war's front lines, I had been almost certain that it would not have survived. To my great surprise, I learned in 2010 that Younous had not only maintained his orchard but that it had never even been attacked! While I never saw him after the war, people said that he had known the *chefs de bandits*, ridden to see them early in the crisis, and struck some kind of deal that gave them something in return for sparing the orchard. This seemed to have worked. The others considered him smart because he knew how to protect his own, a notion with which I would agree: during the war, people had to find ways of protecting what was theirs even if it meant risking siding with dubious figures. Younous had built high walls around the orchard, with locked gates. He also built watchtowers and paid three guards to watch it even at night. Djiti told me that unlike before, when everyone could enter the orchard, get water and share some of the fruit, it was now impossible to enter without knowing someone who worked there. In 2010, Younous was selling most of the fruit—mainly bananas, guavas, papayas and lemons—to a hotel in Adjikong, between the border and El

SO, WE WENT WITH THEM

Geneina (the capital of West Darfur) where they made them into 'tropical fruit juice'. He sold the rest in El Geneina, 'but not in Adré', Djiti added. Perhaps the deal he had been forced to make to survive had also made him *persona non grata* in Adré, and that was why I never saw him again. Unlike Younous, who could pay for security with the money he made from his orchard, most others, like Ashta Ibrahim or Djiti, had been forced to leave their land and their belongings during the war.

In 2011, I also visited the Arab settlement of Tiléha. 'They have seized our land to farm,' Djiti explained to me, agitated: she was alluding to Hachaba and the Masalit farmland. But when I entered Tiléha, this seemed not to be the case. The farms were no larger and they did not span the low hills between Tiléha and Hachaba. What I did notice were the flowers and clean yards outside the houses in Tiléha. A new well had been dug in the middle of the village, making life a lot easier than it had been during my first stay, when the girls had to take their donkeys deep into the wadi to fetch water for their families. I also saw new brick buildings, a small mosque, several storage buildings and some new brick structures in the compounds. The village now even had a shop (also built of bricks instead of wood and straw) where the villagers could buy soap, cigarettes, Coca-Cola and sweets, things that they had to go to Adré or El Geneina for before the war. The women who had left during the war had long ago returned to the village. 'I only left for three months and then returned,' Zargha insisted vehemently, 'and the other women did the same!' But Hamdan also recalled that the times had not been easy. 'We don't want trouble with our neighbours, but three years ago they stole all our cattle, and we also couldn't farm for security reasons.' And while some of the people I spoke with in Tiléha complained about stolen cattle, their neighbours in Hachaba—particularly the old father of Ashta Ibrahim, Daldoum—accused their Arab neighbours of threatening them during the war and claimed that when they traced the footsteps of those who threatened and ambushed them, they always led to Tiléha. As we returned from the villages, we met an old man who had loaded his carriage with something that he hid under a blanket. My travelling companions from Hille Djidíde explained that he was 'a Maba' from Adré, and that he had 'dressed like an Arab to smuggle millet into Sudan'.[14] Apparently, men who disguised themselves as Arabs—obviously another survival tool—also rode to the market with Arab women to avoid being attacked. Meanwhile, these Arab women benefited from having chaperones to accompany them to the markets in Sudan. Along with the lack of evidence that Arabs had seized Masalit fields or were now grazing their animals on Masalit land, as I had heard before going to Tiléha, this convinced me that the customary practice of saying one thing (Djiti grumbling about Arabs taking Masalit land) and doing another (continuing to collaborate in practical matters) had returned after the war. 'We don't let our animals graze on the Masalit's fields,' Mariam from Tiléha asserted as if to counter Djiti's claim against them. 'We don't even have many animals left at the moment.'

With the anxiety that had characterised the lives of the people of the borderlands during the war in decline, it seemed that former differentiations had returned. When people fled, they had momentarily come together as a large group that could be represented by a single list that appealed to aid agencies. Now, the town dwellers of Hille Djidíde could once again be identified as those who had left Chad and were returning from Sudan after a long period of absence, in contrast to those who had remained on the Chadian side. Aid agencies also returned to defining them as 'refugees'. I understood that individuals do not fit into one neat category, even if it is sometimes appropriate for them to demonstrate such unity. In everyday situations of contact, they establish and practise various modes of belonging that affect decisions about their place of residence, housing and use of land. Younous' orchard is a case in point. While most people in his village had to leave their houses and fields in fear of being killed and their property stolen or destroyed, his individual efforts secured his investment, and his property was not seized or raided despite its great value. Younous needed to reorganise his orchard and invest in both social ties and physical defences, but as a result his business had not even suffered during the war years after 2004. My feeling was that he had been able to act in this way because he was the only one who had undertaken this kind of investment when setting up the orchard and therefore was ready to fight for it and take measures not available to the other villagers. This probably meant money to bribe those from whom he needed protection, but also access to information and networks of support. This shows that uncertainties were not always resolved in the same way. For one thing, the spaces in which people lived offered different opportunities and limitations. While the Arab villagers took advantage of opportunities available to them—like sending the women and children to stay with relatives on the Sudanese side of the borderlands and continuing to trade across the border—they lacked the option of leaving the village temporarily for the more secure garrison town of Adré. Leaving the village would have jeopardised their land holdings since they held no official land title, only the usage rights they had been granted by the Masalit landowners. In contrast, the landowning villagers of Hachaba could take the risk of leaving some of their land and going to Adré: in any case, it would have been too risky to work their fields as the war progressed and the attacks grew more frequent. With no alternative means of making a living and unable to trade with Sudan, they went to Adré to earn money.

During my stay in the borderlands, certain structural constraints became palpable over time. Since I had lived in the village before the war, my visit during the war, and continuing contacts and visits after the fighting had ceased, allowed me to observe more subtle developments and modes of belonging and differentiations, but also how certain modalities of differentiation ceased to be important at different times. The most obvious differentiation, I believe, emerged during decisions about where to find security. Most clearly, the villagers of Tiléha and Hachaba differed. Differentiations along ethnic ascriptions such as 'the Masalit', 'the Maba' or 'the Arabs' long predated my arrival, but I discovered that these categorisations, although deployed as useful ascriptions for explaining social relations, did not mirror how people generally viewed themselves. In his analysis of the British strategy of indirect rule that ascribed ethnic belonging to people, Mahmood Mamdani (2014) argues that such ascriptions were used both to grant land titles to those considered 'natives' of the land and to deny these same people the right to vote or partake in political decision-making at the regional and national levels, unlike those the colonisers considered 'citizens'. This system of 'define and rule', as Mamdani calls it (ibid.), entailed administering ascriptions of difference under colonial rule. Land ownership came to represent the largest entitlement that the rural population could claim. But while land was given to those who supposedly had lived on it 'traditionally', Arab families who at that time still practised transhumant pastoralism received no land. Nowadays—but based on the colonial system—the Arab communities claim to be entitled to land as citizens. Unable to play the native card, they resort to the other and potentially more powerful category of citizen, which has been a much more circumscribed and valued category, at least during colonial times.[15] Thus, the people of Tiléha, considered 'Arabs', have been able to frequently cross the border between Chad and Sudan during and after the war with some degree of safety. But they also suffered from war-induced uncertainties, as I showed before. Because they did not officially own the land on which they lived and farmed, they would certainly have lost the land if they had left their village entirely during the war. In contrast to this, the Masalit villagers' 'customary' ownership of their land had been institutionalised under colonialism and they thus found it safer to flee to the town because they retained the option of returning to their village and their land at a later point in time. While these colonial patterns were certainly being replayed in the current situation, the connection was not explicitly invoked, revisited or actively discussed during my stay there and colonialism had not entered discourses on war and belonging. The next chapter will look at another mode of defining belonging and difference: that of kinship and class.

4

IN GENERAL, THEY ARE COMFORTABLE

OPPORTUNITY AND THREAT IN A BETTER-OFF TOWN

The war did not harm everyone in the same way. Long-time residents of Adré experienced it very differently from villagers who had only recently moved there, but they still endured other kinds of hardships and increasing levels of uncertainty. Of all the incidents around an attack on Adré in 2006, the one my friend Khassim's wife Zenaba remembered most vividly was that when her daughter had run for safety, she had kept her shoes but thrown away her bookbag! Zenaba had been working in the hospital and suddenly heard shots, alerting her that the rebels were attacking. Toyota pickups raced through the streets and people fired guns and shouted. Despite her fear, she left the hospital once the trucks had passed and rushed to the school, following the route the six-year-old girl would take home. Meanwhile, an older boy had taken Latifa by the hand and led her out to the street. There, she started to run. She dropped her bookbag and took off her sandals so that she could run faster. Her mother saw her running, carrying the sandals, and took her home, crying with relief. Zenaba could not stop laughing while she was telling me the story. 'Only the shoes, she wouldn't let go of her shoes!', she said, looking at her daughter affectionately and laughing uproariously. The moment-to-moment decision-making and glimpses of the mundane during an emergency are what fascinates and moves me in this story.

Zenaba and I talked about these things only a couple of months later, sitting in the courtyard of her three-room house near the centre of Adré. In 2007, at the height of the war and when everybody felt the tension, the market had moved from its original location on the outskirts to a cramped and dusty site downtown, where there was no shade from trees or fresh breeze from the lake. The mayor wanted people to return to the lakefront site, but Zenaba predicted that the market would remain in the new location: 'Otherwise, how will we get transportation fast enough to carry our things away when we hear that the town is under attack?'[1] In those days, I saw rebel fighters sitting in the back of pickup trucks, many of them only 12 to 15 years old. They looked drunk or high and shouted at people in the street, who looked down or ignored them as the trucks whizzed past and kicked up dust in their faces.

During my visit to Adré in 2007, the situation was dire. When the car stopped in front of Zenaba's house to drop me off, she came out, laughed and hugged me, and then started to cry bitterly. She pointed into her house, and it took me a few moments to realise what I saw: her husband Khassim, one of my closest and dearest friends throughout and beyond my research, lay under a light sheet on a mat in the courtyard surrounded by several women and men who were fanning him. As visitors entered, each sat down and joined in. Khassim barely recognised me, and Zenaba explained that he had a high fever and had developed diabetes-related inflammation. He would die from that disease six years later, despite his wife donating a kidney for transplant surgery in Khartoum.

Khassim's illness lasted two more weeks after I left, so Zenaba could not go to her job at the hospital run by Médecins Sans Frontières. Otherwise, life mostly returned to normal after this attack, only one of several that took place in Adré during the Darfur War. Latifa returned to school and Zenaba continued to work as a midwife. Between moments of terror, their lives seemed relatively unaffected. However, Khassim lived mostly with his first wife, four hours away in Abéché, and only visited Zenaba in Adré on occasional weekends, so she and her children were mostly at home alone. Relatives and neighbours lived all around them, but when they heard gunfire, they still crouched behind the mud-brick courtyard wall as the rebels roamed the city, their trucks loaded with heavy ammunition and Kalashnikovs.[2]

Zenaba and Khassim identified as 'Maba', one of several groups whose ancestors had moved to Adré from other parts of the country. (The others were the 'Haussa', 'Kanembu' or 'Goran'.) They experienced the war differently from villagers who had fled (like the Masalit farmers in Hille Djidíde) or stayed (like the Arab families of Tiléha). However, all these people had known each other since before the war because the villagers had regularly visited relatives in Adré and come to the market.

In this chapter, I look at how this local elite group survived times of crisis by maintaining its status and the perquisites that accompanied it: better housing, higher education, opportunities to marry higher-status individuals, and better-paid business opportunities. I only later understood why they told me so often about how their forefathers moved to Adré, and I came to see these stories as the production of belonging through categorising descent and linked to their maintenance of a certain distance from people living in the surrounding villages. Kinship seemed to play a significant role. By silencing the complexity of their multiple belonging, the inhabitants of Zenaba and Khassim's Adré neighbourhood defined belonging mainly through kinship (both matrilineal and patrilineal) and emphasised a single ancestor whose sons had founded the quarter after arriving in the borderlands with the colonial officials. In part because of their higher social status, this apparently neutral community was less affected by the conflicts around them.

The quarters of Adré: (Un)doing difference by changing placenames

The town of Adré is located on the Chadian side of the Wadi Asoungha, which marks the border between Chad and Sudan in that part of the borderlands. It is located on what was once the main pilgrimage route to Mecca and is today the main road from the Chadian capital N'Djamena to the westernmost city of Sudan, El Geneina. It is unique in the borderlands because a small lake nearby retains some water throughout the dry season. The original French border post when the border between Chad and Sudan was drawn in 1924 (Khayar 1984: 62) was a little further north, but they moved its garrison closer to the lake and founded the town of Adré when they realised there was good water there even in times of drought. Although they never completed a functioning water system (as the German development agency would much later in Abéché), the town had prospered. During the Darfur War, Adré grew even more, absorbing the adjacent villages one by one.

Categories of difference and belonging exist at various levels. According to Brahim (who, although younger, was Khassim's classificatory 'uncle'), the people in town called themselves *nas al-madina*. Literally, this just means 'city people', but he explained that the use of the term suggests that they are 'more open, fairly rich—not all, of course, but in general they are comfortable'. These city people somewhat condescendingly call the residents of the nearby villages *nas al-barra* or *nas al-khoura*, those 'outside'. 'When we go to the villages and call everyone together to inform them about something: for instance, a new policy in development aid,' Brahim added, 'we don't say *nas al-barra*, but rather *nas al-hille*.' *Hille*, meaning a settlement or town, expresses greater respect for the villagers than calling them 'outsiders'.

Adré consists of many *quartiers* (neighbourhoods), of which two were part of the original town plan. Maba from Abéché mainly settled in Quartier Zombo, where Zenaba lived, while Hille Borno ('Borno Town') was mainly inhabited by people from what is now the Nigerian state of Borno, to the west of Chad. As I noted above, Adré was established as a French colonial garrison town to control movement across the border: especially trade, but also pilgrimages and other personal travel. A few kilometres to the south of the original townsite was an Arab settlement called Amkharouba, where the French army's grooms had lived. When Brahim told me about the town's quarters in early 2017, he insisted that the people of Amkharouba were not, as they claimed, 'Arabs' but rather 'Maba and Borno who had arrived with the French and were hired to guard the French officers' horses. They wanted to be identified as Arab but were not real Arabs.' However, he did not know why. Later—and long after colonial rule—this Arab identity became more and more recognised, as other Arabs, refugees from Sudan, settled with them during the Darfur War and Amkharouba became an Arab neighbourhood within Adré. Such (re)formulations of ethnically defined belonging have occurred in different forms throughout the later history of Adré and its quarters. 'The quarters each have their pride,' Brahim told me. 'For instance, during festivals or when high-ranking officials visit the town, each quarter is represented by a banner and a highly respected person speaks for the quarter's population'. Similarly, the names of the quarters have changed: at first, most were named after the previous home of the first settlers or (like Quartier Zombo) were named after their founders. Their current names, however, refer to their locations or other noteworthy characteristics. For example, Quartier Zombo has been renamed Quartier Souhour (Flower Quarter). 'Why did they rename it?', I asked Brahim. 'Because the people who were moving to the quarter were no longer all descendants of Zombo, and the people of the quarter wanted to improve the image of the quarter by having the name refer to something beautiful,' he answered.

But the quarters of Adré also still reflect the town's history. In the years following its foundation around 1925, newly established quarters housed traders or employees of the colonial administration, as well as pilgrims who settled there on the way to and from Mecca. Hille Borno, settled by people from Borno State in Nigeria, was later renamed Quartier Hayachati (Lakeside Quarter). Quartier Claire's name refers to the bright light in the quarter, but it was originally called Quartier Kanembu because its people came from the western Kanem region near Lake Chad. Better-off Masalit and also some Maba families settled in Shig al-Fakhara (Division of the Ascetic), which was known for its *marabout* (Sufi teacher): each quarter had one, but when this one arrived in town, he had chosen an area outside the jurisdiction of the others. Maharadjan, another mainly Masalit quarter, is named after Independence Plaza, the town's main square, but previously was simply called Quartier Masalit. The people of Baguirmi and also some Maba live in Koukaiye, which is named after a landmark tree, while Quartier BET is named after the initials of the far northern regions of Biltine, Ennedi and Tibesti from which its Zaghawa and Goran inhabitants originate. These two quarters have kept their original names. Hille Fog (Hill Town) is also named after its location. During the drought of 1984, many people fled to Adré from rural areas on both sides of the border. According to Brahim, people with leprosy—who were considered outcasts and expected to stay away from other townspeople—had previously occupied the site of Hille Fog. During the drought, 'the government decided to chase them away. And so, one day nomads came on their horses and pointed their rifles towards them. That is when they ran to the other side of the border and moved to the village of Adikong.'

As a colonial and later Chadian garrison town, Adré has always attracted people who moved there for work or seeking a safer haven for themselves and their families. The newest quarters of Adré reflect this continuing process. Hille Djidíde is one of these. It is located on the town's southern fringes, where the Masalit villagers I had lived with earlier had relocated because of the much-increased insecurity during the war. Another is the Quartier Amdjarras, where well-to-do relatives of the Chadian president Idriss Déby have built brick houses. These newcomers, who named their neighbourhood after the president's hometown, moved here because of their positions within the army or national administration. Together with the newcomers from the villages, they represent the most recent signs of such mobility and forms of creating place (Glick Schiller and Çağlar 2018).

War and insecurity are not the only reasons people move into town, though. Some members of better-off communities in Adré benefited from the war due to the job opportunities at international aid agencies and NGOs or by starting a business serving the agencies' staff. Many members of Brahim, Khassim and Zenaba's families left Adré to look for work or professional opportunities in the new city-scale refugee camps like Farchana and Hadjer Hadid. For example, Brahim's sister Fatime worked at UNHCR's Farchana office and her children started businesses trading with the employees and security forces. Brahim himself was hired by an NGO subcontractor of UNHCR, while Zenaba, a licensed midwife, recently returned to Adré with her six children after some years working in the central Chadian town of Mongo.

This chapter looks at the dynamics of foregrounding and backgrounding aspects of difference between people, focusing on Adré's Quartier Zombo (now Quartier Souhour), in order to show that categories not only created a strong feeling of belonging but also raised tensions and encouraged attempts to cross social boundaries: for instance, within class hierarchies or between Muslim religious denominations. However, the privileged position of living in town, with access to employment and salaries and the possibility for bettering one's material conditions even during times of high uncertainty, did not protect people from threats other than war. As the latter part of this chapter will show, such threats and uncertainties were precisely the consequence of this more privileged status and demanded specific ways of processing uncertainty.

The Maba of Adré: Defining difference and belonging through kinship, class and religion

At the beginning of my research as we travelled to Adré in Khassim's chauffeured four-by-four, he informed me that despite the town's location in what was called 'Dar Masalit' it had never actually belonged to the Masalit. The people whom I first met there and discuss in this chapter—Zenaba, my interpreter Brahim, and Djamal, the state agricultural development official and the eldest of his family in Adré after the death of the *marabout* Mahamat Ali Abdalhak Senoussi[3]—are all members of the larger Maba group. The Maba also call themselves *Ouaddaïens* (Wadaians) and trace their ancestors to the Sultanate of Wadai.

In contrast to the Masalit, whose sultanate mostly ended up on the Sudanese side of the colonial border, and the Arab family groups, who travelled widely with their herds in both directions, Maba families originated to the west of the border region or in Abéché.

Their relations do not extend far to the east, let alone across the border, but rather in the direction of the capital of N'Djamena, where Khassim and other influential family members had built houses for their families. When fighting started in the borderlands, no displaced relatives knocked on their doors seeking refuge. They made their living as salaried bankers, doctors, administrators, nurses, teachers and judges or as *marabouts* supported by their congregations. Their relative wealth seemed unaffected by the war: no one was attacking them to seize their land or cattle and the Janjaweed did not dare to come into town and burn their houses. Within the borderlands, the Darfur War has mainly been seen as a conflict between 'Masalit' and 'Arab' groups, so 'Maba' and others in Adré were not directly involved in and felt less affected by the attacks and fighting.

Quartier Zombo and the Barka family

The people of Adré and Abéché held ancestral kinship in very high esteem. (This contrasted with people in the villages, who often could not trace their ancestors back more than two generations.) In fact, many marriages were endogamous: both spouses were direct descendants of a common ancestor. I learned early on that people of the same origin had their own quarter in Adré when Brahim pointed out that the Maba quarter where he grew up was named after one of his ancestors, Zombo. At this point, he did not mention the heterogeneity of the quarter, but proudly stated that 'here, everyone is related'. The more educated urbanites I met in Adré highly esteemed marriages with close relatives, but if I had done research among Maba in the villages, I might have discovered a shallower form of ancestry, like that of the Masalit in Hashaba and other villages I had visited. This distinction in class hierarchies between village and town was confirmed by Abu Souleyman, a Masalit elder from a well-to-do family in Adré whom everyone called 'Seid Reis' or 'Monsieur le Président' because of his military service under the former president Hissein Habré. He was introduced to me as someone who knew about Masalit history. 'I was the first Masalit who moved to central Adré in 1959,' he told me. He had heard about my work in the villages, how I had been asking people 'about their history and where they came from'. 'In the villages, the people know nothing,' he remarked somewhat dismissively, 'they can't tell you even three to four generations back'. He described most villagers as of 'slave descent', a:

> mix of Masalit and the people the Maba had taken as slaves. The runaway slaves always went east. The Masalit found them in the bush and took them home. Then they prepared *la boule* [millet balls], went to the imam and introduced the slave as their brother. The imam ate *la boule* and then gave the former slave a Masalit name. The only thing left is the language, everything else is mixed.

This easy access to belonging, in his opinion, obviously did not correspond to the much stricter rules of kin relations practised in town. Even without being able to trace common ancestors, someone could become 'a brother' in the villages merely by providing the imam with a modest meal. The old man's contempt was palpable: he clearly did not approve of my apparent preference for inquiring among the villagers instead of relative aristocrats like him. Thus, he emphasised how the ability to trace one's descent to a great ancestor indicated high status. Khassim, Zenaba and Brahim's families could provide me with such information, while those in Hachaba could not. According to his account, this was because they were descended not from nobles but 'from the slaves'.

Whether or not Souleyman was right, the 'Masalit' I knew did not consider it so important to marry within their families or care much about knowing and tracing their ancestry beyond their grandparents. The 'Maba' in Adré, on the other hand, prided themselves on being related to everyone else in the quarter, where especially the women repeated the complicated chains of relationships—usually both maternal and paternal—to each other. What I call the Barka family (in their accounts it is Barka rather than his son Zombo who is the common ancestor) is so complex that it took me a long time to understand its intertwined lineages.[4] Khassim narrated that his great-great-grandfather Barka Yakhoub Mahamat came from the village Kourgnon Mallan, near Kodoï in the Biltine region north of Abéché. A *grand marabout,* he relocated to Abéché to advise the sultan, and when the French passed through in the mid-1920s on their way to establish Adré, he sent two of his sons, Senoussi and Zombo, with them to become interpreters. These two sons were the origin of the entire Maba family network in Adré. As Barka had established the line of the Maba living in Quartier Zombo, everyone sought to trace their connection to this famous and respected man and a direct line to Senoussi or Zombo, whether male or female, was usually most important.

The Maba settled in what would become the centre of town, opposite the mosque. Senoussi became a *grand marabout* like his father and prayed with the people, delivered judgements, and was sought out for advice. Over the years, the family relations confused me. For instance, Khassim originally referred to Djamal as his uncle and then said that, strictly speaking, Djamal was his classificatory grandfather despite being only eight years older. Meanwhile, the much younger Brahim, whom he had recommended to me as an interpreter, described himself as Khassim's uncle. Recounting the lines of descent is a matter of pride—but also a way to avoid complicated tensions.

Maba kin relations are constructed and maintained through various techniques that seek to keep them 'clean'. These highlight more direct connections to the favoured ancestor, affirming belonging, but also downplay or simply omit ties to less favoured ancestors, diminishing differences. The account I will present next describes how I gathered that knowledge and what I made of it. Family histories are confusing and the universal inclusion of individuals' fathers' and grandfathers' names on their own does not clarify matters: at least to untrained ears, the same few names repeat over and over. This mode of categorising the self, the other and the modalities of belonging demonstrates how differences are temporarily foregrounded and backgrounded in discourse and practice and how speakers can bend belonging in various directions according to what they want to highlight.

Khassim, for instance, could trace his position in the Barka family on both sides of his family. But while his father was only connected to Barka indirectly,[5] his mother, Tassa, had a very direct link: Barka's eldest son Senoussi was the father of Azzia, his mother's mother. Meanwhile, Khassim's 'uncle' Djamal is Barka's direct great-grandson: his father, Ahmat, was Senoussi's youngest son. So while Barka (via his mother's line) was only Khassim's great-great-grandfather, he was Djamal's great-grandfather, even though the two men were roughly the same age. This was possible because Khassim's grandmother Azzia was born when Senoussi was still a young man, and Djamal's father Ahmat was born when he was 70 and, as Djamal put it, 'could barely walk'.

The ancestry of the residents of the Quartier Zombo actually included a rather large number of people from 'outside' the direct line to Barka. For instance, Djamal's mother was, notably, of Zaghawa origin and thus not part of his father Ahmat's preferred kin group. He explained that this was not merely a love match: marriages between members of different groups could establish or reinforce relationships, particularly among influential families. Djamal was one of this couple's younger sons and had remained in Adré while his elder brothers moved to N'Djamena where they became bankers or worked for international organisations and continued the family line. As Djamal traced his ancestry to Barka through the same line as Khassim's grandmother Azzia, he was his classificatory grandfather. And because Khassim's paternal line to Barka's cousin (another Ahmat) contained even more generations, he traced his relationship to Djamal along his more direct maternal line to the founder of the clan.

Just as categorisations of belonging can be situationally foregrounded or backgrounded, kin can be traced along many routes and marriages with 'outside' spouses situationally highlighted or silenced in each generation.

Khassim's success story: Belonging and differentiation within the family group

Such connections between people along kin and ethnic lines can bring about alliances or reconciliation but, as Abdul-Jalil (1984), Barth (1969), Flint and deWaal (2005) and Kapteijns (1985) argue, they can also lead to future division and conflict. Family relations reinforce positions within the community in good times but can also lead to separation when times are bad. Especially for richer and influential people in Abéché and Adré, descent also implied internal differentiations based on historical circumstances in each town and within the Maba community.

Khassim presented himself as a self-made man. He had eventually become a successful contractor and built dams, storages, garages, wells and school buildings for many international development organisations but had to struggle to get there. That story of struggle is also one about internal differentiation and a successful attempt to move beyond the confines of ethnicity and family. During one of our later meetings, he told me that he had been his mother's only son. After her husband left her for another woman, she had struggled to feed him and his two younger sisters and as a young man, he had stayed at home to help support the family. In the late 1970s, once his sisters were old enough to take care of themselves, an uncle who had studied in Russia and lived in France paid for him to go to Algeria to study construction engineering. However, the uncle only gave him enough for his travel and he arrived with two pairs of trousers and four shirts that had to last him the next the four years. He also had to feed himself, so he mostly ate French toast made from stale bread. He laughed, telling me how he was nostalgic about the food of his student days: he never let his wives Zenaba and Suleikha throw out stale bread and, in rare moments when he had time to relax with them, liked to show them how he could soak it in beaten egg and fry it in a pan. During the summer breaks, some of the students had illegally crossed the Mediterranean by boat to work on tomato farms in Italy. He recalled sleeping outdoors in the fields and enduring sun, rain and poor treatment, but the money he earned there helped him complete his studies and to start his construction business back in Abéché.

Khassim's remarkable career as one of the first people in the area to become rich by making contacts with international development and humanitarian aid organisations began with construction contracts for projects that were administered by a German named Peter. Khassim met him after returning to Abéché where they built a relationship of friendship and trust and Peter (who later died of heart failure in Abéché) supported Khassim by giving him contracts for a number of years. An emotional man, Khassim wept when he remembered this friend, one of the first employees at the Abéché office of the German development agency GTZ (Gesellschaft für Technische Zusammenarbeit or Corporation for Technical Cooperation; now Gesellschaft für Internationale Zusammenarbeit (GIZ) or Corporation for International Cooperation).[6] He credited Peter with permanently changing his own life and the lives of his extended family members. Every subsequent GIZ representative in Abéché has worked with his business, which is now run by his son. Khassim applied to every request for tender and his company (which he named after his mother Tassa) was very often awarded the contract, demonstrating to many other aid agencies, like the World Food Programme (WFP), UNHCR, and UNICEF, that he was a capable contractor. Khassim was reliable, friendly and very hospitable. He would invite strangers into his house, arrange plush cushions and carpets for them, let them rest and serve them what seemed to me like the best food in town. I am not only telling his story in detail to memorialise him but also because it displays another way of dealing with uncertainties day to day that is particularly useful to those for whom education has opened a wider range of possibilities. It is also a survival skill that Khassim has passed on to his extended family.

Khassim's reliance on international supporters was definitely risky. Aid was always considered a temporary measure and the uncertainty of how long international agencies would stay must have been a constant concern for his new business. On the other hand, he knew very well that he could not count on state-owned Chadian companies for contracts as his family lacked close relations with either the president or the local authorities connected with the sultanate. In the event, taking his chances with international projects paid off very well. The stature he later gained inside his extended family was based on his perseverance, which had allowed him to complete his studies, and on his openness to strangers, which had gained him the trusted support of international aid managers. The fact that he could personally cross categories—a family man who supported two households, a liberal Muslim, and a welcoming and generous host and reliable business partner, but also a stern or even harsh patriarch—had to do with his knowledge and expertise in construction work, his familiarity with international agencies, and the finesse with which he presented himself and his work to a world of sceptical and goal-oriented aid agencies.

Lifeworlds of the better-off townspeople

Being rich where most other people were poor and remaining a respected family member in the face of general jealousy and mistrust was a central challenge in Khassim's life. One solution, as previously mentioned, was lavish generosity. Another was following the religious laws on ownership and sharing. Women played a particular role in this as although men bought most goods, women were their official owners and custodians. Sometimes, however, they kept this secret. Khassim laughed when he told me about his cattle. He said that when his grandfather died, he left him a heifer that he had entrusted to a friend some time before.[7] However, Khassim was not informed of this even though it would have served him well during his difficult student years in Algeria—by then, the heifer had reproduced and he could have sold the calves—and when he returned to Chad and asked his old aunt in Adré to help support his young family. Instead, she neither gave him anything nor mentioned the cattle that she knew he owned. It was only when he had become wealthy through his contracts with Peter that she told him about the cattle. By then, the herd had grown to about 50 head, including bulls that were each worth 250,000 CFA francs (400 euros). Khassim reacted like a true businessman and immediately sold ten bulls and used the money to buy more cows, but almost all of these died in an epidemic a few years later. When he told me the story, he still had about 20 head of cattle, but he continued to keep them a secret. Even close relatives did not know about them.

With little trust in the banking system, people protect their wealth through various kinds of investments. The most favoured are parcels of land, which (at least in the towns and cities) are enclosed to mark ownership once they are purchased and registered. This strategy explains the large expanses of empty walled lots that I saw outside Abéché and Adré. These walls are built before any other structures. Both men and women bought land, and women also invested in (or were given) gold, which they put in jugs and buried in secret places under the dirt floors of their houses. Brahim told me that they would get up in the middle of the night, dig a hole, and clandestinely bury their gold. This gold is bought from well-known, trusted traders, who keep it out of view inside their private houses. Khassim explained the various underlying principles for preventing jealousy or open envy because of differences in wealth: 'Men aren't allowed to own gold,' he told me, 'only women. And each year, you have to show your gold and weigh it, and if it exceeds a certain measure, we split it among the family so as to not own more than they do.' He told me this last thing when he visited me in Germany with Brahim: we went to a large electronics store where Brahim surprised me by buying an electric iron and Khassim an electronic scale for weighing gold.

Khassim was also generous towards the larger community in which he lived. I interpreted this generosity in several ways. First, I saw it as an essential part of his character and religious convictions to give and help others. But this generosity may have had practical dimensions to it—it created relations of reciprocity, as I learned one day when I arrived at Abéché airport without the right documents. At the time, hundreds of international aid workers were flying in and out of Abéché daily and I had failed to observe the stricter rules for travel. When I landed, a security officer held me in the transfer area and threatened to send me back to N'Djamena on the next flight. I called Khassim for help, and he asked to have a word with the officer. When I handed the latter the phone, his cold hostility turned to first surprise and then mild friendliness and he said: 'He told me that you are his sister, no matter what the skin colour. He will come here. Rest assured, everything will be fine.' Khassim arrived in his flowing cotton robe, hugged me dramatically, and said simply, 'Let her go now. *Halas*!' And off we went. Later, he said that this officer was one of many people whose school fees he had paid, guaranteeing his thankfulness and support for life.

During my visits to Khassim's houses in Adré and in Abéché, I heard many stories like this, in which unexpectedly needing a favour revealed a mixture of distrust and envy combined with a deep commitment to supporting members of the community inside and outside the family and sharing one's wealth. As everyone was related in one way or another, not all expectations in matters like marriage arrangements or who would get sent to school could be met. Some, like Brahim, had to end their formal education prematurely when their main supporter (in this case, his father) died. On other occasions, one branch of the family's disappointment about a choice of marriage partner led to lifelong mistrust towards family members or to secrecy and dissociation, despite a superficial veneer of community being maintained. Here, categories of difference and belonging again overlapped situationally and in everyday practice as closer and more distant family members met to discuss certain issues: personal support, family relations, marriage, and child fostering but also ownership, business relations and the ways to guarantee a better future in times of increased uncertainty. These practices changed when people outside the community or family group were involved. And although they still followed the pattern of doing and undoing differences according to the situation at hand, a much clearer separation and high degree of caution was needed, especially when dealing with members of the president's coterie.

Negotiating survival in times of crisis

The Maba preference for endogamy, their frequent references to direct descent from 'one family'—in Adré, especially that of Barka—and their geographical concentration in the Quartier Zombo suggest a closed network that kept apart from other residents of Adré and the people in the villages, the *nas al-barra*, alike. However, two of their practices—marrying into other communities and connecting the children to the most important ancestors (like the brothers Zombo and Senoussi) using either the paternal or maternal line and sharing wealth and other help with the wider community—complicated the picture. While the rhetoric of kinship certainly maintained boundaries, the ways of categorising belonging were flexible in everyday encounters and in the practice of kinship and interethnic, interreligious, or international relations.

Often, individuals formed ties with members of other communities during their lifetime and thus gained knowledge about them. For example, Brahim's mother Izze was of 'Maba' origin but due to her father's cattle herding had grown up in an 'Arab' village on the Sudanese side of the border. Therefore, she not only spoke the same dialect of Arabic as most of the Arab groups in the borderlands but also knew many Arab women, particularly in the Arab village of Tiléha, south of Adré. Similarly, Djiti, my Masalit host's daughter in Hashaba, was an occasional guest in Zenaba's house in Adré, and (due to my connection to her and her mother Ashta) received financial help from Khassim after they moved from Hashaba to Adré. And when Brahim started to work for the aid agencies in Farchana, he came to know the mostly Fur residents of the Farchana refugee camp well and could tell me, in detail, who was married to whom, which part of the camp they were staying in and what categories of deservingness or vulnerability they had been placed in by the aid agencies. Still, the war had exacerbated social differences. The Maba of Adré went from being small town elite to profiting from the wartime situation as traders, aid workers, electricians or contractors for aid agencies, like Khassim. The only exception was Djamal: as he worked for the National Office of Rural Development (ONDR), he was part of the national institutional structures although the rest of his family avoided getting involved with the state in favour of international collaborations.

Still, the Maba's relations with the other local groups were characterised by their history as a historically hegemonic group in the area since the time of the Sultanate of Wadai. Already privileged due to their education or religious reputation, the sons of Senoussi had come to Adré alongside the French colonial administrators. Similarly, during the Darfur War and at the height of the crisis, members of the Barka family also left Adré to work for international agencies at various locations. For instance,

Brahim's elder sister Fatime went to Farchana early on to work as an administrator for the UNCHR. With her wages, she and her husband built a large house directly opposite the UN compound. Her relatives sold food to the organisation's international staff and mobile phones at the local market. Brahim himself was hired by one of the agencies to work in the aid sector, rented a house with his wife Sureiya, and acquired material goods including a satellite dish, a television, several mobile phones, a motorbike and furniture. Sureiya learned to sew with the women living in the camp at its educational centre and the couple sent their sons to private schools for their education.

These privileges, which offered opportunities to gain more and suffer less from the war situation, also illuminate the Maba's current relations with other groups and the national government. Even before the war, Khassim told me, the Masalit of the borderlands had expressed resentment towards his Maba family members because they had not supported them against the cronies of the national regime or supported the young Masalit men's rebellious endeavours when the Darfur uprising started. The disappointment was particularly pronounced as they had lived as neighbours with friendly relations for many decades. Instead, Khassim's business opportunities increased through his good relations with the international agencies and their greatly increased presence during the years of war. Even though his company was only one of several such companies that received a share of the aid agencies' lucrative construction contracts, he built many guest houses for the UNHCR and truck depots for the WFP and continued to build dams in the wadis for GIZ. However, Khassim's business was limited to specialised construction: he had no access to the more lucrative contracts available for private buildings and hotels.[8] He thus did not profit directly from the war-related humanitarian situation, which primarily demanded private housing, but primarily from his older connections to the development aid milieu in Abéché. There, he continued to secure good contracts and make more money. However, this exposed him and his extended family to new risks, those of becoming too wealthy and too visible to those who enjoyed impunity. Impunity can be defined as a generalised exemption from punishment due to a generalised position of power, resulting in a threat related to Massumi's (2010) concept of 'affective threats'. In my understanding, these imminent threats are just as intimidating as actually occurring acts, including violence, as they loom constantly and create an 'atmosphere of fear' that is felt with 'tendential infinity' (2010: 61).

On the long drive from Abéché to N'Djamena, Mahamat, a younger relative of Khassim, explained the difficulties in managing a business under threat. A community with close ties to the state's current hegemonic group intimidated everyone whose belongings—or even wives or children—they might come to see as objects of desire. Just outside Abéché, I noticed a large herd of camels and wondered which group of nomads was passing through. With a contemptuous snort, Mahamat dryly remarked: 'No one around here owns camels any more except *the* family. Nomads no longer pass through here. *The* family takes every camel they can find and if you reclaim it, they will kill you.'[9] As a full-grown camel was worth about 550,000 CFA francs (800 euros), the men we passed could have gotten quite rich by guarding a large herd of camels. Mahamat had worked as a mechanic for the UNHCR and had only recently started his own business. But he said that as a businessman he had to be on guard constantly and take precautions diligently. If a member of 'the family' took a car to him for repairs, Mahamat usually suspected he was going to be cheated. He said he had to drive around with the car owner for about two hours first and take note of every sound and every little problem with the car. 'Why do you have to do this?' I wondered. 'Because otherwise he won't leave me in peace until I've repaired his whole car, put in new parts and worked for days and weeks—and then he still won't pay me.'

While the people of the borderlands have learned over time to create belonging and difference by situationally defining belonging according to ethnicity, place, kin or religion, the possibility of undoing differences between categories of people is limited in an atmosphere of the affective and actual threat caused by the impunity granted to some people. Where power meets greed and a certain form of brutality, the only options are tinkering and manoeuvring. Mahamat's stories show that, particularly during the war years, even those who seemingly profited from the ruptures of war had to face threats and risks that were specific to them as better-off city folk. Once again, people maintained categories of difference through interaction, but such categorisations were flexible in situations of both conflict and generosity and allowed space to negotiate survival in times of crisis.

PART II

WARTIME IN THE BORDERLANDS

AID AND EMPLACEMENT AT THE CAMPS

5

CLEARLY, THEY ARE 'INTERNALLY DISPLACED PERSONS'

AID AGENCIES AND THE MAKING OF 'REFUGEES'

Since the Darfur War began in 2003, the UNHCR has instituted elaborate measures to categorise those in eastern Chad seeking the aid and refuge guaranteed by international agreements. The 1951 UN Convention on the Status of Refugees[1] designates people who cross international borders to escape violence or other threats to their lives as 'refugees'. This broad category includes many subcategories, like 'vulnerable persons' 'disadvantaged' due to physical or mental disabilities, old age, lack of family support, and ill health as well as temporary conditions like pregnancy. Meanwhile, aid organisations designate those who seek refuge without crossing an international border as 'internally displaced persons' (IDPs). This category includes similar subcategories but the support available comes from different institutions.

Categories are not just efficient means to describe realities: they actively shift and shape subjectivities (Bowker and Star 1999; Breckenridge 2014; Desrosières 1998; Hacking 1995, 1999; Lakoff 1987; Li 2007; Rottenburg et al. 2015; Star 1999). Through the process of registration, people wittingly or unwittingly internalise such ascriptions (Krause and Schramm 2011, M'charek et al. 2013), which changes their senses of self and belonging and limits or extends the range of actions available to them to access services or even experience reality (Hacking 1999). However, this process also allows for new modes of self-definition that open the space for creative adaptation, particularly in situations of displacement and emplacement. Attributing an internationally meaningful, highly institutionalised and legally based category like 'refugee' to a person changes the rules of the game from various perspectives. In an environment where some people are grouped together as refugees, those excluded from this category are affected as well.[2] Once international aid institutions have intervened in national policies using instruments ranging from contracts to international conventions on human rights, efforts to define 'refugees' become political actions[3] that entail processes to define eligibility and facilitate access, even as some people seek to avoid being categorised this way.

The outbreak of the Darfur War in 2003 attracted many aid agencies that imposed new requirements and definitions on the Chad–Sudan borderlands. To understand the various mutual expectations, experiences, resistances and agreements between them and those who received their aid, I will add my own observations since 2000 to those of others about the aid situation during an earlier crisis in the borderlands in the 1980s, when drought and war by proxy devolved into comprehensive violence and direct war (de Waal 1988; Maxwell 1986; Ruiz 1987). I argue that aid agencies and the population they targeted each generated different kinds of knowledge over time: on the one hand, that collected by aid staff and government employees as well as rebels and military; on the other, that learned from experience by a war-afflicted and war-weary civilian population. All such notions were progressively mobilised to develop different aid practices (Glasman 2017, 2020). Part II of this book thus looks at processes through which different kinds of knowledge, codes and categorisations interacted. While Part I addressed the ways of categorising that manifested as flexible definitions of belonging within and among the people of the borderlands—between villagers and townspeople, between and among 'the Masalit', 'the

CLEARLY, THEY ARE 'INTERNALLY DISPLACED PERSONS'

Arabs' and 'the Maba'—this part addresses another prominent kind of actor: aid organisations ranging from independent non-governmental organisations to multinational agencies like the UNHCR, World Food Programme or UNICEF. The policies and activities of these organisations influence and are influenced by the lives and decision-making processes of the borderlanders.

During my visit to the borderlands in 2007, during the Darfur War, I responded to local requests to intervene as an active mediator and translator of the borderlanders' situation in the context of war, displacement and emergency aid. As I described in Chapter 2, I took part in producing a list, which the villagers ultimately compiled, and which was interpreted as an attempt to be included in international aid measures. This list's journey continued, as did its concomitant themes: sustainable interweaving aid, development and security measures along with governance in a region that has seen very little direct intervention by the civilian state. Categorising, here, was not only about different modes of belonging: it became a fundamental political act that went beyond the local hierarchies within which individuals imagined themselves. It was about access to international agencies, no matter whether this access is desired, achieved, mediated or denied. Access to aid became a factor for understanding how political belonging is forged in the borderlands—from both a historical and a current perspective, and whether carried out consciously or unconsciously.

My understanding of the power asymmetries generated by the structure of aid among its recipients differs from some of McFalls' (2010) findings about the logic of humanitarianism's therapeutic domination (comparable to Agamben's 'structure of exception') more than other studies that focus on how aid imposes categorisations upon the recipients of aid (for instance, Bornstein and Redfield 2011; Fassin and Pandolfi 2010). McFalls describes aid as 'the uncontested and uncontestable radical biopower of our age' (2010: 317). In place of this extreme view that aid agencies single-handedly produce new forms of citizenship or even dictatorship, I argue that an influx of aid agencies, military forces and so on instead provokes various attempts at maintaining lifeworlds. This is especially true during states of emergency, when people constantly and flexibly redefine categories, often through mutual adaptations, and even though these adaptations and their effects may only become evident much later, when experiences from 'within the actual social fields and formations in question' can be accounted for (Bjarnesen and Vigh 2016: 9). A lifeworld perspective, which focuses on the everyday even in situations of severe crisis and uncertainty, refutes the idea that displacement and war result in 'bare life' during states of emergency, large-scale humanitarian aid and military deployment (see also Beckett 2013; Schiocchet 2014).

War's emergencies and traumas are real, but everyday life continues even during the most urgent situations. Managing the extreme uncertainty produced by forced mobility and displacement requires knowing about possible modes of access to necessities like land, housing, food, work or health services. People who have been displaced and their hosts, as well as international agencies and other actors, all rely on this kind of knowledge and its connected practices of categorising who qualifies for what kind of access to the resources needed to survive. International practices of categorising often are not congruent with local practices of identification and (self-)ascription, so that categories derive from situative, local, mutable and negotiatory social processes. Looking at both providing and claiming access to aid brings the political and internationally entangled aspects of categorising to the fore.

Delivering the list

I will now return to the story of the list, as its conclusion sheds light on the ways the information in it became adapted, (partly) accepted, rejected or something else—which I define as 'modes of translation'—by those who encountered it. This story began when I returned to the village in 2007 after six years away. Through the list, the villagers, who had decided to not move to the camps in 2007, had documented their case for international aid; next they considered how my visit to the borderlands might help them get it. As I departed with the list for the aid agencies in Abéché and N'Djamena, it became an object of translation, and I became a mediator. Djamal's calculations of the amounts and qualities of seeds based on the number of affected people and amount of land available for farming had prepared me to communicate their needs and respond to the requirements of aid infrastructure, even though I was a complete newcomer to this field. Once I was in Abéché, then the main point of distribution for aid, I inquired whom to meet with and how to present the evidence I had brought. This form of evidence, as Rottenburg et al. (2015) discuss, is a construct: a representation of reality that directly addresses the framework that analysts seek to reveal. As the temporary representative of the people of Hille Djidíde, my task was to make their numbers speak and enable the list to perform. On my way home, I brought it to Abéché, signifying the third act in the staging of the list. The largest city in eastern Chad, Abéché had since 2003 become the aid hub of the borderlands war zone, and more than a hundred organisations had set up offices there to coordinate interventions.

Abeché: The list translated

Once I arrived in Abéché, I considered where to start my inquiry. Where would the list make an impression? How could it best state the villagers' demands? I did not know many people at the aid agencies, so on the first day I visited various offices to look for contacts who did. I started with two German organisations: Gesellschaft für Internationale Zusammenarbeit (GIZ) and the development bank Kreditanstalt für Wiederaufbau (KfW). There, I recognised some acquaintances from my previous research in Chad, who promised to bring up those whom they called 'internally displaced people (IDPs) in Adré' at a meeting they had with the WFP that afternoon and I realised that in future meetings I would also have to use this term to describe the people who had written the list in Hille Djidíde. I then made a copy of the list for them to bring as evidence. They also pointed out that international organisations might have reservations about our suggestion of placing Djamal in charge of distributing any seeds that might arrive in Adré: 'international agencies generally don't trust Chadian national institutions' like the National Office of Rural Development (ONDR).

Next, I went to the UNICEF office in Abéché and sought out Nanyalta, a graduate of Chad's National School of Sanitary and Social Agents (ENASS) who had grown up in Abéché and N'Djamena with parents of mixed Arab and Hadjerai[4] origin. She had devoted her entire career to 'bringing assistance to populations in crisis situations', was known to everyone, and was appreciated for her dedication to her work in the borderlands despite traversing the sandy ground there with difficulty due to a childhood case of polio. Unfortunately, Nanyalta turned out to be in N'Djamena for business when I arrived, but her Chadian colleagues were also interested in the 'case of the IDPs from Adré'. One explained that 'these displaced people in remote places like Adré don't have anyone to speak for them' and added that 'nobody was really aware of their situation' because all the rebels and fighting made it difficult to get to Adré safely. These responses were exactly what Djamal had expected when he adapted the list to the requirements and programmes of the aid agencies. At that point, I was happy that the list seemed to be appreciated.

This happiness did not last very long. One of the GIZ employees, Axel, returned from meeting with the WFP and said that the person in charge there 'did not want to even touch the list', as if any physical contact with it would confer not only visibility but also significance and the need to act (Behrends 2020). He suggested talking to the UN's Office for the Coordination of Humanitarian Affairs (OCHA), which had set up a field office to coordinate all the aid activities in the borderlands. He also was the first to break the news that 'no one' could do anything in the border area, 'particularly in Adré', owing to the 'unconditionally strict safety regulations' handed down from the organisations' headquarters. As I listened to him, I grew discouraged. I also got the impression that many of the international organisations—despite their official cooperation—were fierce competitors over programmes and funding, a situation I had seen even before the Darfur War.

By my last day in Abéché, I had given up hope for the list, so when I entered the busy OCHA office I was much surprised when

CLEARLY, THEY ARE 'INTERNALLY DISPLACED PERSONS'

the dynamic head of the US bureau agreed to see me within an hour. Everywhere, people were talking loudly and assertively on the phone, regardless of whether it was just to complain about a broken computer or if they were ordering an emergency measure affecting a hundred thousand people. While waiting for him, I dropped by the UNHCR office, where I had arranged a meeting with its local head, a woman from France.

She turned out to be an impressive personality, radiating energy and vigour, and exuding a no-nonsense attitude when dealing with situations. However, she did not seem interested in the list. Due to the problem of categories, she could not help me: her organisation dealt exclusively with 'refugees' and according to her (and UNHCR's) definitions, the people of Hille Djidíde were 'clearly' 'internally displaced persons'. Therefore, she was unable to help, but she was happy to comment on the overall refugee situation. With an impressive torrent of words and in an insistent voice, she enumerated the themes she considered most important and provided me with some basic facts about the UNHCR-assisted camps, the only camps for displaced people in the borderlands. 'The camps are like cities,' she said: each housed more than 20,000 people. 'We have a refugee population of 230,000 and 170,000 IDPs'. And while the agency was responsible for the security of all these people, the aid workers also felt themselves in great danger and had to provide for their own security in the current war situation.

Reviewing the situation with camp residents and the 'local population' (another of the international agencies' categories), she continued that between November 2006 and March 2007 the refugees had faced an interruption in UNHCR funding during which they had to take the initiative and survived by forming close bonds with nearby villagers. But by the time the FAO resumed aid provision to the camp dwellers, five months without aid and a year of bad harvests had led to severe malnutrition among both the 'host population and the IDPs' who had not received any kind of aid and for whom food was getting ever scarcer. Meanwhile, tensions were rising, and the host population took up arms to protect their farms and food supplies.

This situation taught the agencies several lessons. Clearly, they saw that reducing aid would increase self-reliance—a mindset that I encountered later during my repeated visits to the region after the 2008 signing of the Chad–Sudan peace agreement—but they also learned the importance of coordination between the many aid organisations present at the height of the war. Summarising the situation, she insisted, 'That is why it is now up to the OCHA to define the gaps and fill them, particularly as we have rising numbers of IDPs: 150,000 people since March 2006.' Before I left her office, she surprised me with an offer to fund a short-term study about the demographic dynamics in the area: the history of the 'Arabs', the meaning of land, the possible reactions or expectations towards an international military intervention, the possibilities for reconciliation. 'We know nothing about these histories,' she sighed, 'and I have a hundred thousand dollars I need to spend by the end of the year!' I departed and decided to think about making a proposal.[5]

The UNHCR officer's appeal for more information 'about the people' was echoed in many other conversations I had with aid experts around that time. Most had trouble distinguishing the different groups, sides, factions and alliances. To the local population and to the camp dwellers, the aid organisations were very visible, not only due to their physical presence at frequent meetings, briefings, emergency negotiations, and so on, but in the numerous white four-wheel-drive vehicles parked outside these gatherings. The organisations constantly referred to their proclaimed intentions to appease, reconcile, negotiate or reintegrate and meanwhile also moved or resettled populations. This state-like (or alternate state) attitude was, of course, buoyed by acts like those of the Tama rebel Mahamat Nour, the leader of the Rally for Democracy and Freedom (RDL) movement.[6] A large contingent of rebels passed through Abéché on their way to attack N'Djamena and oust President Idriss Déby in April 2006. (This was the attack where Latifa lost her bookbag.) Bypassing all the Chadian government offices, Nour went directly to the UNHCR office to announce that they were targeting neither the international aid community nor the population of Abéché, only the institutions of 'the Chadian state'.

CLEARLY, THEY ARE 'INTERNALLY DISPLACED PERSONS'

After my interview with the UNHCR director, her young American office manager explained that the organisations working in this 'crisis area' followed what they called a 'cluster approach' that allocated a particular area of work to each agency. UN bodies should together head a total of 11 clusters that they would distribute among them. These bodies—WFP, FAO, UNICEF, WHO, UNDP—would then coordinate their work with the Chadian ministries. All participating organisations would be invited to sector-based meetings. The UNHCR was the only organisation considered 'multi-sectorial' within the confines of the refugee camps, where they were responsible for 'site management, emergencies, and protection'. Until recently, the overall coordination of all aid activities had also been in the hands of the UNHCR, but in 2006 OCHA had taken it over. Since then, all organisations had been required to meet weekly to discuss security. A bit further to the city's north, the office manager recounted that 'no movement [was] possible without a military escort. Since January 2006, 70 cars of aid organisations [had] been stolen, and five in the last month alone, all during the daytime.' And while the Chadian army did not hamper aid operations, it did not help them either. On the contrary, rumours that the government had provided arms for rebels in 2007 had rendered the situation even more volatile, causing tensions to escalate.

The OCHA's field representative in Abéché was a man from the US who raced from one crisis to the next and from one end of the world to the other. He introduced himself to me as a 'long-time expert on questions of aid organisation'. He started our meeting by telling me that he had been charged with opening the OCHA office in Chad for 'capacity building' and would then be transferred to the next place where his expertise was needed. When I offered him the list, he explained that OCHA coordinated all humanitarian activities in eastern Chad but the work along the border was divided. The only international agency historically and officially allowed to work on the 'frontline'—including the area of Adré and Hille Djidíde—was the International Committee of the Red Cross (ICRC). The security situation would 'not allow for any other organisation to move into this area'. During the last five to six weeks, large numbers of Chadian troops had been observed being deployed along the border with Sudan. The strategy had been 'written' based on these reports and any further activities had to be announced at the Tuesday meetings with fixed agendas. 'For instance,' he said, 'we have to deal with the case of the *chef de canton* of the Kado region, who owns most of the land rented by the HCR in Farchana. And the newly arriving aid agencies, like Islamic Relief or the Birmingham Lutheran World Federation, which need to fill gaps in assistance'. As we drank tea, he kept talking for quite a while and I saw that he had done his homework and was conversant with the latest intelligence about the region's complexity: 'the current Sultan of Goz Beida was a big intellectual in the FROLINAT' or 'the president of the Association of Chadian Chiefs studied geography in the Soviet Union'. He also talked about policy changes that he had to implement during his three-month mission to the area—'We have a new approach where we don't give goods and food but money, so that the people can decide themselves what they need and simply buy it'—but felt that we should talk to the ICRC about my concerns and region of interest. Although he briefly looked through 'my' list and, in passing, asked his assistant to make a copy, as far as I know nothing came of it.

N'Djamena: Controlling aid

I ended my journey in 2007 in N'Djamena, a few days after my stay at Abéché. There, I visited OCHA's Chadian headquarters, where I was met by a small group of friendly people. This would be my last attempt to deliver the list and kick-start an intervention in Hille Djidíde. My hosts took notes as I retold the story, asked questions, and said they looked forward to seeing the 'paper or book or whatever' I would write about the situation. They again reassured me that 'no one will be left out of aid' but that they were 'not the ones who can intervene in a situation like the one you describe'. However, after seeing my disappointment when I realised how little chance I had of helping the villagers as their chosen mediator, they invited me to a 'meeting with NGOs'. This meeting was about the new 'cluster approach'—now well established in the aid world but very new at the time—and marked my last point of entry into the aid world during that trip to Chad. It gave me an insight, however small, into the aid world's complexity, competition, negotiations, and the challenges involved in reconciling the different strategies and ethics underlying the organisation of aid: the aid workers' lifeworlds. It also revealed how the aid world had taken on the role of government as a process-oriented, ideological and legally framed intervention project possessing infrastructures and technologies, making its own policies based on its own ideas, and engaging in politics. Autesserre (2009, 2014) has studied how such aid structures, in the person of individual aid workers, actively separate their sites and activities from the intended recipients of their aid. And although this meeting at first seemed to confirm that aid workers construct and maintain solid boundaries between their operations and any national or local involvement, my observations of how international aid and local measures for survival, and the flexibility of belonging, adapt to each other, contradict her analysis. This will be the subject of Part II of this book.

The meeting in N'Djamena brought together the key agencies that were to intervene in the 'Darfur Crisis', as the war has become known in aid circles. It was convened by OCHA and included representatives of the WFP, CARE, the ICRC, Médecins Sans Frontières (MSF) and some smaller organisations. The participants seemed to know each other already, and those who did not were identified primarily in terms of the organisations they worked for. During the meeting, a representative of MSF tellingly looked down while the UN representative of the WFP—the highest-ranking attendee and the chair of the meeting despite having been the only one to arrive late—explained the structure. Aid clusters would lead all aid work and position newly arriving organisations in the 'gaps' where assistance was still needed. Each cluster would be headed by a UN agency active in the Darfur Crisis (the FAO, WFP and HCR) and cover sectors like food, health, education, and the environment. Except for MSF and the ICRC, every organisation had accepted this approach.[7] His PowerPoint presentation on 'humanitarian reform' was addressed to an audience of 14 men and only three women (including me). A slight majority came from outside Africa. Despite the heat, many were dressed in suits or in shirt and tie; others wore the safari-style outfits so common among aid workers—khaki trousers, many-pocketed jackets and sturdy boots—a professional, down-to-earth and practical costume (if also one reminiscent of colonial soldiers) that showed that they were there to tackle a 'serious situation'.

As I listened to the debate, I understood that the aid sector was preoccupied with the problem of *who rules*. The cluster approach had been proposed to manage more than 400 international aid workers in Abéché alone. They were employed by organisations with very different funding sources and ethical standards and responsible for different causes and communities.[8] Direct conflicts of interest among the participating organisations seemed rather rare, not only in particular fields of aid (such as trauma, housing, food security, hygiene, women's rights, children, water, schooling) but even about general approaches. However, there was an overarching problem that lay not with those being regulated but with where the rules were set, and the meeting's participants protested that this necessarily resulted in the centralisation of 'more power'. Whoever decided about the clusters could influence operations within the intervention arena as well as the standing of the participating organisations on a global scale. The representatives therefore demanded that the structures that had been built up over the last three years had to be respected as at least a basis for future operations.

They could already see signs indicating that their interests were neglected: some complained that 'only one head of an international organisation [was] present' (the WFP representative) or that 'the coordinator (UN/OCHA) [could] impose himself!' 'No,' the OCHA representative responded, 'the coordinator only coordinates!' To include organisations that aimed to operate across them, the meeting's participants argued that 'clusters should not become exclusive circles but must remain open to the outside'. In particular, the representatives of Chadian NGOs operating in the borderlands stressed their desire to 'move ahead together, there should be no exclusion'. Others complained that MSF would not join the clusters—'why do they get to have a special place?'

In short, although the cluster approach itself seemed reasonable to the meeting's participants, they remained sceptical about its implementation and acceptance by either the organisations or aid recipients. Particularly from the UN representative, there was talk of a 'spirit of participation' and an affirmation that 'the UN does not impose itself' but would have to justify all moves to the Interagency Committee (IAC).

To my understanding, this struggle was about power and mainly concerned processes of categorising: who would assign the subordinate organisations to categories? By delineating lines of categorising, the leading agencies could also influence financial flows and priorities on a much larger scale than the intervention within a particular situation. What I observed were the local outcomes of a broader encompassing mode of sorting out (Schramm and Beaudevin 2019) in which smaller agencies had to abide by the dictates of larger ones at least grudgingly if they wanted to remain in the aid landscape of eastern Chad.

Looking back at the time since this eventful journey, I never got to observe whether the cluster approach was applied as anticipated during that meeting in N'Djamena. In the years that followed, a failed 2008 coup attempt in Chad[9] that led to the rebellions in both Chad and Sudan successively fading out and a 2010 peace agreement between the two countries' governments both had significant impacts on the aid climate. With neither the urgency of war nor the attention of the international media, more and more organisations seemed to be leaving the area. The UNHCR camps still existed, but clearly, the eastern Chadian aid machinery had to be cut back after 2010. The expanded aid infrastructure, which included air traffic, big new offices and luxury villas for international aid staff, new roads, technical equipment, and internet and mobile phone infrastructure had fewer and fewer users. As the Darfur Crisis faded in Chad, the cluster leaders of UNHCR, WFP, UNICEF and others faced the new problem of finding organisations to take over the diverse tasks of planning, realising, managing, and—not least—finding ways to exit the protracted post-conflict situation. As it turned out, they (re-)turned to the organisations that had been there before the crisis made the headlines and before increased funding had drawn other aid organisations to the region. Secours Catholique du Développement (SECADEV), which had the longest local history in both development and emergency aid, took over the camps and once again became the most prominent subcontractor of UNHCR, still the unquestioned flagship institution of the aid world in the Chad–Sudan borderlands.

As for my mission from Hille Djidíde, I failed to obtain the needed funding for the former borderland villagers, at least officially. The non-intervention clause was legally binding and could not be circumvented so long as the only organisations active in the war zone focused on providing urgently needed medical care and had no means to distribute food or seeds. Two members of the ICRC I spoke with in N'Djamena certainly regarded this policy as most critical: 'At the moment, a lot of money is being dedicated to measures to assist internally displaced people,' one German representative explained to me, mentioning the amount of USD 130 million. 'The French government ordered transport flights, but they came to little more than very effective advertising.' French airplanes could transport no more cargo than the WFP's trucks already did and were more expensive. Moreover, he added,

> there [was] such an enormous amount of aid supplies on the road that [the trucks] had to be specially protected in the middle of the bush with tents and armed guards, to prevent large-scale theft. Because of the legal limitations to provide aid to war zones, much of the food intended for IDPs [was] thus left to rot on the streets.

He sighed: 'As usual, aid causes displacement too. It is the attraction of goods that inclines people to move, when before they had not decided if they should stay or move.' In view of such well-known paradoxes of aid, his colleague maintained that 'most certainly, a lot of decisions made at higher international levels lack knowledge of the situation on the ground'. In a critical study of this very phenomenon of the creation of new displacement and famine through the installation of aid measures, to which I will refer in the next chapter, Alex de Waal (1988, 1989) has examined the 1980s situation in the Chad–Sudan borderlands.

CLEARLY, THEY ARE 'INTERNALLY DISPLACED PERSONS'

But the story of the list still has a happy ending of a kind. Although I failed to find aid even when I returned to Germany—the reasons there ranged from 'funds are allotted for the whole year' to 'no chance to spontaneously alter allocations'[10]—it later turned out that my contact at GIZ had unilaterally decided to use his remaining funds for 2007 for this purpose. He was known for his daring and unorthodox measures and after my departure he loaded a pickup truck with about 250 euros worth of seeds and gardening tools and set off for Adré alone. He gave the supplies to Djamal, who distributed them among the people of Hachaba, just as we had planned during our long deliberations on how to distribute what little we anticipated receiving. Although this was far less than we had hoped for, it was highly appreciated. When I returned in 2010, I was invited to attend a meeting where speeches of praise were showered upon me and the GIZ representative, who was not present but had remained in touch with Djamal. Later, after the 2008 peace agreement that started the peace process in Chad, he also got Hille Djidíde added to GIZ's official list for seed distribution. By that point, international organisations no longer considered the area to be a no-go war zone, and other agencies started to assist. Thus, the former villagers managed to survive by raising crops while living in the town of Adré.

My journey into the aid world provides some insights on how aid is related to processes of categorising, or as Glasman (2017: 18) puts it, how the capacity to control the 'means of classification' made aid as much about the distribution of power and the production of social technologies and forms of establishing structures as about saving lives and furthering development. And this holds for both ends of the aid chain: those providing aid and those intended to receive it. It turns out that 'aid' is interpreted very differently depending on the position of the person encountering it. Both the categories introduced and applied by the aid organisations and the categories of the people living and staying in the borderlands interacted and mixed. During the meeting of aid agencies in 2007, I learned that approaches to aid necessitate certain forms of knowledge about the how, when and where of intervening: knowledge, in effect, that becomes visible and palpable through practices, procedures, and legal regulations that expose the ways categories interfere and interact with those that already existed in areas where the organisations intervene.

The argument that every intervention produces diverse responses is not false, but the question remains of what lines such responses are produced along and which categories they fore- and background. Categorising people as 'refugees', 'displaced people', 'locals', 'the vulnerable', 'Sudanese', 'Chadians', 'Masalit', 'Arabs', 'Europeans', 'Americans'—but also 'men', 'women', 'young', 'old', or 'horse owners', 'farmers' or 'herders'—displays certain ways of understanding the specific environment which agencies also seek to regulate through aid provision (see Bowker and Star 1999; Mosse and Lewis 2005). Individuals and communities observe, study, and interpret other communities—whether international aid agencies, rebels, villagers, herders, farmers, people who had to leave their home environs, hosting communities, the land-owning class and those who live on other people's land, people who claim to belong or not to belong to a particular place—and adapt their self-understandings to them.

6

THOSE ARE THE ONLY REAL REFUGEES

AID AND COMPETITION IN THE CAMPS AND VILLAGES

Very few international agencies were providing aid in the borderlands before the Darfur War began in 2003, even though UNCHR had characterised the situation as an 'emergency' as early as 1997. For about 40 years, eastern Chad had received some limited development aid, mainly oriented towards agriculture and pastoralism. German agencies focused on water and built tanks and subterranean dams in wadis to capture rainwater for gardening, while French ones often organised and constructed transit corridors for cattle and camels to reduce water competition between herding and farming communities. Two global organisations were operating when the crisis started in 1995, the World Food Programme (WFP) and UNHCR, and had been present intermittently since Hissein Habré's regime and the Chadian civil war of the 1980s (Burr and Collins 1999). As de Waal (1988) and others describe, many borderlanders moved from Chad to Sudan during that era to escape drought, famine and war. They retained vivid memories of uncertainty, of the experience of crossing an international border, and of aid distribution and its effects. This chapter looks at the aid situation before the war to shed light on why and how people responded to aid. I argue that these differing reactions were based on their personal memories of the 1980s, but were also related to how foreign development aid immediately before the war had increased competition among villages in the borderlands.

The pre-war humanitarian aid programme was intended to provide blankets, tents, soap, food and basic medical care to Sudanese people who had fled violence and who had settled in Chadian border villages. But even when I first arrived in 2000, it looked as if that integration programme would soon end. Some of the 'refugees' had already begun to make their way back to Darfur, intending to return permanently or temporarily so that they could cultivate their old fields and care for relatives who had remained through the period of uncertainty. Violence seemed to have decreased significantly. Unaware of the impending storm, UNHCR was preparing to enter a development phase to help the many people who did not want to return to their former homes integrate permanently into the villages. This attempt to withdraw after the so-called integration phase later turned out to be extremely important as the response to it partly anticipated the greater unrest and resistance that emerged in the refugee camps after the war escalated in early 2003.

The pre-war era differed from the wartime period in its lack of camps. The various groups of people I saw in the villages all seemed at first glance to live under very similar circumstances; however, on closer examination they varied in occupation, place of origin and residence, ethnic belonging, and family connections. They referred to themselves with categories introduced by the aid agencies: 'refugees', 'first-wave' or 'second-wave' newcomers, 'Sudanese', and so on. Moreover, the pre-war period was hardly peaceful, as it was punctuated by small skirmishes that resulted from and fed back into major conflicts.

This chapter looks at how the borderland population experienced this time and focuses on people's relation to international aid. In 2001, the aid agencies regarded all the people who had already crossed the international border and settled in border villages as 'spontaneously settled refugees'. In the main office of Secours Catholique du Développement (SECADEV), the

Catholic organisation that worked most closely with the UNHCR, I saw hand-drawn maps showing all the villages where people had settled along the border. The UNHCR offered three programmes for this population of about 10,000: repatriation, integration and resettlement. If the conflict ceased, people would be given assistance so they could repatriate. For many, this would not be a simple option: their former homes had changed with regard to the larger political and economic situation and the security situation and there was also the risk of tense relations with former neighbours who might have been adversaries (or worse) before they fled (Allen 1996; Allen and Morsink 1994; Leutloff 1999). If people agreed to return home, the UNHCR would usually provide transport and a basic supply package including food, blankets, soap and a small amount of money. But few people in the borderlands chose this option; the majority remained in Chad.

The second option, 'integration', was offered to those who did not consider it safe to return to their former home and planned to remain in Chad. The option to integrate was characterised by a shift from emergency aid, which provided people with basic foodstuffs and other supplies, to development aid, which was given only under the condition that recipients no longer considered themselves 'refugees'. Those applying for the third option, 'resettlement', needed to prove that neither of the other options fit their situation: that is, that they could neither return to their former homes (due to political persecution, for instance) nor integrate into their new village surroundings because of other risks to their safety. But resettlement (in, for instance, the United States) was intended as a last resort, open only to individuals, never groups, and only available if the other two options were impossible.

Like all UNHCR interventions, this one was divided into five phases and was to be applied both where camps had been installed and in situations of spontaneous settlement in villages. Interventions began immediately after the declaration of a specific emergency in which the aid organisation had decided to intervene. As soon as the first people arrived in a village, camp, or other location asking for aid, the second phase would start. They were registered and then given an initial distribution of staple foods like flour, millet, vegetables and sugar, and supplies like blankets, soap, buckets and building materials. Later, they might also receive items like mosquito nets or kitchen utensils. During the second phase, the aid agencies assigned people to categories, ranging from the neediest with no other resources—to those who were better off due to family support or good physical condition. The so-called 'most vulnerable' included old people, single mothers with young children, pregnant women, and people with visible or invisible disabilities. If a protracted conflict prevented people from returning home, emergency aid would eventually merge into the third phase, development, and to reduce people's dependence on aid the distribution of supplies would gradually cease. I later learned that this was the most difficult phase: aid agencies' evaluations of 'security' or the status of 'integration' seldom overlapped with those of aid recipients. At this point, the refugee status was supposed to slowly be undone, as the refugees were supposed to have found their footing, with their children attending school and the adults working at a job, cultivating a field, or engaged in some form of training. The fourth phase would reduce aid even more, as the specific intervention received less and less money from the central organisation and its staff was significantly cut back. This meant that recipients now had to find their own modes of surviving, whether within or outside of camps. The fifth and final phase was marked by the complete withdrawal or exit of all aid staff and the end of the mission. When I had visited the borderlands before the war started, the mission in operation was nearing the end of the second phase. Looking at the logistics of the five phases, it immediately makes sense that during the first three phases it might be easier (at least from an organisational point of view) to control, count, regulate and take care of people inside a clearly demarcated camp than 'spontaneously settled' people who are living among villagers and thus difficult to categorise. The opposite is true for the fourth and fifth: if people have never moved into camps, the phasing out of a development aid situation is much easier, since they have already started to integrate into existing structures and to find and affirm their places in communities.

Redfield (2010, 2013) describes Médecins Sans Frontières' difficulty in defining the end of a medical emergency and judging the sufficiency of aid before leaving with much insight and detail. He shows that the organisation's claim to only operate in direct emergencies contradicts the fact that they have operated continuously in Uganda for more than 20 years. Here, the boundaries between emergency and development merge and Redfield argues that the organisation's approach clearly differs between the groups active in different countries and definitions vary about when an operation is or should be finished.

'Refugees' inside and outside of camps

Anthropologists have extensively critiqued aid agencies' approaches towards people in situations of forced displacement (Agier 2011, 2016; Harrell-Bond et al. 1988; Zolberg et al. 1989). This discussion, as Stepputat (1994) and Turner (2006) argue, has certainly had an impact on the agencies, which have at least partly adapted their approaches based on academic studies. One main line of argument critiques camps as a form of discipline or biopower that reduces the people living within them to 'bare life' (Agamben 2005) and strips them of their personal characteristics, individual experiences, traumas, future aspirations and agency to make decisions about their lives. In contrast to the spontaneous settlement that characterised the phase before the war in the Chad–Sudan borderlands, the camps there did indeed seek to separate those entitled to protection and aid from the local population outside the camp in general, as well as from the specific people or groups regarded as the main threats to their lives. In practice, however, most of the camps were in populated areas and this separation was never quite achieved. Camp residents interacted with aid agency staff and people living outside the camps daily. This provided new opportunities to supplement the aid offered within the camps, so it is surprising that anthropologists have usually focused exclusively on camps, directed their critique only at the restrictive categorisations of aid programmes in situations of war and flight, and consequently also restricted their accounts of 'refugees' resistance to such categorisations to what happens inside the camps. For example, Malkki (1995), Falge (1999) and Horst and Grabska (2015) highlight how people inside refugee camps negotiate their status with aid agencies and state organisations. Horst and Grabska (2015: 15) recount the desire to reduce ambiguity and create situations of 'calculated probabilities', particularly in uncertain situations. Kurimoto (2001) maintains that camps create the boundaries inside which people try to define their 'identities' by, for instance, negotiating separated spaces for different groups: as underlined by Fischer (2017), she observes a sense of hierarchy and class differentiation during the negotiations of certain Tuareg groups in a Burkina Faso refugee camp who rejected the supplies provided by aid organisations, demanding different materials to furnish their houses in the camps. However, Turner (2006) highlights that aid agencies often define such negotiating with aid programmes—which Berk and Galvan (2009) call 'creative tinkering'—as the 'individual pathologies' of a few and accuse them of harming the majority of refugees, whom the organisations expect to remain 'pure, innocent victims' (Turner 2006: 15).

To these insights, I aim to add a focus on the interaction of aid recipients with people both within and outside the camp setting and the additional impact of these interactions on their possibilities of resisting, countering or finding alternatives to the aid provided and beyond the restrictions on personal options that have been criticised in aid operations. To take a closer look at the persistent relationships and options open to those who did not move into the newly opened refugee camps until after 2003, I start with the period before the camps were installed. I argue that it is impossible to fully compartmentalise the significant interactions in camps located in inhabited areas like the Chad–Sudan borderlands, even when the outside population is not large. The borderland communities' very different reactions to the offer of aid were most striking. They concerned both the UNHCR's and WFP's emergency aid, as well as the offer of development aid that was to start the phasing out of aid by more permanently integrating the Sudanese into the borderland villages of Chad.

THOSE ARE THE ONLY REAL REFUGEES

Reactions to aid: Competition within villages and between agencies

During my stay in 2001, some people in the villages seemed to entirely reject the category of 'refugee', even though they had fled Sudan when the fighting started. However, others eagerly adapted to the aid agencies' requirements and quickly organised *groupements*, associations of farmers who agreed to work a tract of land together and use the surplus to ameliorate conditions in their villages. This dominant form of aid led to very pronounced modes of categorising along gender, place of origin, refugee or host status, and ethnicity on the part of both the agencies and the villagers. It also created fierce competition between newcomers and locals in each village, between different villages, and between different aid organisations.

When the war broke out in 2003, different ways of reacting to aid led to different decisions: some stayed in the villages for as long as they possibly could, while others immediately moved to the new camps nearby. In 2001, I had noticed that while some displaced people welcomed the offer of integration connected to development aid measures, others resisted it and insisted that there was still an emergency. Individuals' reactions depended both on how they had been accepted in their new villages and on how far they had moved from their old ones. Some could still walk across the border to their old homes and thus retained a claim to their land, but others could not and their deprivation was more complete. Those who resisted the end of the emergency vehemently opposed the aid agencies' intentions to foster development and described themselves as 'true refugees' who had neither any chance to return nor any desire to integrate in Chad without further aid. Meanwhile, those who had agreed to integrate proved to be extremely adept at meeting the terms of development aid measures: they even fiercely competed within and among villages about which *groupements* followed the aid agencies' guidance most closely. In addition to these internal differences, I also noticed that the 'Arab' villages along the border to Sudan remained highly independent or even autarkic and were not enthusiastic about any of the aid programmes.

It was not just aid recipients who competed with one another: the aid agencies also competed amongst themselves. This competition mainly took place between SECADEV, the Chadian affiliate of a French-based international network, and the US-based Africare. SECADEV had been active in the region for quite some time and managed UNHCR's programmes there. Their aid workers had travelled to remote villages, where their long-term commitment, willingness to endure harsh living conditions in remote areas, and knowledge of conditions in the borderlands helped them inform people about the advantages of *groupements*. SECADEV assisted people in many villages—both women and men and young and old—in forming *groupements* but, significantly, provided no direct material support. However, around 1998, problems at their head office in N'Djamena (some said a loss of funding; others mismanagement) had almost completely halted their work. Their local assistants had thus been very happy to join the UNHCR emergency programme and they now focused exclusively on villages hosting 'refugees'. To carry out the UNHCR programme for the 'Sudanese refugees', including forming 'refugee groups' and distributing supplies via their chiefs, they had suspended some of their former projects but had also not permanently resigned from their jobs at SECADEV. In 2001, with the emergency phase ending, they were eager to return to their old *groupements* and address the UNHCR's new focus on integration.

Around the time of SECADEV's original emergency intervention, but before UNHCR's integration phase began, Africare had initiated a food security initiative in the same area. This was not exclusively directed at 'refugees' but was a development measure addressed at all people living in the region that took a clearly goal-oriented approach. Like SECADEV, Africare employed Chadians as development assistants, but not ones with the same long-term knowledge of the region or connections to villagers and villages. With much more funding available, Africare began with an evaluation of village histories, population structures and the village's organisational status and selected the villages that they considered most capable of fulfilling their agricultural performance expectations. They notified each village chief of their arrival and asked him to call a meeting at which the Africare assistant then asked how the village was organised and about its problems, aims and possibilities and what *groupements* had previously been formed there. Based on this information, they then selected villages to assist. Importantly, this approach and SECADEV's were both based on *groupements*: the difference was the material resources that Africare provided. If a village managed to produce a surplus by the end of the farming season, the organisation would build a depot or a well, buy farming tools, or fund something else based on the priorities the group had expressed at the beginning of the collaboration, and would continue to sponsor successful *groupements* activities. The catch was that new local groups from other villages could not join the programme as cooperatives once the initial evaluation phase had ended: after that, the only way to enter was for individuals to join existing cooperatives. Not surprisingly, Africare built their activities partly on disappointed *groupements* that SECADEV had set up and later abandoned.

As a result of this situation, the local assistants of SECADEV harboured considerable animosity towards this new 'rich' NGO. When the UNHCR's integration phase started, SECADEV's assistants attempted to rebuild their relationships with the *groupements* they had previously initiated but found that Africare had taken over. While the competition between the agencies had little direct effect on the villagers, competition between the villages for Africare's assistance led to hostility between those it selected and those that had already joined the UNHCR integration programme managed by SECADEV. They regarded Africare as more effective because it offered faster development through material assets like wells, storage facilities called *magasins*, and machinery. The villagers who were excluded complained that the selection of only some villages put the others at a disadvantage.

Africare's administrator in Abéché, a man from Senegal, gave me some basic facts about the organisation's procedures. However, I learned about the competition between organisations mainly from SECADEV's assistants—especially Nanyalta, whom I had already met during my first journey to the borderlands—and the villagers themselves. When I was looking for the 'refugees' along the border, the UNHCR head office in N'Djamena had directed me to SECADEV's representative in Abéché and then their office in Adré. The director and his staff there were more than ready to assist me and accompanied me to different villages, first during the second phase of registering and counting people, later in distributions of food and supplies, and finally in the third phase of forming *groupements* to integrate into villages when the UNHCR was about to move out. There, I met 'their' clients, the 'refugees' who profited from and cooperated in their endeavours, and I learned about how the emergency support and later integration into villages had had unintended consequences. One of these was the competition among the villagers and between villages, and another was the vehement resistance of some 'refugees' to the UNHCR's integration programme.

Ready for development: Competition between villages

It is not surprising that competition results from emergency and development aid, considering the different experiences, varying relations to land and property, and contrasting perspectives on the role of the state prevalent in Masalit and Arab villages in the borderlands. Only Masalit villages with recent arrivals from nearby villages across the border ended up responding to the offers of development aid, because their inhabitants neither had access to governmental resources in Chad and Sudan nor the ability to resist the assaults that the president's people carried out with impunity. Arab villagers rejected the aid agencies' process. They did not compete to join food and supply distribution networks and only half-heartedly formed *groupements* of any kind. Masalit villages competed both internally and with other villages for access to aid and supplies. Every village where there were registered 'refugees' participated in the UNHCR distribution programme during the second, emergency, phase of interventions and many now joined the agency's efforts to integrate the newcomers during the third phase, development aid. This aid was distributed by SECADEV, the agency that had previously started to organise *groupements* in the villages.

In addition, a small number of villages qualified for similar development aid provided by Africare. Hachaba was not included, unlike the slightly larger neighbouring village of Guilane. 'When Africare built the four community granaries for us, we had a big celebration. They came with four cars to hand over the keys. There was even a man from Canada,' the village's chief, Dahab,[1] recalled. He had participated in the ceremony and was proud that his village had qualified but added that they 'no longer trust[ed] SECADEV'. 'Before, they were active and committed. They founded and supported *groupements*. But for a few years now, their commitment has been shallow.' There were also rumours of embezzlement and he told me that 'we even wrote a letter asking the prefect to withdraw SECADEV as a development agency'. Although the villagers had become disenchanted with SECADEV's development activities, they still applauded their UNHCR-related activities. 'Every village has elected a chief of refugees,' Dahab said. 'But we don't otherwise differentiate between 'refugees' and others. They all live here with their families now.' By highlighting that people were only defined and categorised as 'refugees' in order to work with the agencies, he underlined the situational use of this category: while useful for accessing aid, it did not matter much in everyday life in the village. However, 'not differentiating' did not mean that the newcomers were not bound by certain village procedures and rules set up before their arrival. In particular, gaining access to land close to the village and the coveted wadi gardens meant taking whatever the villagers offered.

Guilane could boast of 12 *groupements* supported by Africare, and the agency was open to funding more if the village was selected for the next phase of the programme. Although I had originally been told that their selection procedure followed a rigid evaluation process, it turned out to depend partly on personal preference. Abdullai, a former SECADEV employee who now worked for Africare, explained that 'actually they follow the recommendations of the *chef de canton*'. Full of praise for the agency, he continued that

> the *chef de canton* tells us which villages should be selected for the first appraisals. One important factor for appraising their

> eligibility is that they can prove that they have established fully operational *groupements* with a president, secretary, treasurer, and vice-president ... They have to prove they have made a common profit from farming, entrusted it to a treasurer, and formulated development goals. Then, Africare can step in. Once all the preliminary steps have been taken and if the *groupements* have continued to function and earn a profit, Africare comes with their masons and mechanics and they build a well, a road, a storage facility, or whatever the villagers asked for—totally free of charge ... Our organisation demands a lot

he conceded, 'but we keep our promises.' He disparaged his former employer, SECADEV, insisting that Africare's organisers provided better support: 'We are there for the villagers, all the time. Meanwhile, the other organisation's employees leave the people on their own while they sleep in town.'

Yakhoub was president of one of the Africare *groupements* in Guilane. He remembered that the organisation had come to their village 'because we didn't have any military bases here'. When they arrived, the people from Guilane invited their neighbours from Hachaba and Werwerita to join them. 'We said that we'd only participate if all the others took part as well. But when they heard that the storage facilities, tools, or wells would only be built in Guilane, they declined.' It was only after this event that the boundaries between the villages had been drawn, he remembered: 'Before we were considered one village, and now we are separate.' But it was still possible to join the programme. 'I remember that the people from the village of Ardébé joined our *groupement* in Guilane,' he told me, 'and when we finished the work Africare built them a storage facility, not here, but in Ardébé!'

Hachaba's version of the story was quite different. Younous, who had planted the large wadi garden,[2] was also part of a gardening cooperative, a *groupement*. 'In Hachaba, we have two *groupements*, one for the Chadian citizens and one for the refugees.' When I accompanied Younous to the field of the latter group, of which he served as president, about ten men were tending peanut plants there. 'Once we are ready,' he said, 'Africare will come and build a storage facility (*magasin*) for us.' After this allusion to the group's requirements, he continued: 'We were motivated by the example of Guilane, but we don't want to join their *groupements*, we want to develop Hachaba!' He himself had been born in Hachaba but had moved to Sudan during the 1980s crisis and stayed 'because I liked it better there'. Based on a very simplified categorisation that did not take individuals' multiple cross-border movements into account, SECADEV ignored both the house that he still maintained in Sudan and his birthplace in Chad and considered him a 'refugee'. So did the UNHCR: after all, he had fled his home in Sudan due to violence and crossed the border seeking safety.

Mahamat Ismael—who would later organise the compilation of the villagers' list—was the most active man in Hachaba in forming, heading and managing *groupements* and motivating others to help develop their village. He also promoted the various aid agencies. At first, he was wary of me but became friendlier after a while. Wanting to enlist me in his efforts, he asked for a contribution to the *groupements* to help fund a motorised pump.[3] I donated 20,000 CFA francs in cash (about 30 euros) and then saw this money give rise to suspicion between the various *groupements*. People asked who had received the money, what it would be used for, whether it would benefit all of them or just Mahamat Ismael, and so on. Nanyalta of SECADEV had once told me, 'The refugees are much more active than the local population', as Mahamat Ismael seemed to demonstrate. Like Younous, he categorised himself as a 'refugee', even though he had only lived in Sudan for eight years. Like Younous, he had been born and raised in Hachaba and returned after attacks on his Sudanese village threatened his family's lives. When the UNHCR started to distribute supplies in the villages, he became *chef des réfugiés* of the second group that arrived from Sudan. He claimed to have organised three different *groupements* while in that position: one mainly for male 'refugees' (which also admitted 'local' men), one for 'refugee' women and one for 'local' women. His categories included a separation along gender and origin while Younous only mentioned two *groupements* to me, 'one for the locals and one for the refugees'. Throughout my research, I kept encountering Mahamat Ismael organising funds and assistance for his groups or demonstrating how they could cooperate successfully. I also continuously heard accusations that he 'had more than others' or 'did not distribute the profits fairly'. Eventually, I also heard about internal struggles within various *groupements*: that someone had embezzled membership fees or donations, or how 'that group split up and they formed their own group' after some event or another. The definition of categories of belonging along different lines could change quickly. When new modes of affiliating emerged, they caused people to reinterpret how they and others belonged or did not belong to one or the other group. Meanwhile, outsiders, like the long-term aid workers employed by SECADEV, got yet another impression.

For Nanyalta (who later worked for UNICEF) and Aimée, two women who worked for SECADEV, neither Mahamat Ismael, nor Younous, nor even the 2001 'refugees' from Hachaba, Guilane and other villages were 'real refugees': they had only jumped on the bandwagon when the WFP and UNHCR started to distribute supplies. 'The only *real* refugees are the ones in Wandalou,' said Nanyalta when the two of them came on their horse cart to visit me in Hachaba one morning. 'They came from far away, unlike those others who have lived here or a few steps across the border their whole lives.' Still, she conceded that, whether 'real refugees' or not, the 'Sudanese [were] more active than the Chadians. They want schools, they are economically productive.' Even the houses looked different on the other side of the border: 'They have flowers, fruit trees, and the soil is better. Every last hamlet in Sudan has a telephone, something you won't find here at all.'[4] In other words, she considered people from Hachaba, Guilane and the other villages more or less the same, whether they identified as 'locals' or 'refugees'. As in Abdul-Jalil's (1984) findings quoted in the introduction, people found different ways of connecting and disconnecting according to the situation—in this case, the outside interventions. Nanyalta had a very pragmatic explanation for Africare succeeding where SECADEV had struggled. 'While SECADEV used to work with individual *groupements*, Africare works with villages. We have always tried to motivate the *groupements* to do their own thing. Africare not only pays the advocates more but gives equipment to the *groupements* for free, whereas we asked them to work and pay for it themselves.' It was Nanyalta and her colleague who would later introduce me to the Wandalou group of 'refugees' whom I agree were different from everyone I had met in the borderlands so far.

The Wandalou group: Resisting 'integration'

'They're terrible!' exclaimed Henri Marcel when we met in N'Djamena at the end of my second visit to Chad in 2001. The only UNHCR representative in Abéché, this tall Ivorian was visibly upset when I described meeting the 'refugees' living in Wandalou, about 18 kilometres south of Adré on the Chadian side of the border. He had been responsible for aid to about 10,000 people who had fled after their villages in Sudan had been violently attacked and his hostility to the Wandalou group stemmed from their unwillingness to integrate into that village. Unlike in Hachaba and Guilane, where the differentiation between refugees and locals had an imposed and artificial character that was belied by the feeling of belonging most 'refugees' actually reported, a fierce competition had erupted there over how aid had been limited at first to the new settlers and not distributed to the village population. Some people classified as 'refugees' by the UNHCR office in Abéché had moved to the centres of existing villages, as I had seen in Hachaba. In Wandalou, however, they had been given a patch of land that was clearly outside the village proper. There were no shade trees and no nearby fields or wadi gardens. The UNHCR emergency intervention programme's terms placed them in the most complicated category. According to Henri Marcel, they had 'spontaneously settled' but were not 'integrated' into the village. Given this situation, they demanded international assistance as their main survival practice. Meanwhile, Wandalou's long-time residents thought it unfair that the WFP and UNHCR provided supplies to 'refugees' while those who had given them land, food and other support had received no international aid of any kind. Meanwhile, the UNHCR's main intention at the time was to integrate 'refugees' into villages and then leave. As Marcel informed me, 'we are trying to pull out by integrating refugees into the existing villages. And from 2002 onwards, for those who want it, repatriation into Sudan will most likely be possible.' This meant they had to reduce the level of competition between villagers and 'refugees' and eventually the villagers were also included into the distribution of supplies.

The deputy head of the Wandalou group of 'refugees', Moussa Mahamat Saleh Youssif, was an active and outspoken man. He cracked jokes and liked to start drinking early in the afternoon. A former teacher, he considered himself 'political' rather than a 'simple refugee' and had become a thorn in the side of the aid agencies in the region. Instead of agreeing to transition into the development programme, he insisted that the aid agencies continue distributing supplies—in other words, that they continue the emergency aid. He and his people were in no way ready to integrate. With a serious expression, he showed me Arabic documents to prove that 'the Sudanese government is trying to clear Darfur of all other people than Arabs'.[5] Marcel charged the Wandalou group with being particularly:

> unwilling to accept our offers of assisting in repatriation or integration. They want to remain in the state of urgency. They neither want to return to Sudan nor accept lasting integration into the existing villages. All they want is aid, in the form of supplies and assistance in dealing with the other villagers, or for the government to protect them.

He sighed. I smiled. I liked the Wandalou group and had fond memories of visiting them, to which I will return later. They were rebellious and active and seemed to know what they wanted: they insisted that 'we will not go back to Sudan if the UNHCR Sudan does not pay repatriation money or at least money for integration and compensation for what we lost! If we accept their meagre offers now, we will never regain the life we had back in Sudan.' Among other factors—lack of land and of the ability to return—their resistance also seemed to reflect class differences: they were not ready to settle for less than what they felt they deserved. To the 'refugees' in Wandalou, the UNHCR's integration strategy of forming *groupements* mainly meant one thing: the aid programme would end, and they would be 'left alone'. Because of this, they started to resist this programme fiercely, as Fadoul, another young aid worker for SECADEV, vividly recalled to me in long conversations at their office in Adré that same year.

One of Fadoul's parents was Masalit, and he seemed to have good connections with the people in the villages. Still, something had happened shortly before our conversation that almost made him quit his job. By late 2000, the UNHCR had announced that they would withdraw from the emergency programme and move to the development phase. 'The refugees north of Adré were cut off from those south of it, and those in the south organised themselves under a leader. The leader came from the group in Wandalou. They started by claiming that the emergency should continue, but we only could offer them integration, which meant working on farms and forming *groupements*,' he told me. 'When they heard that, they started to demand "safe repatriation". When the UNHCR couldn't guarantee that, SECADEV suggested that they might have a chance if they could prove that all "refugees" wanted the same thing.' The Wandalou group had quickly organised all the villages south of Adré, he continued, shuddering to recall a meeting in Wandalou where hundreds of armed people had shouted that they 'never wanted to hear about *groupements* again'. Apparently, Fadoul and his colleagues had barely escaped with their lives. After that, Henri Marcel had travelled to N'Djamena to see if they could change the programme to meet these 'refugees' demands. It was this dispiriting experience that had inspired his critical comment about Moussa and his people, who were still waiting eagerly for a response. Fadoul also remarked that no one in the Arab villages (unlike the Masalit villages) wanted to return to Sudan right then. As long as they could easily get to the markets and pastures across the border, they only wanted to integrate into the Arab village communities on the Chadian side.

The last I heard about that episode on that trip to Chad was in November 2001. SECADEV's representative in Adré at the time, Batram, told me about an 'incident [that] totally changed our perception of the situation in the borderlands'. The NGO had started to implement the UNHCR's development programme, but the international agency intended to 'exit the situation about a year's time from now'. This was bad news for him and his colleagues as it was the UNHCR that had saved their jobs following the alleged mismanagement at SECADEV's main office. While he did want to implement the UNHCR's toolbox of measures—or aid technologies—directed at 'spontaneously settled refugees' and move on to development, Batram also seemed interested in demonstrating the region's continuing vulnerability and need for emergency aid. He had just heard a story that would give the UNHCR a plausible reason to again categorise the situation as 'insecure' and 'life-threatening'. This would help everyone: it was not only sufficient cause to keep aid personnel in place but also to continue emergency aid measures.

What had happened? 'Recently we heard about a vehicle that crossed the border from Sudan,' Batram told me. 'It looked like one of our cars, but the UNHCR logo was clearly a forgery. I called Henri Marcel, and he called the Khartoum office. Bingo, we were right: they had no knowledge whatsoever about the situation!' He was excited about this obvious 'attempt by the Sudanese government to lure the refugees back into Sudan', assuming that they intended to 'gain the upper hand regarding their people'. He thought this particularly likely in the context of the recent September 11 attacks and George W. Bush's ensuing condemnation of Sudan alongside the so-called Axis of Evil. Indeed, in October 2001 the Sudanese government had seemed to attempt a display of cooperation with the West. It might well be that they had encouraged 'refugees' to return to demonstrate that a volatile situation was again safe—but there are other possible reasons why a 'fake aid car' might have been sent into Chad to 'get the refugees to return'. But whatever was behind it, this incident gave rise to hopes, particularly among the Wandalou group, that the situation might not be declared safe or returning to the homeland be prudent any time soon. It also enabled SECADEV's staff to continue working for the UNHCR, a win-win situation for everyone (except the people in the car, whoever they might have been).

THOSE ARE THE ONLY REAL REFUGEES

Ideologies of hosting strangers in the borderlands

It turned out that newcomers who (were) integrated less into their host villages were also better organised among themselves and knew more about what the aid programmes offered. However, none of the applicants fully adhered to the requirements and rules about who was eligible for their programmes, which meant the agencies also needed to interpret situations to adapt to people's claims, even to the point of being flexible about categories and whether a situation called for emergency or development measures. Recent scholarship is far from condemning this line of thinking and shows that this logic is typical of aid distribution: as every situation is necessarily different, aid workers must adapt categories to the situations they encounter. This requires great flexibility in defining emergencies, transitioning to a new phase in an intervention, and declaring a mission accomplished (Redfield 2010).

The host villagers also had different registers of newcomer integration at their disposal. Next, I will describe the impact of new arrivals on host villages in cases where the newcomers were previously known to the village's population—as in Hachaba and Guilane—or completely unknown—as in Wandalou. For a closer look at local policies of integrating and hosting strangers, I will turn to de Waal's (1988) analysis of the conjunction of war, drought and famine in 1980s Darfur. During this period, many people moved from Chad to Sudan because international aid was being offered on that side of the border due to protracted warfare in Chad's easternmost province, Wadai. De Waal identifies several ways to host and integrate people besides international aid and calls them the 'three ideologies of "refugeehood"' (1988: 133). He argues that the first of these, the 'Sudanic ideology', 'has no place for refugees as we understand them' (ibid.) and categorises migrants as 'misplaced persons' who by staying long enough can integrate with or be 'absorbed by' the people they have moved to live among. They do this through 'moral inclusion into the community, becoming fictively a member of kin' (1988: 134), an act they usually accomplish through referring to various modes of belonging, as in Abdul-Jalil's description (1984) of the village of Dor in Darfur. Sometimes, this might involve movements of sizeable communities, but de Waal maintains that people normally 'move in small groups or as individuals' that can be given a piece of land outside the village. Eventually, they can decide to become part of the people they moved in with and thereby gain 'entitlement to local forms of assistance and relief' (1988: 134).[6] Within the Sudanic ideology, de Waal also mentions a 'complementary phenomenon': people can physically move 'without political or ethnic displacement' (1988: 133), bringing their homeland (Arabic *dar*) with them. For example, the regional denomination 'Dar Masalit' simultaneously applies to several distinct places, including not only the original 'homeland' along what is now the Chad–Sudan border but also Gedarif in northeastern Sudan, to which many Masalit have migrated to work in the government's large-scale mechanised farming schemes. However, it must be said that not all groups can create a homeland, particularly in the Chad–Sudan borderlands, as is shown by the case of the Arab populations there. 'Arabs' in the borderland villages usually belong to branches of families like the 'Mahariye' or the 'Walad Zed'. Some had homelands further up north, at least in Chad, but due to droughts and war they have left them. When they started to arrive in the borderlands, they were considered 'nomads' and not all gained title to their land, especially during British colonialism in Sudan. Many groups, particularly in Northern Darfur, have no *dar* and many consider this an obvious cause of the recurring conflicts in the region.[7]

The second ideology de Waal discusses is the 'Islamic' mode of hosting strangers. This practice is implicit in religious duties such as the Hajj, the pilgrimage to Mecca that every Muslim is expected to undertake at least once in his or her life. In this context, generosity towards fellow Muslim strangers in general is obligatory, with no distinction between those who have come to stay and those who are just passing through. In a universalist manner, this practice does not distinguish between those who are entitled to charity and those who might not be: while the Sudanic mode leads to joining the host community and becoming one of them, the Islamic mode is generalised and does not make such claims. Moreover, 'the type of assistance to be given is different. The Islamic *zaka* [sic] is usually given in the form of grain. The Sudanic absorption of outsiders, by contrast, means submission to the norms of the group, and merely that they will be treated in the same way as everyone else' (1988: 135).

The final ideology de Waal identifies is the 'nationalist'. This is the most recent one and only developed during the second part of the twentieth century once people in the borderlands had become citizens of different national states. Although this situation may be new, de Waal claims that it was not totally alien: the people of the borderlands used to claim allegiance to one of two powerful sultanates, the Fur and the Maba (Wadai). But it is significant that these changing alliances and modes of political belonging (Behrends 2007; Behrends and Schlee 2008; Kapteijns 1985) were, in order to create adherence to national values, replaced—often by eliminating minor differences—with what Appadurai (2006) has called a national genius. For example, since independence in 1957 the Sudanese national government has connected nationalism to the ideology of 'Arab' supremacy. While becoming Fur or Maba was once desirable because it could integrate someone's occupation with their place of residence (Abdul-Jalil 1984), de Waal (1988) shows that it became preferable to be more like the urbanised Sudanese Arabs in the north of the country. Under this ideology, the treatment of newcomers fundamentally changed. Before independence, foreigners had generally been accepted as newcomers, but after it—and particularly during the 1980s period of drought and war—they started to be identified as 'bandits, thieves, lazy and most tellingly Chadians' (de Waal 1988: 136). Especially in urban areas, this led to the denial of 'relief to people who did not belong to the urban community' (ibid.). During the 1984–5 famine, the aid agencies took on the responsibility of caring for misplaced people with 'intermittent successes', according to de Waal (1988: 138), but this had the unintended consequence of reinforcing nationalist hostility towards strangers. The 'new ethnicity' of 'refugee' provided the hosts 'with a new way of categorising and excluding them' that cut off the possibility of integrating by crossing various modes of belonging and 'becoming the other' or by relying on Islamic hospitality toward strangers (ibid.). De Waal criticises the concentration of aid distribution along the border for keeping the people in an 'area of economic fragility' (ibid.) and eventually causing a famine when the drought had already begun to ease. It also further antagonised hosts against the strangers by creating a new form of 'refugee citizenship' that (at the time of de Waal's analysis) made it impossible for Chadian newcomers to become Sudanese, especially when the allocation of international aid favoured 'refugees' over 'locals'. This resulted in the category of 'refugeehood'—a requirement for receiving aid—and also led Sudanese citizens to move into the camps and—in a Sudanic mode of changing their belonging—to thus become 'refugees'. The aid agencies considered this cheating, but,

> in fact, they were merely changing their ethnicity in a time-honoured Sudanic way, in recognition of the power relations in society. By 1986, a large proportion of the camp populations were 'really Sudanese'. Most of the 'real Chadians' had in the meantime managed to obtain land nearby ... and were ready to assimilate and 'become Sudanese'. This made the two groups virtually indistinguishable. This attempted typecasting of ethnic categories on the basis of alleged origin by UNHCR will be familiar to students of the creation of ethnicity by colonial authorities earlier this century (1988: 138).

De Waal's poignant analysis of the 1980s situation in Darfur is extremely helpful in developing an understanding both of the various ways in which villagers hosted strangers and in which newcomers integrated into existing villages. However, I did not observe his nationalist mode of rejecting strangers by deriding them as Sudanese: on the contrary, Chadian villagers seemed to view coming from Sudan rather positively. Still, some newcomers from faraway places had to emphasise their status as 'refugees' more, another result of not being able to integrate according to the Sudanic or Islamic mode. While de Waal attributes the turn to refugeeness during the 1980s drought and famine to the nationalist mode of not integrating strangers, I offer a slightly different perspective: it was only the Wandalou group who became 'refugees' and were rejected under the 'nationalist' mode, and this was *because* aid had at first been provided only to them.

Thus, nationalist sentiments did not cause people to turn to aid agencies; rather, it was the aid agencies' offers that motivated people to invoke nationality. Instead of relating this move to a nationalist agenda that excludes those who do not fit the nationalist project—as highlighted by Appadurai (2006)—my analysis recalls Ferguson's (1990) and Ferguson and Gupta's (2002) accounts of internationally based aid assuming national responsibilities. In the villages of Hachaba and Guilane, the newcomers' kinship and even their proximity to their old villages across the border enabled integration according to de Waal's Sudanese mode of changing affiliation. However, de Waal's categorisations make it possible to speak of a switch, especially for the group in Wandalou: while the Chadian villagers there seem to have first adhered to an Islamic or even Sudanic mode of sharing even limited goods, they became increasingly angry as they realised that the aid agencies were favouring the newcomers 'because they were from Sudan'. Only once the villagers began to feel excluded due to their local Chadian nationality did they rebel and define new modes of belonging and (non-)integration. The next part will summarise the consequences of this switch.

Kin and 'real refugees': Switching between modes of hosting

The newcomers in villages like Hachaba and Guilane were more or less known to their host communities because they had previous ties to the villages or had been close neighbours across the border. The villagers integrated them, providing land to farm and places to build houses within the villages, but when the aid agencies started to distribute supplies the newcomers still declared themselves 'refugees'. Unlike Moussa and his Wandalou group, they did not demand that emergency aid should continue. Instead, they volunteered for the development programme and convincingly presented it as a fantastic option for all the villagers, newcomers or not. They were most active in trying to direct different versions of this development aid into their village, thus proving their commitment and loyalty: as de Waal might argue, according to the 'Sudanic' mode of taking on the interests and values of their current residence. They were happy to receive farming assistance from the integration programme since farming was what they would have been doing in any case. The local villagers also accepted this form of integration, although it later led to competition over the relative quality of aid from SECADEV and Africare. In Wandalou, however, the newcomers were welcomed more according to the Islamic mode but not integrated and consequently took the 'refugee' route early on. As I mentioned, the Wandalou group were a special case: unlike 'refugees' in the other villages like Hachaba and Guilane, they could not return to their previous farms across the border. They also considered the land given to them by the villagers inadequate, too far away or of poor quality (although I was unable to verify this at the time). They supported their status as 'real refugees' with all the means available to them: political pamphlets, demanding English education for their children, and testimony that showed their lives would be in danger if they returned to Sudan.

In the following chapter, I will look at the period of the war itself. During this time, the differences between the more and less integrated groups of newcomers, who were all defined as 'refugees', became more evident. While Moussa's Wandalou group moved to the UNHCR's refugee camp in Farchana as soon as it opened, the people who had settled in villages like Hachaba and Guilane stayed with their new neighbours. Later, both the 'hosts' and 'refugees' left the villages and moved to the new quarter of Hille Djidíde in Adré. Because development aid ceased during the war, they sought other means of support and the former categorisation of 'refugees' and 'locals' temporarily lost its primary importance. Now, the refugee camp in Farchana will be the main site of my investigation.

7

THE CAMPS ARE VERY DIFFERENT

NEGOTIATING SECURITY AMIDST UNCERTAINTY

I followed the Darfur War from a distance, online and in the newspapers. In 2003, the previous aid dynamics—including the competition and negotiations between villagers and newcomers I described in the previous chapter—ended abruptly once the huge influx of people fleeing extreme violence in Sudan had eliminated any question about whether the emergency or development phase of aid was appropriate. Aid distribution was now divided into only two phases, an emergency declaration and then providing people with shelter, food and medical care. The situation in Darfur was internationally described as a genocide and briefly attracted the world's gaze, until other disasters displaced it in the headlines (Prunier 2005). Hundreds of thousands of people from Sudan arrived in Chad and were immediately caught up in a hastily constructed system of aid that was fine-tuned over the years that followed. In 2008, a European Union Force (EUFOR) was deployed in eastern Chad. In February of 2008, a joint force of rebel fighters attacked the Chadian capital. After a week of heavy fighting, the government, supported by French and West African forces, successfully countered the rebels[1] and resumed negotiations with the Sudanese regime. In early 2010, EUFOR was replaced by MINURCAT (United Nations Mission in the Central African Republic and Chad), but a few months later the two countries' presidents signed a peace treaty establishing a bilateral military force along the border and the Chadian president ordered the new mission to leave only a few months after it arrived.

This chapter follows the connections between aid, displacement and emplacement at the UNHCR camp in Farchana, a 50-kilometre, two-hour drive from Adré and the Sudanese border. The camp's population increased exponentially at the height of the war, and it was there that I observed the interactions between providers and recipients of aid and learned about their lifeworlds or lived experiences during this time. In explaining the trajectories these followed and the conflicts and changes they caused for all involved, I will describe three separate visits to the camp: the first during the war in 2007, the second in 2010 just after the governments of Chad and Sudan agreed to end hostilities and stop supporting the other country's rebel groups, and a third in 2011 once the international forces had left and the effects of the agreement were more clearly felt. In 2011, there were also clearly noticeable changes in the regional organisation of aid. At first, it had been centrally coordinated from Abéché, but decision-making was later delegated to separate administrations at each of the twelve camps in the extended borderland area. Throughout the chapter, certain protagonists appear, including representatives of both the camps' inhabitants and of aid organisations and NGOs. I will especially focus on how three people explained their own or their organisations' experiences between 2007 and 2011: from wartime to a time of relative peace (at least on the Chadian side of the border). Each person described the situation inside the camp differently, so I treat their narratives as representative of how their lived experiences of uncertainty and of aid were perceived and how they interacted, affected each other, clashed and gave rise to new processes.

My three protagonists are Moussa Mahamat Saleh Youssif, whom I introduced in the last chapter; Abdallah, a rebel-turned-refugee who became the new leader of the refugees in the Farchana camp; and Idriss Saley Adjidey, the regional director of Secours

Catholique du Développement (SECADEV), which took over the camp's management in 2010. Further voices include various UNHCR representatives, especially my friend and interpreter Brahim and his sister Fatime, the UNHCR's office manager in Farchana since their arrival in 2003. Fatime and her family—including Brahim (up to a point)—found professional success and a measure of wealth through the refugee situation, while Moussa, Abdallah and Idriss Saley Adjidey were more involved in advocating for their positions on how to deal with the emergency.

I first met Moussa in Wandalou, where he had stayed before moving to the Farchana camp during the war. He was one of the people who had no relatives in Chad and thus could not smoothly integrate into village communities. To the villagers, he and his people had remained foreigners, even though they spoke the same language(s), adhered to the same religion and identified with the same ethnicity. The main factor they lacked was close kinship with locals. The consequent lack of support, combined with the expectation of more dedicated humanitarian aid, led them into the camps. There, Moussa soon became known as 'Cheikh Moussa' and became the first *président de réfugiés* for the camp's 20,000 people. There, his history of resisting the UNHCR's attempts to switch from 'emergency' into 'development' mode in Wandalou led in yet another direction and was ultimately turned against him. The complex interrelations between aid agencies and the people living in the camp affected his image, which changed from 'leader' to 'spy' to 'vulnerable person' and from 'friend' to 'foe' to 'old man'.

Abdallah, a rebel-turned-refugee, had not arrived until after the peace agreement was signed and the rebels considered defeated. Unlike Moussa, he turned away from the international agencies and towards the local administrative level of the Chadian government. His local-political approach derived both from his unfinished formal education in Sudan and his experiences as a rebel during the war. His perspective highlights the extent to which categorising is contingent and not permanent—and how the perspectives and experiences of new actors transform the logic of a situation when new experiences and practices must be taken into consideration. His personal trajectory led from alleged former rebel to chief of refugees and finally a private person with very clear opinions about what needed to be done within the camp and what security meant to him and the camp's inhabitants.

Idriss Adjidey, SECADEV's regional director during the war, shared with me his reflections on his organisation's involvement both in the sector of urgent humanitarian aid as well as in development measures. I will relate these to the comments of national and international aid and military personnel and of my friend Brahim, who became a salaried aid worker to support his growing family during the war. I will also show how ways of perceiving the situation's urgency and security sometimes led to fierce negotiations of differing realities. When people told me about their own actions and intentions and about what they made of other people's, I captured insights into how these actions, intentions and perceptions interacted and affected change. But I also saw how the profound knowledge 'refugees' have about possibilities for aid often contrasted with a profound ignorance among international staff at the agencies about the people to whom they were dispensing it.[2]

Once people moved to Camp Farchana, their movement within Chad was officially limited to the camp's premises. Leaving required a travel permit from the camp's office and returning to Darfur was considered too risky and left those who attempted it stuck in limbo. Many studies on this restrictive aspect of camps have highlighted the better and faster integration processes of 'refugees' who decide to survive war and displacement on their own compared to those who decide to move to camps (Malkki 1995; Spittler 1989). In this chapter I argue that, even if survival depended on adhering to the aid agencies' terms and regulations, the camp residents showed how they not only negotiated these terms in practice but formulated very clear positions about what they needed (or did not need) and how they actively set out to find it. Glick Schiller and Çağlar (2015) have called this process emplacement.

THE CAMPS ARE VERY DIFFERENT

Idriss Adjidey: Making refugees in Camp Farchana

By 2010, the first years of the war were over and the pace of SECADEV's activities was somewhat less intense. Idriss Saleh Adjidey and I sat down for a long interview in his Adré office and talked about the war and refugee camps, as well as the organisation's earlier history in the region, particularly his understanding of the '*groupement* approach' that the Wandalou group had so aggressively opposed. He told me that 'SECADEV first came here during the terrible urgency of the 1980s drought. The idea was to help people get out of that situation. But afterwards, SECADEV thought it more prudent to help people contain the catastrophes on their own terms. In this case, we needed to orient the people towards development activities.'[3] This decision was made after the war in the 1980s and remained in place until another state of emergency was declared in 1995. From then on, he explained, the organisation wore 'two hats', humanitarian assistance and development aid. For the developmental activities, they worked with *groupements*, which he described as 'ensembles of persons who think about their problems, know their villages and seek out means to solve them. For us, it is much easier to work with a category of people instead of only working with villagers who might not have future visions of development for their villages'. In other words, he considered the formation of *groupements* a preparatory stage: aid interventions were easier to organise once the villagers themselves had decided what they needed, and his organisation could respond with a range of possible actions.

While SECADEV's development measures were nominally separate from the most recent emergency developments, its international administration and humanitarian assistance were, as I have noted, among the aid programmes coordinated by the UN. All these organisations were grouped into clusters to efficiently manage not only the many people arriving from Sudan but also the many aid organisations seeking to establish a presence in the crisis zone during the war. Before Adjidey described the process by which people who had made it to the Chadian side of the border became official 'refugees', he emphasised his dissatisfaction with the

Chadian government agency that he said was already responsible for many of the tasks taken on by external organisations. This *Comité National d'Accueil et Enregistrement des Réfugiés* (the National Committee for the Accommodation and Registration of Refugees, CNAR)[4] should have welcomed and registered the 'refugees'. But he stressed repeatedly that this state agency was 'absent' and the international agencies—in particular SECADEV—had taken over. 'In the absence of CNAR, SECADEV and Médecins Sans Frontières were at the forefront. We organised the refugees and registered them, because the CNAR wasn't around. So, we did CNAR's work at the border.' After MSF conducted medical examinations, a third agency joined the process. 'It was the Red Cross that accompanied the people from the frontier to the camp.' At the camp site, SECADEV, UNHCR and CNAR 'welcomed the refugees and gave them their cards', a second medical screening took place, and SECADEV provided them with bedding and other non-food supplies. The Red Cross then accompanied them 'to their particular space in the camp, because the German Gesellschaft für Technische Zusammenarbeit (GTZ) had already installed housing for them there'. Initially, supplies were distributed daily, but the amount and frequency of aid significantly decreased over time and only came monthly once people were 'stabilised' inside the camp. Adjidey proudly emphasised that, 'once the refugees are settled', SECADEV was responsible for 'all the changes they go through, the hygiene, the sanitation'. To transform them into camp residents, they had established a regulated rapport by 'recruiting' and nominating *chefs* who were 'qualified for each field'. Such a programme of aid is far from spontaneous. According to Adjidey, it meant being 'well prepared', communicating along hierarchies of 'programme directors and their coordinators, as well as refugees' committees with facilitators inside the camp'.

This complex ensemble of organisations dealing with the camp logistics was specific to Farchana. In other camps, different organisations took on specialised tasks and expertise like those of SECADEV and no two camps looked the same. Each camp drew its residents from a different combination of areas and their organisational approaches varied despite generally following the model instituted by the lead organisation, the UNHCR. Adjidey explained that SECADEV followed an 'integrated development approach'. This meant, above all, that they were a single organisation that worked in multiple 'sectors' of intervention and thus cut across the clusters designated by the UN. Their staff also recruited chiefs from among the camp's residents to accommodate their opinions and promoted education for women and children within the camp. In this situation, their previous experience within the region proved valuable: 'In the eyes of the UNHCR, SECADEV was their saviour!', he exclaimed. These fine-tuned measures for organising the camp and the cooperation between aid agencies from the smallest NGOs to the largest UN bodies clearly had evolved over time. Adjidey explained that cutting across the UN's cluster categorisation and offering expertise in various fields had allowed SECADEV to maintain its regional office and solidify its presence under the volatile conditions of war and displacement. Providing both emergency aid and development enabled them to outcompete their former rival: Africare's energy had all gone into development projects that ended when they could no longer work in what the International Committee of the Red Cross (ICRC) and the UN agencies categorised as a war zone.

Living inside the refugee camp meant a whole new set of categorisations. First, the newly defined 'refugees' were assigned to blocks, areas of the camp that were named according to the letters of the Latin alphabet. By 2007, Brahim, who was then managing the construction of shelters in the camp for the Lutheran World Federation, could differentiate a local from the town of Farchana (this category included people like himself who had recently moved from Adré) from a *réfugié* from the camp, even though they were indistinguishable to outsiders. This categorisation into 'locals' and 'refugees' was obvious to Brahim, who knew exactly who had been assigned to which block. 'You see those women over there? They're refugees from Block C,' he would explain to me. Senior managers for UNHCR and the World Food Programme, who normally only stayed in one place for a few months at a time, were usually utterly confused by this strange mix of people in and around the camp. It was obvious that they knew (about) each other in minute detail, but they still lived under very different circumstances: some were registered as refugees and others were not. Such flexible belonging was also a problem for the rotating heads of mission, who did not stay long enough to grasp the details of the situation or were only marginally interested in them. To remain mobile and face the greatest uncertainty with the same ease, those living in and around the camp had to consistently dance to the tune of the aid organisations and *also* negotiate their differing realities. These new ascriptions—like being or not being a 'refugee', living in a particular sector of a camp, or participating in one or more of the activities offered by aid agencies within the camp—provided new modes of belonging that also intersected with older ways of categorising established long before the camp. Sometimes, this happened in unpredictable ways.

Moussa: Resisting and appealing to international agencies

Camp Farchana had existed for only three years when I visited in 2007, and I was impressed by its finished appearance. There were neatly fenced yards with round houses and enclosed toilets for each block, sometimes even individual rows of houses, and bridges with water pipes beneath them spanned the minor wadis cutting across the area. These orderly arrangements contrasted with media reports showing people living in tents and shacks or even with only trees for shelter. Nanyalta, who had worked for SECADEV when I lived in Hachaba, now worked for UNICEF's Abéché office and oversaw children's welfare in the camps. 'In Farchana you have mainly the Masalit people,' she told me. 'The camps are very different! In the south they garden, harvest vegetables and sell them on the market. Their houses are very well maintained. In the north you have a lot of Zaghawa from Sudan. They're often highly educated and influence the atmosphere in the camp in that way.' But she had nothing good to say about Farchana. 'Farchana's one of the most difficult to manage,' she told me. 'The Masalit are hot-headed. Remember your friend Moussa? Just like in Wandalou, they continue to resist all the efforts to organise them in *groupements*.' Organising collective farming by *groupements*, as I explained in the previous chapter, was a measure that the aid agencies had first applied within the borderlands' villages to integrate and render the newcomers self-sufficient. For aid recipients, this practice had now come to signify the first step in stopping the flow of aid. In contrast to my perception, Nanyalta therefore did not consider the camp particularly well organised. 'They still think that if you form *groupements*, the international aid will come to an end.' Whenever she entered the camps, she met people who knew her from the time she worked for SECADEV in the villages. 'They ask me to provide more meat and fruit for them to eat,' she concluded laughing, 'but I tell them, if they give you meat and fruit, I'll move into the camp, too!' This also reflected an image of the camp held by people living outside it.

Moussa positioned himself within the logic of aid with his claims: he argued for his and his people's needs and concerns in the language of the aid agencies. As Nanyalta's explanation shows, it was especially the group of people who had experienced aid before arriving in the camp who had their own ideas of which of the range of aid measures they needed—and which they intended to resist. In 2007, Brahim's sister Fatime arranged for us to drive inside the camp and meet with the former teacher and self-declared political activist. Remembering my 2001 conversation with Moussa in a makeshift hut in the cramped settlement at Wandalou, I was excited to see him again, almost six years later. I expected him to be hard to find, considering that the sprawling camp's population had swollen to 20,000 people, but it turned out that he was famous. After checking in with the main administrative office at the centre of the camp, we were told to wait for Moussa in a specially designated area while they sent someone to find him. Finally, he arrived, walking slowly towards us, and smiled, opened his arms and called my name. Then we sat down to catch up and look at photographs, including some I had taken in Wandalou back in 2001. Like Brahim, he had adopted the camp's habit of categorising of people by the block where they lived. Casually, he indicated 'Block A', 'Block C', or 'Block Y' for each person in the photographs.

Moussa told me that once the conflict in Darfur had escalated into a full-blown war, he and his mother had waited at the gates of the camp until they were admitted. Their access to food and other goods improved once they got inside, but they also experienced severe difficulties there. First, they lived in temporary huts covered with tarps; then these were replaced by adobe buildings with tin roofs. The camp's regulations at that time did not permit me to go further in or see the houses, but he described how each had a small courtyard for cooking, a living area, and minimal space around it. According to Moussa, their former hosts from Wandalou had not joined them in Farchana: they had at first remained in the village and later moved to Hille Djidíde like the people from Hachaba and Guilane. When we told Moussa about our experiences with the settlers there and their list and need for seeds, he explained that many in the camp had also kept trying to find work in the fields. Some tried their luck around Farchana, but unused land was scarce there, especially since the UNHCR also provided firewood that was gathered near the camp. By the time of our conversation, they had managed to get seeds to plant in the fields outside the camp and official permission to leave the camp to farm. But Moussa had calculated that there were not enough seeds for the farmers to plant the one-hectare fields they needed to be financially independent. While the camp management and its associated NGOs provided camp residents with basic needs—food, firewood, schooling, and vocational education—he insisted that this could not provide a path toward greater self-sufficiency.

This goal of self-sufficiency was obviously high on his list, but the aid agencies' strategy for making camp residents more independent—'forming *groupements*'—continued to be an explosive issue: according to Moussa, it had led to him resigning as *président de réfugiés* and nearly being beaten to death! Based on their experiences in the villages and again confronted with the prospect of aid measures ending prematurely, Moussa and his people had fiercely resisted any measure of forming cooperatives in the camp. As he explained, 'we came to Chad in 1999, and it is true that the aid agencies came here to help us. But afterwards, they left us in the lurch. They said that now we had to take care of ourselves with what we had.[5] We did that, until the second event. New refugees arrived and we went to Farchana with them.' The second event was at the beginning of the Darfur War in 2003. He later realised that in that case, there had been a misunderstanding: the measure of forming groups was not, at that point, connected with any immediate intention to close the camps. The aid agencies aimed to protect their environment, but the camp's inhabitants misunderstood this and interpreted the measures as another preliminary move to exit the situation. This misunderstanding may have been exacerbated by the high number of aid organisations competing to become active within the refugee camps—a side effect of the great publicity the Darfur War had attracted during its first years—which made it difficult to inform the camp residents about the respective aid measures and rendered individual measures opaque to the people affected by them.

Resistance emerged in the camp because each new organisation that entered had to find a field it could work in to improve the situation without duplicating aid already offered. Many agencies sought to reduce the environmental impact of the concentrated refugee population and particularly of cutting trees for firewood. Therefore, they proposed a tree-planting programme. According to Moussa: 'Now we had the problem of planting trees. They said this would be for a *groupement*. Before, in Wandalou, as soon as we formed *groupements*, they left the area. So here, if we were to form *groupements*, it would be certain that they will leave us. So, no one did it (*alors, on n'en fait pas*).' Moussa explained to me that later he realised that the measure was not an exit strategy.

> I, Moussa, told them that the planting of trees is not a *groupement*. It is something that will last. You have not reached the status of a *groupement*. A *groupement* is something that will last, but if you just come like that, it is not yet a *groupement*. The state has said that we have destroyed trees, now the state suggests that we replant them, but this is not a *groupement*.

Trying to explain the temporary measure of planting trees, Moussa referred to the Chadian state, although Idriss Saley Adjidey later told me that the measure had been initiated by an NGO from Japan, which saw replacing trees that the camp's inhabitants had used for firewood or building materials as a gap in aid provision that could be an opportunity to become active in this type of emergency. Adjidey remembered that the NGO's organiser had convinced some of the people to help him 'and they dug the holes for the young trees he was about to deliver'. But then, many camp residents agitated against the measure and 'when the trees arrived, the mob said that the organiser should fill all the holes or one of them would be his grave'. Adjidey sighed and finished his story. 'So, he filled them all and left. The agitators had said that "they were not here to develop Chad".'

Moussa's incorrect statement that the Chadian state had initiated the measure of planting trees caused his people to see him as a government spy. His repeated explanations did not help, even though Moussa obviously hoped that his people would understand the message. But they misunderstood his explanation for why he had switched sides. He said that now they regarded him as a pro-government traitor who had tried to trick them into acting in favour of the aid agencies' exit. They came to his house with sticks and beat him up so badly that he needed to go to the hospital. 'They thought you were with the Sudanese government?' I asked disbelievingly. 'No, with the Chadian government,' he corrected me. This entire incident had happened in 2005 and turned into a big enough uprising that the Chadian state actually did intervene in the camp. 'That day, the governor arrived from Abéché, and the prefect came from Adré and even our subprefect from Farchana was there. They came here, and they were also beaten up—the subprefect from Farchana, a colonel and me.' After the perpetrators were imprisoned for three months, Moussa used his position as *président de réfugiés* to petition the prefect. 'They are poor, and they don't deserve this treatment. I asked for them to be freed. It was because of these politicians who came from afar and said that 'you have to do this and this and this'—this is why the poor citizens came to behave like that.' 'So, you defended those who beat you up,' I asked. 'Yes,' he said. Fear of regulations beyond those of the aid agencies, demands for tree planting, rations that included no meat, and the fear of being abandoned in what still seemed a desperate situation had all infuriated them. In this situation, Moussa had no space to mediate between the tree-planting initiative and

THE CAMPS ARE VERY DIFFERENT

the camp's inhabitants who thought he had switched sides. Thus, he came to be perceived as a government spy. That this incident took place in 2005, soon after the war began and when more and more people were arriving daily, also suggests rising fears among the camp's inhabitants that forming *groupements* would lead to the international agencies departing prematurely, after which it would become impossible to survive the war. The aggression this fear led to resembled that organised by Moussa himself in Wandalou when the UNHCR had first announced it would leave the area.

But the misunderstandings based on the respective actors' past experiences and the fearful prospect of the Chadian state replacing the international agencies as their protector were not the only reason for conflicting interpretations. The Wandalou group, and eventually the camp's whole population, saw tree planting as conflicting with their need for more land to farm. Although wanting land to cultivate contradicted the logic of resisting development measures that would lead to the aid agencies' departure, it also shows how people fought for any option they saw threatened, including access to land as well as aid. When switching between camp demands and people's experiences and understandings became impossible, violence increased. Eventually, Moussa was seen as a treacherous chief who was colluding with the subprefect and colonel, the representatives of the government.

Among various possible causes, this aversion towards the Chadian state points towards the Farchana camp's residents' desire to find allies more powerful than the Sudanese state they had fled. Thus, they appealed for the support of the UN—an international agency that represented a mightier (and perhaps more neutral) power than the local one. Moreover, the large number of international organisations and visits from celebrities including the UN Secretary-General Kofi Annan himself made this international option seem within reach. SECADEV's Adjidey understood this desire, but it annoyed him. His agency was ready to negotiate the access to farmland that Moussa had previously demanded, allowing the camp's residents to supplement their aid by growing millet, but now the offer was rejected. 'It was Moussa again. He said that they were now protected by the United Nations, they have come to meet Kofi Annan, and that it's Kofi Annan who has brought them here.'

The struggles during those first years at Camp Farchana show that the camp's people had a clear priority: making sure that international aid remained in place. They did not want the Chadian state to interfere with that aid, and (at that point in time) did not want to integrate with the Chadian population. However, they actively sought access to farmland outside the camp, at least until they thought that it might interfere with getting direct aid from the UN. Adjidey, who had laboured for three decades to develop a region that the government seemed to have completely neglected, took this as a defeat and felt misunderstood. Nor was Moussa satisfied with the course of events. In fact, when I returned to the camp in 2010, he told me that the situation had changed for the worse. His mind was fixed on two issues: how the US had dealt with the 'Sudan problem' and the reduction in food aid, which had affected most people in the camp. Meanwhile, resuming their former lives in Sudan was still inconceivable. Moussa attributed this misery to international politics: 'Only God knows if we can return. I can't answer this question. Before, Bush was the American president, and the UN were there; the situation was better. Since the African is president of the United States, if they tell us what he says, we don't like it here.' 'You mean Obama?' 'Obama. We don't like it. He can't tell us to go back tomorrow or the day after tomorrow. He did not manage the problem of the Sudanese elections well. Because of that we don't like him. He should have decided something, but he couldn't decide whatever it was.' His disappointment was about the fact that the political situation in Sudan had not changed since the war. In his accusations, he took on the voice of the feared and hated Sudanese president Omar al-Bashir:

> 'I have brought my Janjaweed relatives to Darfur to occupy the land. With their animals. I have made Darfur the pasture for the Arabs.' And on top of that, they had to take our animals as well. Even now, our cows are there with the Janjaweed; some of them may well be dead by now. But even if the US does not want to negotiate our return to Darfur (with the Sudanese government),

THE CAMPS ARE VERY DIFFERENT

> I am sure that we cannot live in Farchana. Maybe they will bring us to another camp, but in Farchana here, it is very difficult.

Abdallah: Making local alliances

After the Chadian government defeated the rebel attack on N'Djamena in February 2008, a new population flooded the camps: former fighters from the various rebel movements. On my 2010 visit to Farchana, I found a new *président de réfugiés* with a new approach to international aid. SECADEV's Adjidey recalled that the arrival of former rebels in the UNHCR camps had 'brought a lot of turbulence!' Wanting to control their new situation, they 'first of all' took power away from the 'old people, among them Moussa'. Dissatisfied with what they found upon arriving, the newcomers demanded new elections for refugee representatives. 'And so, UNHCR, SECADEV and CNAR organised that election and, as the young people are active, they make themselves heard. This is how Abdallah got elected.' Adjidey described Abdallah as 'young, educated, he understands. Among the young, they get along. He stabilised the camp.' The aid agencies seem to have been happy to find fresh adjuncts who were less set on resistance and making claims than Moussa had been and who sought, rather, to demonstrate their capacity for leading groups. But Adjidey added that the new top man, Abdallah, might also have overreached his power. For example, he was said to have broken the arm of a young woman accused of being a sex worker at a Farchana bar frequented by foreigners. 'He served some time in prison because one human rights NGO could not accept his behaviour. They took him to prison, and someone replaced him as *président de réfugiés* for the time being. But when he returned from prison, he took back his position. He fought with the *Toroboro* and can still contact them anytime.' In different ways, both Moussa and Abdallah aimed to move beyond the role of passive aid recipients whose only option was to open their hands. They had ideas and knowledge about what they needed and what they were able to claim—whether it was access to resources like land or food or enforcing their moral standards inside the camp. However, the response to Abdallah's act of violence shows that the refugee representative's behaviour and punishment was also subject to the rules of the international actors, who demanded that the national government imprison him.

Abdallah and Moussa not only had different aims and understandings as leaders but also different attitudes towards the aid agencies and how they negotiated claims. Abdallah turned out to involve himself in local politics much more than Moussa had ever considered doing. In 2010, the subprefect would not allow me to enter the refugee camp to meet with him and even warned the camp's manager, a woman from UNHCR, not to let me enter the camp and not to provide me with the necessary access papers. But I was lucky: as Brahim and I were leaving the subprefect's office, Abdallah, who had just been elected *président de réfugiés*, happened to arrive. Brahim spoke to him in the Masalit language—which he knew the subprefect's staff did not understand—and arranged a discreet meeting at a friend's barbershop. It turned out that Abdallah's presence at the government's office was not as coincidental as it seemed: he had been much more active in building up a regional network with local power holders and administrative agents of the Chadian government than Moussa, who had distanced himself from all local affairs and instead placed his case in the hands of the UN.

Abdallah was indeed an impressive man. His reputation as a former rebel seemed to give him some standing among not only the 'refugees' but, as Brahim confirmed, his neighbours in Farchana as well. I was careful to observe the advice of these neighbours, who also worked for international NGOs. 'Don't ask him any questions about his life as a rebel,' they said, 'and don't take pictures of him.' Young, dynamic, with a dark beard and a very serious manner, he came into the barbershop's back room and sat down. He had learned English in Sudan but felt more comfortable in Arabic and he constantly had to answer the telephone during our meeting because of the demands of his position as *président de réfugiés*. He turned out to be quite displeased with the general situation, but he seemed less concerned than Moussa with either the international agencies or the individual needs and concerns of the camp's inhabitants. Instead, he was more intent on leveraging

THE CAMPS ARE VERY DIFFERENT

their large number to gain power and build close connections with local governmental authorities.

Abdallah's political ambitions, unlike Moussa's, did not preclude integrating in Chad. As a former Sudanese rebel, he had found the Chadian state helpful: after all, Déby had supported the Sudanese *Toroboro*. Instead of putting all his negotiating efforts into dealing with the aid agencies, he invested in the links he had established with local politicians. However, he did not stop at the village level and looked for contacts with those whom he perceived as his peers, considering that he was the leader of 20,000 camp residents (and probably also a former high-ranking rebel). Thus, he took to meeting with the region's subprefects (the central government's representatives at that level) and the *chefs de canton*, their counterparts in the hierarchy of 'traditional' leaders. He complained of 'a difficult relationship between the projects [aid agencies] and the refugees. They don't ask us what we need. One would think that when they have their budget for the next year, they would come to us and ask, "What is it that you want?", but this coordination does not exist.' His frustration was that they would only come to him when 'they have done something'. In the opposite case, 'if we want something to be done', access was harder. One of the problems he was most concerned about was the food supply. 'For the last four or five years the people here have only eaten millet,' he said, repeating a complaint I had already heard three years before. The camp residents wanted more meat but it was expensive and they had no opportunities to earn money to buy it.

Abdallah resisted the unspoken policy of the aid agencies of generally excluding Chadian politics from their aid regime and forged an explicit link between life premised on international aid and connecting to national governmental institutions. However, he did not necessarily do this on behalf of the camp residents, but rather for himself. Although aid agencies needed the consent of national governments to operate in war zones, their decisions regarding the internal management of the camp were more independent. Thus, issues like choosing what food to provide or negotiating access to land for the refugees might bypass the state altogether.

But Abdallah considered himself an *homme politique*, and the state and its local institutions were his milieu. He assured me that 'the Chadian state is there to help us, more than the organisations. If the Chadian government wants something, they inform us, they invite me as the refugees' president and tell me that "we want to do this and that, and you, as the president of the refugees, are invited".' He felt neglected by the aid agencies, who only informed him after the fact. In his view, 'the organisations have their own laws and don't involve us'.

Although he was a former rebel, Abdallah's approach was less confrontational towards the aid agencies than Moussa's. Adjidey, the SECADEV representative, confirmed that Abdallah readily accepted development measures and did not resist forming *groupements*. In our conversations, however, Abdallah confessed to his utter lack of understanding of the intentions behind the 'laws of the projects'. Unconvinced of their efficiency, he grudgingly accepted the aid agencies' measures to render people eligible for aid and to issue refugee cards (as he believed) randomly. He accepted the camp as it was, played along with its rules, and, unlike Moussa, did not instigate an uprising against the camp's management. As far as the aid agencies were concerned, he had brought peace to the camp. On the other hand, he never fully submitted to what he considered the logic of the projects, only seeing the camp as a provider of food, housing and security. He knew little of international figures like Kofi Annan or Barack Obama: his ambition lay in expanding his political networks with the local administration of the Chadian government. This reflected his desire to build his standing in regional political networks, with the refugee issue only serving as a starting point. Regarding the aid world, he only sighed in resignation: 'I don't really know about the NGO's plans. They didn't inform me. We're only happy that they're here with us, they work. Even if we sometimes think that they don't know their work very well.'

I have argued that aid measures and how they were or were not embraced depended on the recipients' expectations and experiences—for instance, their desire for better food, meaning more meat and less rice. Abdallah considered aid basic security from harm and hunger, but he still thought that the camp residents were dissatisfied with it and that some of its basic assumptions needed to change. But to the aid agencies the new representative brought stabilisation in comparison to the hot-headed Moussa and his agitation against aid measures. Forming *groupements* was no longer a contested matter. Seen from the side of aid recipients, however, new concerns had emerged. During my conversation with Abdallah, I mostly felt his lack of trust, not only of aid but also of me, a foreigner he had never heard of before. He was willing to talk to me, but did not know much about me or how much he should or should not tell me. Thus, I took what he told me as representing a distancing from aid and a perception of insecurity in the larger region that others did not seem to feel in the same way.

Negotiating 'realities' through notions of 'security'

In looking at the issue of security that Abdallah raised, the concepts of situational categorising and of flexible belonging can serve as indicators for the regulations, experiences and perceptions of the interacting communities in relation to crisis and aid. Isabelle Stengers (2005) had similar concerns from a different epistemological background when she developed the concept of 'ecologies of practice'. To conceptualise the interaction of what she terms ecologies, she starts with the 'demand' that 'no practice be defined as "like any other"' (Stengers 2005: 184).[6] The notion of 'regimes of practice' extends beyond individual or communal practices of interaction and includes a diversity of backgrounds, of experiences, knowledge and expectations. Thévenot (2001: 38)[7] maintains that 'pragmatic engagement' accounts 'for not only the movements of an actor but also the way his environment responds to him and the way he takes into account these responses.' Different regimes, in this definition, involve different realisms that interact and respond to each other. Using knowledge to adapt to such interrelating regimes in a situation of displacement and aid enables one to focus on eligibility and on processes of ordering, steering and allocating, to which various organisations have a claim. In this kind of analysis, no one actor is privileged over another;

each is understood in its interactions within a field, opening the possibility of seeing the interdependencies between them, how they shape processes, and how actors emerge and consolidate (Eckert et al. 2012). Departing from Bourdieu's understanding of practice, Thévenot regards pragmatism not as a stable force, but as 'the capacity demanded by contemporary societies to shift from one pragmatic orientation to another, depending on arrangements specific to the situation' (Thévenot 2001: 71).

In 2010, security practices and how the situation was perceived varied, but I did observe a general sense of insecurity among both workers and camp residents. In fact, things felt tenser to me, even though the fighting had ceased over the last couple of years. The rebels were no longer visible like in 2007, when they drove around openly in Toyota trucks and sat outside restaurants, hair in dreadlocks and Kalashnikovs at their sides. Some had retreated to Sudan or elsewhere, and many had even moved into the camps as 'refugees'. Security had been a major aspect of the aid agencies' operations in the borderlands during the war and remained one after the violence in Darfur had significantly decreased. When I came to Abéché in 2010, I was told about recent abductions of international aid and construction workers, but the hostages had so far always been released after a few days. I felt that an underlying threat had always been present during my travels to Chad, whether from highway robbers, government soldiers who acted with impunity, or young rebels who were often also high on drugs. Even some townspeople in Adré and elsewhere would throw stones at strangers and call them names, something I had experienced during my first trip to the borderlands.

The coexistence of multiple 'regimes of practice' regarding security became clearer to me when I compared my own standards with those of international aid workers. On the way from N'Djamena to Abéché in 2010, I met Mansour, a young employee of the ICRC—one of the few organisations with a mandate to work within war zones. He had to follow particularly stringent security measures. When he was driving outside their compound, he was expected to keep in constant radio contact with headquarters and report where he was and who was in the car with him. His team stayed in heavily guarded residences with radios in every room. Each building had a panic room into which to retreat in case of attack. There were guards, constant check-ins, secret codes, and alerts about which places it was or was not safe to go. In comparison, security was low on the list of research standards for a working anthropologist: I lived in a neighbourhood they did not consider safe, apparently because of a recent kidnapping.

Moreover, security threats had become a way to attract the attention of national and international governments and thus entered the level of diplomacy and politics, making the issue even more prominent. During this period, President Déby had announced that the borderlands were safe and directed the international MINURCAT mission to leave the country, only a few months after its installation. For the international agencies, the departure of the international military presence was not good news: MINURCAT provided security for their ground convoys. On the other hand, Brahim and other inhabitants of the borderlands felt that it would 'not make any difference at all for us if MINURCAT stays or leaves—they haven't changed one thing here'. When I asked Brahim if it was safe to travel to the borderlands in 2010, he told me it was 'very safe, nothing to worry about'. He had just bought a new motorbike and his wife had given birth to his third son. In contrast to negotiations about the provision of and eligibility for aid, decisions about the area's security seemed to have been left up to the actors themselves. The differences between these coexisting standards were striking and it was difficult to grapple with how such different 'ecologies' or 'regimes of practice' came to exist side by side and only interacted sometimes.

Gabriel, a Farchana-based member of the MINURCAT security team from Burkina Faso, did not share Brahim's opinion about the security of the region at all. When I met him in N'Djamena before I went back to Abéché, he told me the withdrawal was happening much too soon. 'The situation isn't safe at all,' he told me, citing a recent Amnesty International report entitled 'We too deserve protection' (Amnesty International 2010) that quoted local and international voices against the withdrawal of the international troops. 'I think Déby only wants to get rid of international militaries,' he continued, 'he distrusts everyone but the French.' The Amnesty International report argued that the Chadian troops that were intended to replace MINURCAT could themselves make the borderlands insecure as neither the people in the camps nor the international agencies trusted them to keep them safe. In Gabriel's opinion, the situation in Farchana (where a couple of hundred troops were still stationed) was 'the most dangerous', as there was constant 'civil unrest'. On the Sudanese side, he knew of continuing attacks on villagers by 'the Sudanese army and the Janjaweed' and he was convinced there was no security. Furthermore, he regarded the mixed Chadian and Sudanese troops that had been installed to prevent further rebel attacks as a threat to the region on their own terms. 'They rape women and steal people's goods.' The displaced people around Adré who were trying to reclaim their land in the villages risked confronting these troops after the rebels had been repelled. After our talk I was eager to proceed to Farchana and see the situation for myself. (This was the visit in 2010 when I had not been allowed to enter the camp and when I first met with Abdallah, then *président de réfugiés*.)

Before I went to Farchana, I took a detour to Adré, where I talked to the current prefect to get his opinions on the regional security situation and the president's order for MINURCAT to pull out of Chad. 'MINURCAT have been very slow, they did not achieve much during their mission,' he began to explain, and then contrasted them with their predecessors. 'The EUFOR troops were effective, they were fast! If you needed them, they arrived right away.' He then told me a story about the relationship between the international troops and employees of the national administration. As I listened, it seemed to me that the problem was not with the international troops but that the Chadian government had slowed down the international army's movements to demonstrate its own efficacy. The story concerned a rebel hideout on the southern edge of the canton of Asoungha, next to Sudan.

> One time, I ordered MINURCAT's presence for a problematic situation in the canton's south. I wanted them to go there by helicopter to demonstrate a military presence. So, I initiated the demand, but it took fifteen days until the governor in Abéché

approved it. Then, he ordered the villagers to prepare a space for a helicopter to land—three more days. When everything was ready, the governor was replaced, so the approval had to be newly given by the new governor.

If I understood him correctly, he then went there with the Chadian army. 'Now, everything's better down there,' he assured me, concluding that 'we're now disarming those rebels who are still around'. However, 'there are still too many weapons around. Everyone has a machine gun hidden under the sand somewhere to pull out as soon as they have to defend themselves.' I could not confirm this, but of course hiding weapons was not something people would readily tell a stranger about, even one they had known for some time. As I left with Brahim, three men from Tunisia came by to let the prefect know that they were nearly done surveying a new paved road between Adré and Abéché. 'We're almost done, only three kilometres left,' they said, 'and we're told that we will need a different kind of protection so close to the border.' 'This's right,' the prefect told them, 'I'll accompany you myself. Let's have breakfast and then move on.' They declined the offer for breakfast, but I saw as I left that they still had to wait for the prefect to finish his own breakfast. 'Breakfast is really the least of our worries,' they grumbled: they were certainly not pleased with the Chadian administration's speed and effectiveness right then!

In retrospect, the continued existence of threats seemed to mean different things to different actors. For the government, they justified measures of control of people's movement; for international aid agencies and military forces, they justified their continued presence in the area in order to support the remaining camps. The MINURCAT officer made the bilateral Chadian and Sudanese military force sound like the worst perpetrators, while the prefect in Adré made it sound as if rebels were still roaming around the edges of the border cantons. My friend and translator Brahim made it sound like there was no reason to worry about security whatsoever. 'The situation's peaceful!' he insisted. In his view, I could walk down any street at any time of the day while visiting Farchana. In 2010, I asked Moussa, the former *président de réfugiés*, what he thought about the region's security, now that the rebellion was more or less over, and he blamed the issues on the government at the national level. This was the position he had adopted very early on: not dealing with national agencies and representatives but focusing all his efforts, claims and analysis on the international organisations. He was convinced that the Chadian government had its own interests in, and advantages derived from, the concentration of refugees and international agencies. In his view, the so-called rebels around Farchana were 'the people of President Idriss Déby', not 'the real *Toroboro* from Sudan' and the security problem was their impunity that allowed them to steal people's cattle and sheep without ever facing punishment. But, he concluded, 'we are not responsible for resolving Chad's problems. Chad itself knows its own affairs'.

As I indicated earlier in this book, returning to peace in the borderlands just meant returning to an unstable pre-war situation. The insecurity posed by the president's people and their exemption from punishment concerned both the local villagers and the aid agencies in their four-wheel-drive vehicles. Here, the camp residents and the local villagers were on the same page: both perceived people who were fully supported by the Chadian president as the worst threat.

Through looking at their situations, providers and recipients of aid and also local borderland residents demonstrated to me what they perceived to be the highest uncertainties of war, how they intended to act accordingly and how they negotiated about what they expected of the respective others. That these intentions differed, adapted and changed over time is one of the main stories I intended to tell in this chapter: by looking at what each of them perceived as urgent, whether defining needs, activities or relations, or finally, threats, the realities of the involved persons and their institutional groundings came to the fore. I have tried to show this in relation to the political approach of Abdallah, the aid-based approach of Moussa, and also the perspective of the NGO representative Adjidey. It surprised me to see how different uncertainties interrelated and opened new pathways for the future, and I will focus on this theme in the following chapter—how the aid agencies finally prepared to leave the area of intervention by recategorising 'refugees' as 'refugee citizens'.

8

THEY ARE OUR RELATIVES NOW

EXITING AID, BUT EXITING DISPLACEMENT?

The Darfur War began suddenly, but it is impossible to pinpoint the exact moment that it 'ended', especially in relation to aid. Many have described this period as protracted and complicated, with no clear end in sight (Long 2010, 2011; Chatty and Mansour 2011; Horst and Grabska 2015; Sassen 2013). After the 2010 peace agreement between Chad and Sudan (which was renewed in 2020), the refugee camps in Chad were still full of people, though many who were looking for ways to support their families independently had temporarily moved out to farm or trade. (Often, people who left made sure to obtain temporary leaves of absence from the camp to ensure that they would still be eligible for food rations if they returned.) Although the rebel attack on N'Djamena in February 2008 represented a significant break that led to a de-escalation of the rebellion and other military conflict in Chad,[1] a sense of insecurity persisted in the borderlands. The camps and aid agencies continued to operate, the rebels roamed freely, and no one gave up their weapons. I therefore speak of a 'post-war' phase of the Darfur War characterised by three significant moments. This periodisation is also applicable to aid, which was still provided as of 2023.

The first of these moments was on 15 January 2010, when the Chadian and the Sudanese presidents agreed to normalise relations between the two countries, to reopen the border and to install a mixed border force of 3,000 troops to protect both the borderlands and the international presence there. More importantly for the aid agencies operating in the borderlands, the Chadian president formally ended the two-year-old United Nations Mission in the Central African Republic and Chad (MINURCAT) on the same day, despite the general expectation that it would be extended when its first mandate expired on 15 March 2010 (Amnesty International 2010: 22). The second moment was marked by the international aid agencies' responses—especially those of the UNHCR: to significantly reduce aid, to close its regional office in Abéché, and to start to prepare its exit. While President Déby's termination of MINURCAT's international military presence in the Chad–Sudan borderlands was key to this transition to a 'post-war' phase, an Amnesty International report later that year expressed strong doubts about the country's capacity to provide such protection, even though the organisation recognised the Chadian government's 'duty and right to protect people living on its territory' (2010: 6). The third moment concerns the country's new oil wealth, which I will discuss in the book's third part, and its link to Déby's decision to end MINURCAT's presence in Chad. The knowledge that Déby had spent his first oil dollars on security and counter-insurgency rather than the long-deliberated and internationally coordinated plan to develop the country led many long-term development agencies to strike Chad from their list of countries most in need of development aid. The aid agencies thus started to reduce their operations or even (like the German Gesellschaft für Internationale Zusammenarbeit—GIZ) to end some longstanding projects in the country.

Although open rebellion and rebel recruitment ceased in the borderlands after 2010, other kinds of instability and insecurity increased again. Incidents of theft, homicide, rape, arbitrary arrest, extortion, expropriation and illegal business practices were widespread, with impunity for the perpetrators. This form of insecurity affected everyone within the borderlands: especially the population of the camps and local villages, but to a lesser degree the national and international aid agencies and even the city and town dwellers, who had so far been affected less by the war. The withdrawal of MINURCAT had a major impact on the borderland's population, but less on security than on the economy. New retail establishments—mobile phone stores, beverage outlets and restaurants, as well as construction businesses that built officer housing, hotels, barracks and so on—that had sprung up to serve the international soldiers lost their customers. But at the same time, more resources supported the refugee camps. The UNHCR's decision to decentralise its presence in eastern Chad meant significantly increasing the number of on-site staff at their 12 remaining sites, which called for building more housing, storage buildings and garages, as well as improving transportation to N'Djamena and between the camps. The airport in Farchana now had two daily arrivals and departures, three on Fridays. In this new 'post-war' situation, both aid agencies and the people living in and around the camps combined modes of doing and undoing the refugee category in relation to both policy and everyday practices.

During this period, I travelled to Chad repeatedly, sometimes to the borderlands and sometimes to N'Djamena for conferences and meetings with Chadian colleagues.[2] Brahim's role in my research also changed during this time. At the beginning of my research in 2000 and 2001, he had been a young teacher who came to the borderland's villages as my interpreter and informal consultant. Through years of working for a Lutheran NGO in the refugee camps (first at Farchana and later further southwest at Hadjer Hadid), he had become an expert, a mediator of knowledge with a position 'in the middle', as Merry (2006: 39) refers to those who 'translate the discourses and practices from the arena of international law and legal institutions to specific situations of suffering and violation'. As Merry points out, brokers or translators 'refashion global rights agendas for local contexts and reframe local grievances in terms of global human rights principles and activities' (ibid.). They could thus be compared to catalysts, but unlike a literal catalyst the translator-middleman significantly also changes in the process of translation. Brahim was both a translator and middleman in the truest sense of the words.

Based on their local rootedness and long-term engagement with international agencies, Brahim and his colleagues applied the UN policy of dealing with refugees, particularly the most vulnerable ones, to people living both in the camp and in its surroundings. At the same time, he also applied his knowledge of the situation and people in the borderlands to adapt the UN code of conduct to what he saw was needed and might work on the ground. He also conveyed his insights to me and carefully explained the most recent 'new way of dealing with the refugees'. Although I sometimes suspected his take on events of being too optimistic considering the dire situation, I could not help but agree that many of the measures taken to integrate the camp dwellers into the Chadian borderland villages and towns seemed to have worked reasonably well. My conversations with Brahim as we looked through his many photographs and discussed his occasional reports, as well as with international and Chadian UN staff, have helped shape my conclusions in this chapter. An ongoing situation of emplacement has developed since the 'refugees' could not or cannot return to their former homes in Sudan. '*Les réfugiés? Ils sont nos parents maintenant!*' (The refugees? They are our relatives now!) Brahim told me one day. He no longer saw them as in any way different from the local population (although many continued to insist on their 'refugee status', at least while the international agencies were still around). Some became very successful traders; others farmed in the general vicinity of the camps, and quite a few moved further away to Abéché, N'Djamena or the south of Chad. Building on the previous chapter's insight that everyday practices of providing and receiving aid adapt to one another—even if through conflict—I argue that, after years of intervention, humanitarian and development activities eventually converged, with each other and with the people's livelihood practices. I will now turn to the everyday practices of living in and around the UNHCR camps, starting with how the protracted situation came to be managed.

THEY ARE OUR RELATIVES NOW

A protracted refugee situation: Managing from day to day

'The market in Farchana is still a village market', Brahim explained to me during my visit to the borderlands in 2011, 'but the refugee camp has become a city!' This city-within-a-village at first glance seemed to survive only through the continuing efforts of the aid agencies. However, I later noticed new activities and a new mindset emerging among those I had come to know both in and outside of the camps as they turned from focusing on what aid could provide to a mix of activities geared towards regularising their lives under the circumstances. This was compatible with how the aid agencies' fourth phase, 'integration', had been described to me. But to achieve it, the agencies, the camp's population and the local village population turned their everyday activities into a finely tuned performance of mutual adaptation—an emplacement—that was still marked by the international agencies' aim to control the situation through repeated counting, registration, categorisation and making other attempts to adapt life around the camps to their various programmes for resettling, repatriating or integrating people.

The camps could not be closed because their inhabitants could not return to safe homes across the border. 'A peace agreement isn't enough to ensure the people's safe return. Its measures also need to be clearly implemented,' said Perikles, a senior UNHCR programme officer in Farchana, about the agency's intentions at the time. 'The refugees must have access to land, a secure income in farming or trade, access to health, education, rule of law. All that is not a given—particularly not since their former land has by now been occupied by others.' He was certain that the people in the camps would not disperse easily, or even any time soon. 'Some have registered as returnees in our office in El Geneina, over in Sudan, and they're supposed to live in secure pockets. But when we systematically compared the names of the people, none of them corresponds to the refugees we have registered here ...', which meant, as I was told, that perhaps none of the returnees has been registered there. While I was at first surprised by his meticulous insistence on people's registration instead of their actual movements, I soon understood his subtle insinuation that he could never really know what people were in fact doing. The refugee agency's forms of registration were supposed to document practices, but Perikles obviously saw that they could do so only to a limited degree. To achieve its clearly formulated aims, the agency had flexibly adapted its evidentiary practice and its measures to the practice of their protégées. To confirm this, he concluded, 'it's fortunate that the people in this region, refugees and locals, are more or less the same people. That makes the situation so much easier.' He compared the situation to his experience in Somalia, where the people in camps were so different from the surrounding population that mixing them caused 'immense problems'. On the same day, incidentally, Brahim showed me some photographs about his work in the camp, where he always pointed out who was a *réfugié* and who was not. The sameness Perikles had seen turned into categorical differences in Brahim's eyes. He built houses for the *vulnérables*, assisted not by (mere) construction workers but *réfugiés*. He even called his *groupe mobile* (the small group who moved around with him and worked permanently with him) 'refugees', not 'colleagues' or 'co-workers'.

Once they had begun planning to phase out aid, the agencies' earlier attempt to categorically distinguish between 'refugees' who were eligible for aid and 'locals' who were not now yielded the exact opposite result: undoing the differences between and highlighting the sameness of the people in the camps and those outside. Brahim's reaction, however, showed how such differences had taken on a life of their own. The 'refugee' category, while needed to provide aid, should necessarily have become defunct once the situation called for 'integration', but that move inevitably reified the category at the very moment it was called into question: the category could not be undone without assuming that it was based on a sound premise in the first place. After the passage of so many years, and when the situation had become protracted, how did international agencies and people categorised as 'refugees' or 'internally displaced' manage their situation in the Chad–Sudan borderlands in general and Farchana in particular?

THEY ARE OUR RELATIVES NOW

In early 2011, the UNHCR was still evacuating those considered 'vulnerable' and their families to other countries, mainly the United States. Several categories of vulnerable people qualified for this measure: elders with no family in the camp, blind people with other physical or mental disabilities, children with no adult caring for them, pregnant women, and widows. Apparently, the agency had been flying out about six *vulnérables* per month with their families but the Chadian government eventually ended this practice. According to Brahim's sister Fatime, who worked for the UNHCR's office in Farchana, the Chadian government's decision was related to its intention to no longer categorise the situation as insecure. The move coincided with the demand for the international military mission MINURCAT to be pulled out of the country; the situation had to appear secure whatever the facts on the ground, and the government thought that resettling people was sending the wrong signals to international observers of the situation. For all involved, managing a protracted situation meant taking everything into account that appeared to be of importance and the agencies had to obey the Chadian government's decree banning resettlement. On the other hand, the camp's managers had to coordinate their residents' movements within and outside of the camps and the residents had to be careful not to lose their places there. Their informed practice was to comply with the agencies' various attempts to record their movements as proof for preparing the following aid measures. Both sides, the camp residents and the aid agencies, continued trying to apply their ideas about how to manage the situation. But the vigour of their resistance, their anger at not getting what they needed, the fear they felt due to constant new registration measures, and their sense that they needed to frantically seek out ways to be eligible for particular allocations of food or for spaces in occupational training programmes had all clearly declined.

Brahim and I also saw Moussa in 2011, on our last visit to Farchana. I wanted to find out how life had treated him. How had he been coping with the camp situation and the protests against him? Did he still want to return to Sudan? What prospects did he think he had for the future? I had followed him in my research since my first journey to Chad in 2000, when he was a 'spontaneously settled refugee from Sudan' in the village of Wandalou, and later as *président de réfugiés* in the Farchana camp. Although I did want to do a follow-up interview for my research, he had also become someone I cared about. He looked older, and instead of his habitual turban and *jellabiya* he wore a beige suit and a baseball cap. He had just returned from teaching in one of the camp's schools and had stopped to buy some meat, which he was about to take home before heading to his favourite spot to drink. About this, he was as frank as always. 'I now prefer Castel or Guinness, not locally brewed beer anymore,' he explained, smiling. I took this as a sign that he was doing better financially, which he later confirmed. Impulsively, we sat on the ground under an awning and started to talk. For a long time, he had been in hospital in Adré with gastritis and his health was not good. Later, he told me that 'now, I've become a *vulnérable*'—this was due to his age, 63. Brahim had even built him a house in his compound of the kind typically provided for the *vulnérables*. But even though he could now 'qualify' for resettlement to the United States, he no longer wanted to move there. He seemed less agile and less fierce to me than in the old days and was mourning his eldest son's recent death. 'He fought for Abdelwahid and was killed. Just recently, when the government bombed the villages where they thought the rebels were. They are still around!' he insisted. 'Fighting will break out again very soon,' he asserted. 'It's not over yet.' 'How do you make a living?', I asked. It turned out that his teaching paid him 45,000 CFA francs (about 70 euros) per month—a good deal more than he had made in Sudan. 'Is that enough to buy you drinks?', I continued. His eyes sparkled as he added, 'I have a few chickens and some sheep to sell for beer.' The aid agencies had given him the animals when he became officially *vulnérable* to provide him with a small supplement to his income.

To me, Moussa's story represented not only an individual biography but also an example of combining a life in a camp with a parallel one that corresponded to his personal values and aims, even if these mainly concerned his *marigot* (Chadian French for daily tippling, but literally a shallow lake). Like most people in the camp, Moussa combined various practices of *débrouillardise* (resourcefulness). Two of his brothers sent him regular remittances from the US: a hundred dollars, now and then. One had been resettled by the UNHCR and the other had gained entry to the US because he had fought in Syria. Both telephoned from time to time. Another younger brother who had a shop in the Farchana camp handled his finances and gave him money to buy beer. In the sand, Moussa sketched out his plans for the next hundred dollars his brother was about to transfer. He wanted to invest two thirds in his brother's shop and keep one third for his drinks. 'The situation for the refugees is no better than before. The emergency is over, now we have development,' he explained. 'The refugees are supposed to become more and more independent; aid is continuously reduced. The refugees are required to farm somewhere, even if it is far away; it's only the *vulnérables* now who still receive the aid all have received before.' During our talk, some small children joined us. They were neatly dressed and sat quietly to listen to what their teacher had to tell us. Moussa supported his camp zone's soccer team, he told us. They had won against the seven other teams of the camp! 'That day, Moussa was dancing,' Brahim told me later, after we said goodbye to Moussa close to his favourite street bar. This corresponded to the procedure that we had been following for the last three times we had seen *notre vieux* again, 'our old man', as Brahim affectionately called him.

The process of integration that I could observe with the few people I had known inside and outside the camp did seem somehow to be proceeding as planned. But it also seemed to take much longer than the agencies had anticipated. Moussa's account of investing in his brother's shop differed little from what we found when we went to see Abdallah, the former *président de réfugiés* and former rebel whom I had characterised as an *homme politique* because of his alliances with local power holders. Abdallah came out of a small shop and approached us with a broad, welcoming smile. He seemed a different man from the serious and rather sinister person I had met the year before. He told us that after leaving office he had opened this shop and now sold goods from Sudan. He said he was doing better: he was married, had kids and his business was prospering. Brahim later remarked that the office of president had been 'too exhausting for him. He had to be everywhere at the same time: the subprefect, aid organisations. And he did not earn any money in that position, he couldn't make any extra!'

Staying in the camp meant residents had to look for ways to survive while they were unable to return to the more autonomous life they had led before their flight to Chad. Even though some, like Moussa and Abdallah, seemed to have managed to find supplementary income to support their lifestyles, the camp setting still did constrain people's lives and cause tensions and potential violence. Two reporters who Brahim and I met there had been trained by international journalists and contributed to the Netherlands-based Radio Dabanga.[3] 'We report about official meetings between refugees, aid organisations, visitors and the local population,' one of them told us. 'We also address specific incidents inside the camp, like violence, theft or rape. Girls and women are still victims of rape, but neither the local agents of the Chadian government nor the aid organisations want these things to be published.' The other agreed, adding that 'whenever we hand over our reports to an organisation, they cut a lot of information before sending them on'. They feared government retaliation for their broadcasts and felt that they needed to stay anonymous to protect themselves. 'These countries are only paying lip service to peace. But the truth is that the army that's supposed to protect us ... they spy on us and take our wives and daughters as mistresses. Our lives are cheap.' To escape the camp, they considered moving to the newly independent country of South Sudan, but the question was how to move there and settle down without money. They had too many relatives living in the camp to afford to move to another country or outside it. Nor could they hope for a better life anytime soon. They clearly perceived the withdrawal of international troops and the installation of the mixed Chadian and Sudanese force as a threat. 'Who knows whether the mixed troops will just be a nuisance for us? They're drinking and beating up people already. Who knows how far they'll go? There's no one to stop them.' Brahim later expressed similar concerns about his new neighbours, a Zaghawa family.

> Honestly, we fear for the children when they go outside the house to fetch water. The neighbours' children have started to beat them every time they go out to fetch water from the place that's assigned to our house. And if their mothers come to settle things, they beat my children instead of educating their own.

The caravan of aid that had allowed Farchana to flourish also brought some less pleasant effects in its train. Competition over new opportunities for prosperity, the cost of living and extortion were also increasing. 'If you want to marry a girl, the dowry has become very, very expensive,' Fatime told me. 'Now they ask for 500,000 CFA francs! [750 euros]' Brahim agreed, adding that 'if, in the end, you put 150,000 or 200,000 [220 or 300 euros] on the table, they are usually fine with that. But then you have to add what they call the *valise* [suitcase], with dresses for all occasions, jewellery, perfume, several pairs of shoes—as well as dresses and shoes for the sisters of the bride.' The presence of aid in Farchana, both as a resource and as a technology of control, deeply affected the rhythms of life and left no aspect of it untouched.[4]

Making an exit: Mutual adaptation and the need for emplacement

The camp residents seemed resigned to their situation. After surviving the first years of destitution, the excitement of settling down in a new place, the anger over their experiences of injustice and inequality, and the fear of not finding new certainty in life, they had found ways to meet those needs that the aid agencies did not meet or never had. I understand these processes as 'emplacement'. They now regularly moved into and out of the camps and attempted different forms of business ventures, mainly trade, farming, or small-scale animal husbandry. They had found ways to voice disappointment, outrage and demands through elected spokespeople, internationally funded radio channels, and (if necessary) open resistance. Several had found ways to support themselves inside the camp. Moussa taught school, received remittances from family abroad and shared resources with his shopkeeper brother, took advantage of opportunities to glean in the environs of the camp, and eventually received supplemental support as a *vulnérable*. Abdallah kept his shop stocked with goods from Sudan and was close to the local authorities: his approach was to form close ties with those in power and keep up with current events, which might not have translated into immediate income but helped him stay in business and protect his shop from intruders, thieves and other disruptions. However, camp residents who lacked the education to become a teacher or the political contacts to run a successful business without being harassed did not have these possibilities.

The population of Farchana had significantly increased since the camp had opened. First, there were the camp residents themselves. Second, many other people, like Brahim and his sister Fatime, had moved to Farchana with their families because of the employment and business opportunities the camp offered. Meanwhile, the original villagers both enjoyed their hometown's new prosperity and suffered from the high prices and environmental degradation brought by growth, and the insecurity caused by rebels moving into and out of the camps. All of them, however, had found ways to combine their everyday modes of survival with the opportunities offered by the aid agencies. They adapted to each category—'local', 'local NGO staff', 'refugee', 'displaced person', and 'vulnerable', all the way down to 'refugee of zone XY' or 'refugee of the second wave' or 'particularly poor person'—by learning and meeting the requirements each category delimited. In combining different methods of survival, however, they also crossed categorical boundaries. For the people I had met, switching one's mode of belonging from student to rebel to refugee to shop owner, or from village chief to refugee leader to teacher to drinking buddy or vulnerable elder, was a matter of no great concern. If there was no land inside the camp, they would move out of the camp. If they had to register before leaving, they would fight to maintain their place inside the camp and either get permission or have others keep their registrations active. This resembled the felt need to be counted that I had also observed when we made the list in Hille Djidíde. If staying inside the camp was required to continue to count as refugees, they would instruct relatives, neighbours or others to make sure they were counted.

THEY ARE OUR RELATIVES NOW

By 2013, the UNHCR had been involved in two distinct attempts to integrate the camp's population in the Chadian borderlands. The first sought to regroup people, undoing the separation formerly imposed between 'host populations' and 'refugees,' and intended to reorient the intervention to prepare for the agency's exit. Aid providers had to adapt their operations to the dictates of the Chadian government, their parent organisations' new decisions about priorities and intervention policies, and budgetary constraints. A UNHCR briefing that I read in December 2013, entitled 'Strategic Re-orientation: Exploring and Realizing Alternatives in 2014 and Beyond' (UNHCR 2013), seemed to express an intention to move beyond the refugee category by supporting people in moving from camps and simultaneously merged this intention with the organisation's non-negotiable principles of protection.

The international agencies' second attempt at legally undoing the refugee situation involved a large-scale biometric registration process that was to provide the 'refugees' with a new official citizenship status, that of a nationally registered 'refugee in Chad'. A report entitled 'Operation of Verification and Biometric Enrolment of Refugees and Asylum Seekers Living in Chad—2015' (original in French: UNHCR 2015b) was released, which I take to have implied a new form of control that reflected the Chadian government's recent adoption of biometric registering. Now, biometric data like fingerprints and iris scans would 'assure and confirm the identity of each registered person in a certified way and guarantee that only the person who has a right to receive protection and assistance will actually receive it' (UNHCR 2015b: 2). While the first attempt approximated the camp dwellers' own interpretation of their situation within and outside of the camps, the second reflected a desire to make the situation legally controllable or manageable.

Undoing the refugee category: 'Regrouping' refugees and hosts

The 2013 UNHCR report on strategic reorientation took the national situation in Chad into account while also putting it into global perspective. 'The rise in the number of refugees has stretched the capacity of available resources in the camps while needs have increased and [are] becoming more urgent. Furthermore, this coincides with a continuous reduction in Chad's operational budget, coupled with stiff competition with other global emergencies' (UNHCR 2013: 1). This report also addressed differences within the country. Thus, it considered 'the need for assistance in the East' to be 'likely' while other parts of the country seemed to be better off. 'The population in the South has access to a larger and more varied quantity of foodstuff' (UNHCR 2013: 3). As alternatives, the report suggested various ways of 'hosting refugees outside camps among local communities and recognizing/supporting this option' (2013: 1). The clear aim was to 'reduc(e) refugee dependence on aid, including food' (ibid.) and the 'strategy' was discussed at a workshop also attended by 'Chadian line ministries, donors, UN agencies and development organizations' (ibid.). The strategic planning concluded that any transfer of 'refugees' to other places where they could enjoy continued 'access to ongoing camp services or to one of the few nearby villages where refugees are provided with food (WFP) and non-food assistance (HCR), distribution of seeds and agricultural tools' would have to be 'voluntary' (2013: 2) and 'community-based', targeting 'both the refugee and host communities'. The 'sectors of shelter, water, health, sanitation and education' (ibid.) would also have to be continuously catered to— as well as, of course, 'protection'.

This last sector, the report continued, had been discussed at a separate meeting that included 'colleagues from the Protection Programme (including technical units), Logistics and External Relations Sections' (ibid.). The meeting responded to the observation that 'refugees' were 'moving freely, engaging in commerce, accessing land', but also faced 'challenges'. However, the 'UNHCR colleagues holding protection-related titles and others' were nonetheless able to 'provide practical and tangible services to refugees' in view of 'durable solutions' (ibid.). The report emphasised being 'adapted' to 'community-based interventions'. The most striking thing was how difficult it would be to carry out such an exit. On the other hand, the agencies were not quite willing to simply leave, and I was not sure exactly why. Were they worried about the most vulnerable? About being internationally blamed if things went wrong? Or was it just that so many investments, beneficiaries and employees depended on the intervention that it was not possible to let go all at once?

Whatever their reasons—I was never in a position to evaluate the actual need for assistance—the withdrawal measures were certainly elaborate. The UNHCR report mentioned a third 'strategic meeting', this one related to 'self-reliance', where 'following the people' was further explicated. Self-reliance was to be promoted 'with the aim to further define alternative means' (2013: 2). More surprisingly, the report also recognised that the agency had to 'shift attitude', 'reinforce' the community approach, and ensure 'local action plans for localized needs'—as well as 'enhancing attention to gender issues, building on existing refugee capacities and bolstering collaboration between development and humanitarian actors'. 'Self-reliance activities already in place' were also to be promoted (ibid.).

In March 2016, Brahim travelled from the borderlands to meet me in N'Djamena. I was curious to find out how the plan of the aid agencies to leave the area had proceeded and what they had done about it most recently. I was also curious to see what Brahim, with his regional expertise and deep knowledge of the borderlands, thought about these procedures. He explained his perspective on the current situation of the UNHCR camps and the agency's attempt to leave the area. Brahim explained that from now on, categorising people meant regrouping (*régrouper*) 'refugees' with 'host populations'. The Sudanese camp residents were now officially expected to do what many had long ago started to do on their own: settle in villages and at least partly share land with the region's Chadian inhabitants.

The UNHCR had begun this attempt in 2015 with a new integration programme called 'Seeds for Solutions' (UNHCR 2015a). This programme aimed to provide the camp residents with the material basis for two options to become self-sufficient: seeds, hoes, and knives for aspiring farmers and microcredits to buy inventory for would-be traders. For several years, Brahim had helped implement this programme as an employee of the Lutheran

World Federation. He helped me understand how a familiar measure—the *groupements* that had been so vehemently contested during the war phase—had been brought up again in a new form. Now, it was all about categorising and recategorising people. 'Integration is a bit complicated,' he explained. 'To integrate the refugees into the villages, we form *groupements*. Then, there are *groupements* of the refugees and the autochthonous, of widows, of divorcees, and so on. But first, we have to categorise the people. In the camps, we apply the categories of "very poor", "poor", "average" and "rich".' The UNHCR had devised these categories, as I later read in its report (2015), but Brahim and his colleagues were responsible for implementing them. When I asked him how he decided which category a person belonged to, he described the method.

> We talk to the people, and we observe them. The 'very poor' won't even have a mat to sit on. They eat only once a day; sometimes they haven't prepared a meal in three days. They're often elderly or handicapped. The ones in the 'average' category are neither rich nor poor, they're in the middle. Now, we group the 'very poor', the 'poor' and the 'average'; we set the 'rich' aside. We want each group to be in the next [better-off] category by the following year.

Commenting on the naturalness of the categories, he added: 'If you put them all together, they'll each stand apart from the others. You can easily tell them by their clothes. The "rich" will chat, talk in loud voices: you can easily see this category. They don't mix, even before we categorise them.'

This brief statement addresses different positions that allow a nuanced reading and interpretation of the situation of the camp residents. As a translator and mediator between different collective actors, Brahim typifies what have been variously called '*courtiers en développement*' or 'development brokers' (Bierschenk 2000; Lewis and Mosse 2006) or 'people in the middle'—those in a position in between international policy intentions and their localised implementations (Merry 2006). In implementing the UNHCR's new approach, Brahim employed the two categories of 'refugees' and 'autochthonous people' or 'hosts' as they had been institutionalised and defined by the agencies. This categorical distinction between people living in the camps and people living outside of them corresponded to how the international organisation managing the camp represented the situation on the ground.

In applying the categorisations promulgated by the refugee agency, Brahim and his colleagues (who had varying levels of familiarity with the situation in the borderlands), used procedures the organisation provided to categorise the people according to their standard of living: from very poor to rich (UNHCR 2015a). But at the same time, he applied (as he was presumably expected to do to achieve full success) an alternate set of categorisations derived from his specific cultural background and long-term first-hand experience as someone who grew up in the borderlands and knew the lived experiences of their people and how they categorised themselves. This knowledge was based on his observations of how people went about their day, how they ate, slept or sat in their homes, and of their property, health and personal circumstances. His understanding of these basic differences allowed him to translate between ways of defining people along alternate lines, mixing his locally grounded and multi-layered experience with the clear-cut categorisations the agency provided.

But undoing the refugee category did not end there, at least from an institutional point of view. To integrate the camp residents into the local settings, old categorisations were now *remixed* to create new ones. Brahim explained:

> We then mix refugees and locals into one association. Here, again, we always put them together according to one of the four categories. For instance, there are 'autochthonous' who live near the camps—we also regroup them. We do it the same way as with the refugees who already have moved from the camps to the villages. We tell them, 'now, you'll stay together, and work together like brothers'.

This new form of categorising was part of UNHCR's approach of integrating the camps' inhabitants locally. The refugee agency purposely left the task of assessing to which of the new categories each former 'refugee' belonged to local employees like Brahim. 'The UNHCR wants us to categorise the people, but they won't follow up on how we do it. We only give them our reports. Sometimes they'll visit sites—for instance, the fields on which the associations farm together—or they'll come to the markets to visit the trader's associations.'

Without interference from the refugee agency, Brahim and his colleagues not only filled in the content of the new categorisations, but also created processes to implement the new policy of 'integration'. In addition to knowing much more about the people who lived within the camps and their relatives, networks, activities outside the camps and so on, he also knew how to recognise who owned more and who less and who deserved more intensive care and who could support themselves with just a little extra money or other supplemental resources. These were nuanced factors that foreigners might not immediately recognise or take into account, or that they would interpret differently, especially since the agencies' international staff only stayed in the area for a limited period of weeks or months. Brahim told me about the next steps.

> On entering a house and exchanging a few words with its residents, I know which group to place the person in. Once people are sorted into groups, each group has to elect a leader. They have to decide what activity they want to pursue. And they get the money, material, or seeds to start trading or farming after they fill out a questionnaire.

After a couple of months, Brahim and his colleagues returned to the sites to do a follow-up. The idea was to define what elements allowed them to make a new assessment and recategorise the people. 'We want to see if they achieved what they were aiming for,' he explained, 'and if they've found some benefit: if their children are going to school or if they can buy some new clothes. This is how we recognise that they have moved into the next category. We want everyone to switch categories. Sometimes it happens fast, and sometimes it takes a long time.' 'Do you tell them which category they belong to?', I wondered. 'No!' he insisted, 'we never tell them. We would simply tell the very poor "You're suffering a lot", or the average, "You're a bit better off".' At this point, his use of different codes became most evident to me: by translating the UN's categories into the way locals would express such differences, Brahim translated his knowledge and switched from one code to the other. This process might slowly change the boundaries of the category of 'refugee' and, eventually, undo it.

Or will it? The interesting thing here is that this policy-driven attempt at undoing previous categories occurred after a long period of interconnected processes. What seemed to be—and has often been interpreted as—the refugee agency turning people into subjects with categories serving as instruments of power can also be interpreted as a regime of practice that was open to contingencies and code switching, reflected multiple sources of agency, and led to processes of mutual adaptation. With the UN agency's approach of regrouping people, the refugee agency might eventually be able to withdraw based on having succeeded in their mission through turning emergency aid into development assistance, dissolving the camps, and making refugees into citizens who no longer needed aid. For most of the local population ('autochthonous' or 'hosts' in the UN's parlance), however, the former camp residents will remain *réfugiés* much longer. Institutional labels aside, the borderlanders seemed to retain the categorisations created in the context of aid.

As a case in point, I remember a conversation with Mahamat, a young building contractor who worked with the aid agencies (as had his late father Khassim) and described his relationship with someone once categorised as *a réfugié*. When I said to him, 'you told me about the people from the refugee camps who bought houses and land in Abéché. Why do you keep on calling them *réfugiés*, even if they have settled and became rich?', he answered: 'Because we got to know them as refugees.' 'Who started calling them refugees?' 'I suppose that must have been the international organisations; everywhere, they are called refugees.' 'And when did you hear the name for the first time?' I insisted, knowing well that he had been a child of 12 when the war started in Darfur and that the refugee camps had been set up in 2003. I assumed that growing up with the category might have made it real for him.

He said he assumed that 'it must have been when they opened the camps. And I remember the first time I had to buy cement in Adré and there was none to be had. They told me to go to the refugees, they had cement. Since then, I have been in contact with a trader who used to be a refugee. And I still call him *le réfugié.*' When I emailed Brahim to ask about the 'integration process of the camp dwellers', he updated me on a new development.

> As for the refugees in the villages, they are not officially integrated but left to work in agriculture and integrated themselves into the villages. They are also still refugees who return each month to the camps to receive their rations. And if you tell them, 'You are already integrated', they refuse the word *integré*. Therefore, for your information, they are not integrated. But they move with their donkeys to do commerce, rain-fed agriculture and gardening. They have been biometrically registered; they formally exist for the UNHCR as 'refugees'. The biometric verification is not only to follow their integration process, but to follow all the refugees' movements.

The UNHCR's policy matched what the camp dwellers had done in practice for years on their own terms, showing that changes in categorisations do not originate only from established and institutional sources but are also strongly influenced by the categorised themselves (Hacking 1995). The recipients of aid could adopt different categories for themselves depending on their knowledge about aid systems and their policy options. This also included knowledge about the local agricultural seasons, the current availability of land, trading networks, and cross-border business relations. The agency also adopted the camp residents' interpretation of the 'refugee' label as also including those living in the camp who might leave occasionally in search of other ways of supporting themselves. In this way, the 'refugee' category changed, acquired a new locally based meaning, and eventually became open to the possibility of being undone. The process of biometric registration, which I will now describe, further demonstrates this point.

THEY ARE OUR RELATIVES NOW

Undoing the refugee category: Redefining 'refugee citizenship' through biometric verification[5]

Issuing identity cards is one of the primary ways national governments demonstrate who belongs to their populations. The UNHCR's programme of transforming internationally recognised legal 'refugees' into Chadian 'citizens' in 2015 and 2016 thus also implied a transfer of responsibility: by issuing new identity cards, the agency was partially transferring its responsibility for security and care to the Chadian government. The refugee category, while based on national belonging and citizenship, is at the same time a deviation from its logic. Thus, those categorised as 'refugees'—just like cross-border commuters, smugglers, returnees, rebels, enemy soldiers, illegal migrants and others assigned to social categories with unstable relationships to the state—must eventually be given a new, more solid national belonging. The UNHCR's management (in concert with the Chadian government agency the *Commission Nationale d'Accueil et de Réinsertion des Réfugiés et des Rapatriés* (Chadian National Commission for the Reception and Reintegration of Refugees and Repatriates, or CNARR)) of the protracted displacement situation in the borderlands took the form of a large-scale biometric registration initiative.

The UNHCR document 'Operation of Verification and Biometric Enrolment of Refugees and Asylum Seekers Living in Chad—2015' (UNHCR 2015b) described the process's context and preliminary results. 'There are currently 463,000 refugees and asylum seekers in Chad, with most of them having lived in the country for more than ten years' (UNHCR 2015b: 2, my translation). Registration was to 'assure their protection'—a measure developed by the Chadian government in concert with CNARR and the UNHCR—but the report was unclear about how exactly the biometric measures would help the registered people in their everyday lives. The registration measure was conducted first, to guarantee the 'verifying, laying open and completing' of what was already known about each individual: that is, 'every refugee and every other person living in Chad under the mandate of the UNHCR' (ibid.). Once the operation was about to be finalised, a biometric identity management system (BIMS) would 'remain at each site to manage the identities during protection interventions', helping each office 'to avoid accumulations at the end of the exercise in the wider territory' (ibid.). This seemed to confirm two things. First, the Chadian government would eventually receive expensive biometric verification technology to be used at international borders to register people leaving and entering the national territory for reasons of 'protection'. Second, the aid agency wanted to make sure that they could better regulate the number of aid packages given out to the camp residents and prevent double-dipping. To carry out the measure, the Chadian government, through CNARR, had hired 164 'youths who formed the core of two verification teams' (ibid.).

After registering the residents of the first four camps, the UNHCR reported that 'before verification in 17 camps, urban zones and villages' with 463,000 people, they had achieved a 'reduction of 9% in relation to the initial information on the population'. With the 'verification and biometrical enrolment of an average of 3,500 people per day', the whole procedure had, so far, been able to verify '91,678 persons in four camps' (UNHCR 2015b: 2). With this number, the refugee agency not only justified its continued presence but also claimed that the measures taken according to 'categories of vulnerability' would from now on be even more personalised. The large number also supported (at least on paper) the agency's claim that it had prevented fraud that might result in duplicate registrations or in rations being issued to people who had already left the camps.

In March 2016, I attended a conference and a research group meeting in Chad. Brahim also travelled from the Sudanese border region to N'Djamena and again brought digital photographs—this time, about 600. Looking at them on my computer, I saw large, obviously temporary, structures. These were huge halls like hangars, their wooden frames covered with canvas printed with the UNHCR logo, which was visible everywhere. There were photographs showing people waiting outside them or entering smaller structures, as well as of people inside them sitting at desks behind computers, drinking water, and conversing around tables.

Brahim started to explain, telling me how he and his team were involved in building the physical infrastructure to carry out and ensure the smooth operation of biometric registration in four of the twelve refugee camps. And while Western observers have described these structures as cold and impersonal and frequently compared them to machines or at least cited a 'routinisation of processes' (Hyndman 1997, 2000), Brahim compared them to luxury villas whose vast interior spaces were only perceptible after entering.

Breckenridge's book on the South African 'biometric state' (2014) defines biometric identification as 'the automated recognition of individuals based on precisely measured features of the body' or, more simply, 'the identification of people by machines' (2014: 12). However, he shows that this was not the original definition of the term. Far from being a technology introduced in the 'developed West' (2014: 17), its inception can be traced back to colonial India. Breckenridge claims that one political appeal of biometrics is that this technology can 'sweep away the slow, messy, and unreliable paper-based systems of government' (2014: 16). In Chad, the UNHCR's biometric registration of 'refugees' went hand in hand with the government's own introduction of biometric passports, biometric registration for international arrivals at the airport in N'Djamena, and, starting with the 2016 presidential elections, biometric voter registration (see Debos 2017).[6] This process thus contrasted with other measures of the UNHCR, with which the Chadian central government does not interfere,[7] in being closely coordinated with national agencies and based on their common interest in controlling people's movements and national belonging. In contrast to the other UNHCR measure aimed at 'integration'—regrouping 'hosts' and 'refugees' into communities together—the process of biometric registration was more closely supervised and regulated. Since it aimed to make the option of staying in the country of refuge viable for camp dwellers, it was legally responsible to the national agencies involved. The effort to recategorise people thus had a more far-ranging legal dimension than the local measures of organising people into *groupements* of farmers or traders.

The finely tuned structure was intended to create a situation of reproducibility, predictability and order and to prevent manipulation, reinterpretation and other interventions by the persons involved, including both those being registered and UNHCR staff. Nevertheless, both changes and attempts at manipulation took place constantly. Some were minor and had little effect on the registration itself. For example, it was recognised that workers became hungry and thirsty during the long hours they spent in the halls, so both 'refugees' and the surrounding population were invited to sell food there. Encouraging people previously ascribed the roles of 'locals' and 'refugees' to vend side by side and mix with each other could have been a secondary goal here. Later implementations of the process included small locally organised restaurants right from the start. However, more extensive attempts to manipulate the process also took place. Some residents tried to register friends or relatives from outside the camps, even though these were not eligible. 'The young people usually want to get the *carte nationale de réfugié au Tchad* so they can travel freely anywhere. That above all. And sometimes the refugees bring their Sudanese relatives to re-register them on their card, but that is refused,' Brahim told me. Their primary desire—to be registered and able to move freely—was in line with UNHCR's goal, while their secondary desire to add additional family members to the card was not.

In addition to trying to prevent ineligible people from registering, the UNHCR also wanted 'ghost entries' deleted from the files. These included people who had long since left the camp but were still officially receiving food rations and people who had registered in more than one camp. Others, who had already left the camps after being registered and were planning a future in Chad, had nonetheless not given up their 'refugee' status. To update and verify the lists of registered refugees, Brahim sometimes had to follow people to their actual homes in surrounding villages or towns. There, he would remove some from the 'refugee list' and register them as 'integrated' (*integré*). He often encountered resistance to this. The former camp residents refused to give up their refugee status, even when they seemed to have started a new life in the surrounding villages. They insisted they were still 'refugees', thus redefining the category according to their own ideas and needs. According to Hacking (1999: 168), they made it their own by creating some alternative meanings while avoiding others that might limit their access to the services associated with it. The category thus acquired a reality that, according to Hacking, must also be acknowledged by those who believe they hold the actual power of definition.

The registration process was intended to ensure that people who had previously been confined to the camp were now allowed to leave in a controlled manner but could still return for assistance if necessary. However, as I showed before, this mobility had already existed for a long time and had continued up to then, with the knowledge of the refugee agency and its partner organisations. Thus, the new process only legalised well-established everyday practices: residents had been regularly leaving the camps since they had arrived in Chad to ask people in the surrounding villages about available pastures or arable land (Behrends 2014). Their food rations had even become a welcome medium of exchange there. Thus, despite its bureaucratic structure, the organisation did respond to local experiences and environmental conditions to reduce self-imposed differences between people inside and outside the camp. The main goal of this initiative was to ensure the integration of the two communities despite their previous categorisation as 'refugees' and 'host population', and slowly bring them together.

This extensive process took about two hours to complete once people had reached the end of the queue and entered the registration halls. From that point on, they followed a single one-way path until they left the complex as newly categorised 'refugee citizens'. The process had three phases: verifying previous 'refugee' status (Halls 1–6), verifying all statements made up to that point (Halls 7–12), and biometric enrolment in order to prepare and issue the new document (Halls 13–18). The procedure was designed to work—both physically and administratively—in only one direction. However, repeated checking of documents (which I describe below) in practice resulted in disruptions, forced halts, and rejection points that interrupted this unidirectional motion. This shows that the UN organisation needed to assign citizenship-affiliation in as unambiguous a way as possible but also—as its fears of disruption suggest—that the people being registered could, in fact, try to manipulate their registration and use it for self-defined purposes.

The first phase of the process began in Halls 1 and 2 with the verification of each person's identity. The first hall was just a lobby; in the second, two identification cards that had previously been issued to camp residents—the *carte de ration* (ration card) and the *carte de famille* (family card)—were collected and checked for validity. According to Brahim, 'This [was] to prevent fraud.' All those not authorised to undergo the process were to be excluded, while the names of those who were eligible were recorded on a list. Hall 3 was very spacious and could hold about thirty families at a time while they waited to be called to one of the round white plastic tables. These had an air of clean modernity to my eyes, but also one of provisionality, as they could be quickly dismantled at any time and reassembled in another location. Each person was led individually to a table, where assistants collected their cards and took them to the next available table. There, the number of family members present was compared with the names listed on the family card. The initial concern here was verifying continued eligibility to be considered a 'refugee'. If someone was listed on the family card but not present, questions were asked like 'Where is this gentleman here?' If that person had left with a so-called *carte de libération* (authorisation to leave the camp) the name could remain on the family card. If someone was absent and had not been issued this authorisation, the name was crossed out. In Hall 4, all the family members were photographed, and the photographs printed on the registration confirmation form.

In Hall 5, inaccurate cards were corrected—for example, unregistered children could be added here—while those who did not need to make corrections could move directly to the next hall. However, there was a special feature here, a possibility of interruption: 'In this hall only, there is a *porte speciale* [special door]. After a thorough check of all papers, only those who qualified as refugees can proceed from here. All others are dismissed here' (Brahim).

Next, Hall 6 was for registering those who were old, sick, pregnant, or too weak to appear in person—the *vulnérables*, as Brahim called them. 'Here, people can say that someone has to go to them, to register their relatives at home. We call it "*recensement physique*" [physical census taking]. You have to see the person to register them.' Again, the idea was to make sure that no one was registered except in person, even if it meant having to send someone to their home. After this initial, thorough registration and confirmation or rejection of previous status as 'refugees', a review of those previously admitted took place in the following six halls (Halls 7–12). This phase of the process could be considered an intermediate phase, a pausing, reviewing, and possible catching up on processes from the previous one. Only once this review process—which, as mentioned, could reverse the course due to disruption or rejection—was complete could the passage enter its final phase, preparing and issuing the new identity card.

The first form of verification in Phase 2 was an interview, conducted in Hall 7. This concerned a person's biography and regional origin, along with the specific reasons they had fled to Chad. 'About ten questions. To check if they are really Sudanese and not possible Chadians. But there are still some Chadians who know the situation in Sudan very well. Even the NGO people don't know the difference.' Brahim told me that he himself could tell Chadians and Sudanese apart.[8] But however effective he was in determining the nationality of individuals, it certainly was not due to any fundamental ethnic or linguistic difference between 'Chadian' and 'Sudanese' citizens. The Arabic spoken in the Chadian border region is closer to Sudanese Arabic than that of the rest of the country because of long histories of migration to and from Sudan and the other languages of the border region do not differ along the (quite recent) national border. Rather, it was the details that mattered: certain types of clothing or shoes more common in Sudanese than Chadian markets—for example, a popular kind of leopard-print slippers—and small objects like knives or jewellery made by regional artisans. Perhaps Brahim would recognise someone's family history by their patronymics; more likely, he would remember the specific person. I was often amazed by people's knowledge about names, individual histories, and relationships in the borderlands.

In Hall 8, the *chefs de famille* (heads of families) were interviewed separately from their families, again to 'check the truths of one and the other,' as Brahim put it. In addition to comparing the statements for consistency, I think the refugee organisation was also aligning itself with local notions of hierarchy by singling out the elders. The presumption here was that if the head of the family said something, whether male or female, other family members would also have to accept it as official. No one could later question a decision on the grounds that it had been based on suspect information about the family derived from the statements of *un jeune* (a young person).

In Halls 9 and 10 (due to the large number of people, there were two halls for this step), more photos were taken: a group photo of each family and a photo of each individual. Unlike the photos in the fourth hall, which were for internal use, these would appear on the new document, the identification card for 'Chadian refugee citizens'. Moreover (as will be seen in the next hall), this was another means of verification: if the photos on the two documents did not match, the individuals were sent back to go through the process again. These interviews asked the respective heads of families to provide complete personal information about their surname, first name, date and place of birth, card number, block number within the camp, number of family members, and family registration number and these were used to construct a family tree. In Hall 11, the technical staff photocopied all these documents and compared the information 'to see if the current documents matched the previous ones. For example, if someone intentionally destroyed a document inside the halls, they could check it here. Everything that people have received up to here must be complete' (Brahim). Hall 12 was also a place to review the registration process and catch anyone who had missed a previous step. Since each was attested to by a new document, those who had skipped one or more halls could be filtered out. Only once all steps had been completed as prescribed were the cards punched with a small hole to certify that all the steps had been completed. If anything was missing, individuals were sent back to complete it.

The third and final phase of the passage was largely routine: the actual implementation of the (biometric) registration of 'Chadian refugee citizens'. Another waiting area, Hall 13, preceded the actual biometric registration procedure. That finally took place in Hall 14, where fingerprints and iris scans were taken for the *carte d'identité de réfugié*. As Hall 15, which held electrical equipment, and Hall 16, where the biometric files were printed and archived, were accessible only to staff, the soon-to-be citizens proceeded directly to Hall 17, the *'hangar de distribution de dossier'* (file distribution shed). There the printed copies were handed out along with the new identification cards. The former 'refugees' left through Hall 18, which was simply a corridor leading to the exit. After they had passed through these eighteen halls, they had achieved the transitional status that was both imposed by the organisation and also their own object of desire. As Chadian citizens, they now had the right to travel and settle anywhere in the country, but they also retained the right to continued emergency international assistance when needed.

Some procedures varied from camp to camp. At Camp Bredjine, there were no shade trees, so three extra sheds were built for those waiting to enter the process. 'But people didn't use them,' Brahim said, laughing, 'because they were afraid that they'd miss their turn. They preferred to wait in the sun'. Why did people reject these shelters? I suspect it was part of their experience as 'refugees': standing at the end of the line or waiting out of sight might have meant missing a new step in the process. If the process was ahead of schedule, those who arrived early would benefit from it. Sometimes, of course, it was the other way around, but how the people waiting acted indicates their eagerness to anticipate and comply with any changes in the procedure.

While the entire process was designed to enable external scrutiny, it also included some elements that brought together the knowledge of the international organisation and the people who lived in and outside the camps. For example, registering both family groups and individuals and interviewing heads of families separately from the rest of the family showed that the organisation had acquired a knowledge of social structures over years of support in the region. Moreover, one could argue that the new—and restricted—type of Chadian citizenship that the complex recategorisation process led to merely enabled people to do legally what they had done unofficially long before: leave the camp to find land and make a living.

The extremely thorough procedure also clarified the political aspect of the categorisation. Following Foucault's (2007) definition of biopolitics, it involved the body and turned people into subjects of certain forms of governance. However, the fact that such a tight-knit regime *needed* to be established also suggests that the activities of refugees required ever stricter control. After all, it was taken as self-evident that some people would try to get identity cards without being officially entitled to them. The *porte speciale* in Hall 5, through which those unqualified for the new citizenship were ejected, reflected this suspicion. The second phase, from Hall 7 to Hall 12, was entirely devoted to this process of control: everything pointed to the resourceful efforts at establishing eligibility for 'refugee in Chad' status, from thoroughly checking and copying current and previously registered documents, to confirming the proper completion of all the steps by punching a specially shaped hole in these documents, to the repeated and increasingly thorough interviews during which people passed as 'Sudanese' (even though Brahim knew 'they were "Chadians"').

The complex introduction of a new category of citizenship— which could be understood as an instrument of state and refugee organisation power—contrasted with how this new status was dealt with in practice. Later, in February 2017, Brahim explained to me that the *carte nationale de réfugié au Tchad* had unintended consequences. It had been instituted to offer those formerly confined to the camps an opportunity for inclusion through probationary citizenship. Under this status, they both retained their entitlement to camp care and gained citizenship rights such as the freedom to settle outside the camps or to travel within the country without a *carte de libération*. While it was intended as a means of freedom of travel within Chad, it proved to be a disadvantage when, for example, people temporarily returned to Sudan. 'With the ID card, they were taxed differently at the border,' he explained, 'because they could no longer claim to be Sudanese.' As a result, CNARR began distributing temporary passes known as *sauf-conduits,* which were intended to document that travellers enjoyed the confidence of the Chadian state and the UN agency but did not include citizenship rights. But even this limited freedom of movement proved useless, so some of the more enterprising former camp residents—'especially the *big men*'—had acquired fraudulent Chadian birth certificates in order to obtain regular passports. As a result, by 2017 it had become almost impossible to obtain a Chadian passport, regardless of whether one was a former refugee or a 'natural-born Chadian' citizen. Passports became a rare commodity and increasingly tightly controlled by the government.

In sum, the various attempts to reverse categorisation as a 'refugee' brought various actors into close relationships with each other: camp residents and management, the UNHCR and the government authorities in Chad, and the population outside the refugee camps. Brahim and his colleagues played the role of cultural translators in this process. His stories showed me how he had been able to identify with the goals of both the international organisation and its target population. He could both translate the categories and sort through their meanings. In the face of some irregularities, he chose to remain silent. For example, he said nothing when international registration staff believed individuals to be Sudanese whom he knew were from Chad. He and his colleagues could remove people from the list of 'refugees' and declare them integrated if they found that they were now living in the villages they visited—but they could also decide that they still needed food rations and leave their names on the list. When recategorising camp residents, he introduced innovations if he felt it was necessary. These were generally small scale but could have potentially significant consequences for the population inside and outside the camps such as the ability to buy and sell food at the registration complex. The process of having different but overlapping forms of belonging and moving between different codes (Rottenburg 2005) while tinkering with, bending, evading, or resisting the control mechanisms of a refugee regime allows for considerable contingency.

In the following part of the book, I shift the focus from 'displacement' and 'emplacement' within the borderlands to the level of the Chadian state. Shifting the focus to the capital city of N'Djamena, I consider how the Chadian government categorises the borderlands and how, in return, the people of the borderlands and the aid agencies active in this area come to categorise the government.

PART III

THE AFTERMATH OF WAR

STATE AND DEVELOPMENT FROM THE CAPITAL TO THE BORDERLANDS

9

THIS IS NEITHER MY FIRST NOR SECOND TIME SEEING WAR

LIVING THROUGH REBELLION

In February 2014, the UNHCR's top two representatives in N'Djamena told me that after the 2010 peace agreement the Chadian president had decided to weigh in on how they represented the situation in the borderlands. He first demanded that they stop resettling people categorised as 'vulnerable' in third countries. Then, he ordered all the agencies to abandon the category of 'internally displaced people' (IDPs). Déby was already known for issuing orders without fully considering the complexities involved in implementing them. He had already banned plastic bags and cooking with charcoal without offering alternatives, which left thousands with no way to bring their purchases home or prepare their meals. As the UNHCR representatives did not want to abandon the large number of people they had been assisting suddenly, they needed to come up with a solution to this decree's requirement that all Chadian citizens—even those dependent on aid or living in camps or villages and away from their former homes—be categorised as ordinary 'residents'.

When I asked the two UNHCR officials how they would deal with this new situation, they wouldn't meet my eyes. 'Well, yes, it's true that now we can't support IDPs anymore. The people are just here now. We helped them for a while by calling them returnees, but we've also stopped that.' By referring to those displaced within Chad as 'returnees', I supposed that the UNHCR might have meant that these 'internally displaced people' had previously fled Chad for Sudan, returned during the Darfur War to settle in Chadian villages, and then had to flee again to the UNHCR camps. However, this complicated history raised the question of what they should be called then. The agency's logic led to an official label of 'people from Sudan settled in Chad', as one of them told me wryly, well aware of the confusing complexity and wide-ranging political impact of this kind of categorising.

In the next part of this book, I will describe various ideas of how 'the state' could react to how regulation and social ordering happened in practice from day to day. To follow how such practices and ideas of the state were related, I depended on the experiences of my interlocutors, especially those who were key local, regional or national decision-makers. To 'rethink the state' in such a way, Migdal and Schlichte (2005) have outlined how an image of the state can be (de-)constructed through practices. These practices need not 'undermine the state', but 'often are incorporated into the field of power that makes up the state, producing new forms of domination' (2005: 36). Migdal and Schlichte view the state in its multiplicity of forms in order to understand its localised functioning. These forms must be categorised and their dynamic relations studied. Thelen et al. (2017) build on this work, focusing on relationality, and examine state practices within a framework they call 'stategraphy'. Building on Migdal and Schlichte (2005), they 'focus on what happens between actors' and thereby 'shap[e] state formations, images, and practices' (2014: 6) and understand 'different relational modalities' to embody 'past experiences in structural environments that translate into contingent expectations for the future' (2017: 8). In contrast to Migdal and Schlichte, Thelen et al. postulate a 'void between images and practices' that is 'left unexplored' (2017: 5). This perspective is useful in understanding the position of the borderlands in relation to the central government. The Chadian president's image of a country 'at peace' contrasted with the more locally grounded perspectives of aid agencies, who still cared for 'IDPs' and 'refugees' and thus knew that peace had not yet come. The aid agencies now had to come to terms with his decree. Without regard to their current (official or unofficial) idea of the Chadian state, they carefully recategorised the recipients of their aid measures. Such recategorisations and the various future expectations that accompanied them gave rise to some interesting contingencies.

The understanding that images and practices are 'negotiated, approved, and transformed in everyday interactions within webs of relations' (Thelen et al. 2017: 14) is closely related to studying 'states at work', a concept that Bierschenk and Olivier de Sardan (2014) have defined as a practice-related approach to the state (see also Eckert 2003, and Eckert et al. 2012). While Bierschenk and Olivier de Sardan (2014)—not unlike Mamdani (2012)—focus on historical 'sedimentations' of colonial and post-colonial state practices and their creation of path dependencies into possible futures, de Bruijn (2008) gives centre stage to possible modes of resisting state practices. She describes a situation in N'Djamena where agents of civil society like artists, political activists or diaspora citizens 'create the state' by trying to gain authority within it (2008: 104). For her, the images of the state represent an alternative state that serves the people—as imagined by deprived citizens—and the practices these citizens search for ways of making the images come true through wider public accessibility and applicability. Even though the artists and musicians de Bruijn studied feared state aggression, she observed them continuing to develop possibilities to counter the governing regime. She acknowledges that these possibilities do not lead to open rebellion but holds that such actors and organisations 'may develop into political power blocks, which would help to counter the power of the government.' However, she adds that because of Chad's history of violently suppressing any form of resistance 'this still seems a remote and unlikely future' (ibid.). I am inspired by these approaches and the idea of leaving behind 'conventional distinctions between state, civil society and the economy, between public and private … not privilege[ing] one organization or institution, like the state, as the "natural" or "right" centre of governance' (Eckert et al. 2012: 15). Like Bierschenk and Olivier de Sardan's (2014) notion of work and Thelen et al.'s (2017) voids between images and practice, the construction of governing institutions through everyday interaction lies at the heart of these anthropological approaches to studying the state (see also Gupta and Sharma 2006; Hansen and Stepputat 2001; Mitchell 1999).

I take this understanding as my point of departure for this part of the book. In each of its three chapters I will focus on a different aspect of state intervention. This one will begin by relating the concept of 'state of emergency' to experiences within rural and urban lifeworlds following the Darfur War and the rebellion in Chad. I will analyse how the Chadian president reformulated the policy of security from before the 2010 peace agreement as a policy of development and how the images he invoked contradicted those used by Western-oriented international agencies. In the following chapter, Das and Poole's concept of marginality (2004) will help me to analyse images of the state through rebellion and how they might or might not be connected to the country's recent oil production. In this part's last chapter, I will return from the country's capital to the Chad–Sudan borderlands and focus on how the images of the state and development held by the mayor of Abéché and urban residents reflect how they imagine the city's future and their own.

Rebellion in N'Djamena: Belonging in the capital

'As for me, this is neither my first nor the second time seeing war. I have been at the border since my birth, and I have seen many things. I have lived through misery worse than that of N'Djamena', Brahim wrote,[1] ending his story of the game-changing 2008 attack on N'Djamena, the capital city of Chad. This personal afterword, together with the questions that nagged him during the fighting ('Should I too leave the city? Has the president been ousted? Will we have enough food for a prolonged state of emergency?'), reveal the uncertainty experienced during a sequence of rebel attacks on the capital and other cities in Chad during the war. His story

THIS IS NEITHER MY FIRST NOR SECOND TIME SEEING WAR

also sums up how people shifted between images of the state—as, for instance, winning or losing—and between practices of gathering evidence to adapt to rapid changes and to the porous borders between different modes of belonging (in this case, political) as ways of understanding one's personal relation to the governing regime.

During the Chadian rebellion from 2005 to 2008, two different configurations of rebels with different leadership attempted to capture the capital of N'Djamena (Jánszky 2014: 408ff.). During the first attack in 2006, according to some reports, the rebels could not find the right buildings to attack. The second, in 2008, seemed to have been better organised: this time, the rebels knew their way around the capital. People there heard they were rapidly traversing the 1,000-kilometre highway from the eastern border to the western edge of the country and that no one seemed to be stopping them. They entered N'Djamena on 2 February 2008 after speeding across the country for three days. The news of the first battle had spread fast: it took place in Massaguet, only 80 kilometres away from the capital, and the victorious rebels continued towards their main target. During this attack, Brahim stayed in N'Djamena, but in a relatively safe part: his uncle, who worked for a Chadian bank, lived in a Muslim neighbourhood outside the centre.[2] Brahim's family had decided to trust to their good relations with some mid-level government officials to protect them and stayed in the city rather than fleeing across the river to Cameroon, as had many others. They had plenty of food stockpiled and none of them were 'tempted to jump onto one of the rebels' Toyotas and die' in the later battle at the presidential palace (as Brahim put it).

The uncertainty of war—and the general population's uncertainty of how the state would respond to the immediate crisis—elicited various practices for gathering evidence about events. People avidly listened to and repeated rumours about exactly when the rebels had reached which places, their decreasing distance from N'Djamena, and the number of people killed and vehicles destroyed on the way. To estimate how severe the fighting had been, Brahim recorded the exact duration of each attack. He found out that the battle in Massaguet had lasted 4 hours and about 400 people were said to have died. His observations within his own neighbourhood were also a source of evidence: he saw the rebels, heavily armed, drive into the city in Toyota trucks wearing Sudanese uniforms and the people cheer them, jump on to the cars, follow them on motorbikes, and guide them through the city to make sure that this time they would find the important sites to attack. He saw the number of tanks in front of the presidential palace and the fact that the government's soldiers returned the rebels' fire as an indication that, contrary to popular opinion, President Déby had not left N'Djamena. This indicated that the president still hoped for victory and probably had obtained foreign support. But when smoke rose from the palace, people interpreted it as a sign of his defeat. This smoke signified destruction to them: the rebels must have entered the complex and set it on fire. 'Have they really defeated the president?' Brahim wondered at the time. His suspicions were well founded: the people's interpretation turned out to be wrong.

It seemed to Brahim as if the rebels thought that they had won. They roamed freely in the streets, visited relatives and greeted people on the street with their faces uncovered. In the uncertainty immediately after the attack, they knocked on doors to inform people that the fighting would reach their neighbourhood the next day and they should leave town right away. Some followed this advice and left for Cameroon. Others, like Brahim, remained in town and kept watch carefully to see how events would unfold. He wondered if the entire population would leave the city, or only some people. He conferred with his neighbours, who advised him to stay: 'gangsters' had tricked people into leaving so they could loot the empty houses. However, other neighbours said that the rebels had taken those houses as bases for further attacks and that the owners had actually stayed in town and were still hiding in the neighbourhood. Uncertainty took hold in every household and in the mind of every resident.

There was a dramatic moment in Brahim's account when the tide turned, and the government regained the upper hand. As soon as people thought that the rebels had succeeded, they

THIS IS NEITHER MY FIRST NOR SECOND TIME SEEING WAR

started to loot the property of those believed to be part of the president's inner circle. Looting has been a standard practice in every war in Chad so far; it arises from a general aversion to the conspicuous display of privilege by the (former) government's cronies, and is an immediate response during such situations. On this occasion, wealth was seized from everyone believed to be close to the regime—who expected this and had long since fled—but the government was not defeated. The president had received reinforcements from the Central African Republic and more Chadian army troops arrived from the base in Adré, pursuing the rebels. The Sudanese rebels (whom Déby had supported during the Darfur War) and the French military (which has a base in Chad) also helped. Helicopters began to attack the rebel positions on the second day, causing many more people to leave their homes and cross the Chari river to seek safety in Cameroon. The constant gunshots and artillery fire that had marked the attack ceased, and Brahim's report now spoke of 'calm', but the general uncertainty only increased. However, Brahim himself was more curious. When he no longer heard any shooting, he took a walk to get an impression of the situation. He saw dead bodies and deserted cars and tanks—signs of the recent fighting—but no clear indicators of what would happen next. Most people were still staying at home, awaiting the government's response, which soon followed. Now, the government's troops knocked on each door instead of the rebels, searching for them and for looted goods. From Brahim's report, it was clear that the population received absolutely no protection during this time and that it was preyed on by rebels and government troops alike. Neither the police nor radio nor television provided information or advice, so people had to rely on rumours and personal experience to guess what had happened and what lay ahead. Soon, everyone learned that they had reached the wrong initial conclusions: the rebels had failed and the president was still in power. The government troops violently seized anything people could not show a receipt for, leaving them speechless. 'They had no say', as Brahim put it, because 'if you talk, you are considered a rebel', and were risking imprisonment or even summary execution by the soldiers searching the houses. This phase of the war also seemed to give away how the government categorised the neighbourhoods and sections of Chad. Certain 'northern' or Muslim quarters were spared, even as 'southern' and Christian ones were heavily targeted. Despite no evidence that the looters had predominantly been Christian (Brahim didn't even mention hearing that), the president's troops mainly destroyed Christian areas during the war's aftermath, probably because they suspected that most of the resistance and the main opponents would be in these quarters.

The practice of war included several elements that seem to recur in each successive coup d'état: rebels would enter a town or city on pickup trucks, armed to the teeth with guns and heavier weapons. When they arrived, the people would start to clap and celebrate. Brahim saw how they 'jumped on the Toyotas' to lead the rebels to the presidential palace. In a place where no regime had peacefully taken over from a previous one in generations, I wondered if in such situations people pragmatically signal their assent to those whom they expect to be the next to assume power in order to be spared any violence and immediately adapt to the new regime. Another typical element was looting. As soon as people saw smoke rising from the palace and thought the president had been ousted, they started to go to the houses of government officials and take anything they could, right down to the last window frame and floor tile. Brahim recounted that the property and goods of the rich were not only taken but also set on fire. Rumour had it that people had burnt 33 cars at once that belonged to a wealthy man who had been a supplier to the president. As soon as the government's troops had regained the upper hand, the tide turned. Focusing their anger mainly on neighbourhoods inhabited by southerners, the army started to enter houses and take whatever they wanted. On the streets, anyone riding a motorcycle who was stopped might immediately have to turn it over to the police. Later, everyone learned that the government had arrested three opposition politicians on the first day of the attack. Ibni Oumar Mahamat Saleh from Wadai in eastern Chad, the founder of the *Parti pour les Libertés et le Développement* (Party for Freedom and Development, PLD), never returned; he was later reported to have mysteriously disappeared and most already supposed that he was dead. The strongest candidate for the next presidential election, he was said to have had followers among both northern and southern Chadians.

Rebellion in Abéché: Belonging without the state

Nanyalta was working for UNICEF out of Abéché when the rebels proceeded through the borderlands from their Sudanese bases towards N'Djamena. 'First you hear 'tick-tick-tick-tick-tick-tick'—the shooting. But then heavy weapons follow.' She had received a radio message from her head office telling her to remain at home and not come to the office. 'Then we heard the women's 'yu-yu-yu-yu-yu' [imitating a high-pitched voice] when the rebels entered the city.' 'Why did they cheer?' I asked her. In her answer to this question, she translated her experience to me, affecting the perspective of a foreigner: 'Because the Chadians are not normal. They laugh when in pain and cry when in joy. Everyone here thinks that politics is a family affair. If the Goran enter the city, the Goran cheer for them in joy. And everyone else cheers to protect themselves from harm. If Déby entered the next day, they would also cheer him.' When the rebels had first attacked N'Djamena in 2006, Mahamat Nour, their leader at the time, had immediately gone to the head of UNHCR in Abéché to identify himself and declared that he intended to harm neither foreigners nor civilians in the city. He said that he was fighting the state but respected the international agencies present in the area as potential allies and ordered that 'everyone should simply stay at home'. Still, several people recalled that the rebels had looted private houses and also the presidential palace in Abéché and destroyed archives, libraries, pharmacies and even the offices of insurance companies owned by the state.

Like Brahim, Nanyalta recalled that before the attack the city had been filled with Chadian army soldiers. As soon as the rebels entered the place, though, there were none to oppose the attack. People said that they had immediately torn off their uniforms and disappeared. 'There were none to be seen!' Nanyalta recalled, laughing. The UNHCR official later explained that this was why she had declined the Chadian army's protection. 'They do not offer any protection,' she charged. Accordingly, when the attack happened, the French army took responsibility for evacuating international aid personnel. The two things I found most interesting in these accounts were how people welcomed the rebels and that the rebels contacted the humanitarian agencies. Categorising the incoming rebels as their potential new leaders, the people of Abéché—like those of N'Djamena—responded in a manner appropriate to (at least potential) representatives of the state: as cheering masses or hidden from sight. The rebel leader, on his own initiative, communicated his intentions to the humanitarian agencies present in Abéché, categorising them as trusted confidants, and deliberately selected the UNHCR, the flagship institution of humanitarian aid during the Darfur War, as the first. The head of UNHCR, in her turn, immediately took on the presidential role assigned to her, communicated the information within the aid community, effectively circumventing the representatives of the actual Chadian state, and later disparaged them by complaining about the army's failure to provide protection. In retrospect, these actions all look to me like a cycle of adapting to each other's categorisations of who was the most powerful actor in the situation.

Everyday experiences of war and the state: Interpreting indicators for threat

Particularly during the rebellion, which took place on both sides of the Chad–Sudan border, the state was referenced differently in every situation. Before the arrival of mass internet access in the borderlands, no newspaper informed people there about current affairs. The Chadian and Sudanese radio stations did not report on the rebellion and international news very rarely covered the situation in much detail. In order to gauge potential threats, the borderland's population at the time—not unlike those of Abéché and N'Djamena—were forced to rely on what indicators they observed from day to day and on their own experience. Similarly, the international staff of aid organisations, as well as the international military fell back on their emergency plans and depended on a different set of experiences as indicators on which they based their interpretations. I argue that it is in these indicators and their interpretation that the void that Thelen et al. (2017) define as the missing link between state images and practices relating to the state comes to be negotiated.

In 2007, I had seen soldiers roaming in their Toyota pickup trucks in Abéché and Adré; they were especially visible in the latter owing to its smaller size. Some dressed in Chadian uniforms, holding up their guns and cheering, looked only 12 years old. For me and the international staff of aid organisations, this was shocking, but most local people claimed that the boys enlisted voluntarily. 'Their parents and the government do not speak up against it', as a German aid worker, told me at the time. Perceptions of the situation in the borderlands differed in other ways than this detail. It seemed to me, unlike the aid workers, that the people of the area knew quite well what signs and evidence they had to look out for—things that would be less visible to outsiders. Here, I am for example referring to when I was warned not to go into the market the next day because 'there will be war'. But I remember that Brahim also told me about another indicator, what was happening at the markets: 'When the people who are close to the president don't show up at the market in the morning, you'd better wait two to three hours yourself before going there.' As many of the 'president's people', the Zaghawa, were fighting in factions that had turned against the president in the rebellion, they were thought to warn their relatives about both rebel attacks and the government's counterattacks.

Some advice I received later during this visit, on the way from Abéché to Adré, taught me more about everyday practices during war. For instance, I was told not to go out after two in the afternoon or to the young people's dances 'because then the soldiers are drunk'. In particular, I saw young soldiers swaggering around, and they also drove like madmen. I witnessed some of them almost kill a young girl when they couldn't control their car. When I shook my head at them, they started to shout aggressively, even though some of them looked no older than 15. But life had to go on despite these threats. Zenaba, for instance, was seven months pregnant then. She was expecting twins and often had to cross the border to El Geneina for medical check-ups. Based on the accounts I heard, it no longer seemed safe to travel to Sudan, especially for 'Masalit'. So why did Zenaba go? 'It's safer for women', her husband Khassim told me. 'If I went there, they might consider me a rebel, trying to connect with the Sudanese rebels, but for her it's fine.' (The vast majority of those rebels were obviously men.)

Like the movement of people, the movement of goods did not stop during the state of emergency. On the contrary, transport infrastructure actually improved during the war even though I had been told that the border to Sudan was 'closed off' and militarised. The road from El Geneina to Adré was completely paved during that time, and both taxis and trucks constantly travelled back and forth. While the fighting made conditions in the area less predictable, the need for transnational trade—and its profitability—simultaneously increased. The local people adapted to the increased security risks with strategies like repainting their cars. For instance, while most cars were white before the war, Khassim painted his *quat-quatre* (four-by-four) black. 'Black is the colour that the army generally uses,' he explained. Counting on the fear most people had of the army and state officials, he hoped that their reputation would also prevent attacks on him, or at least reduce his risk. In fact, the aid agencies later copied this trick of repainting vehicles. After rebel forces had stolen too many cars, some started to paint their vehicles bright yellow or pink to make them less attractive to them—and more easily identifiable.

This part of the book started with my reading of Brahim's experience of the final attack on N'Djamena and focused on people's experiences with practices they connected to the state and to the state's adversaries. In perceiving and interpreting the threat, they relied heavily on rumours, creativity and their capacity to read the signs, rather than on the protection of the Chadian military. Indeed, one can see in hindsight that the practices of the national government and its forces rendered the situation *less* safe. In these circumstances, belonging worked according to a logic of survival: by siding with the stronger player, the people in

Adré, Abéché and N'Djamena did not confront the situation with resistance, but cheered for those who visibly displayed their power.[3] As Nanyalta pointed out, they would side with the rebels one day and the president the next, if he returned to town. This is not to say that no political opinions or opposition existed in Chad: on the contrary, a number of civil society groups, NGOs, street protests and artists continued to vocalise grievances and dissatisfaction with the regime. In the immediate situation of war and armed attacks, one can only assume that people's fear of violence[4] and desire to lead a better life after a change in government make them cheer on the new authorities. In other words, for the people cheering on the rebel fighters the category of the state—in relation to the question of who rules—came down to their everyday experiences, fears and hopes. In the next chapter, I will turn to the government's perspective on war and the national economy, mainly in relation to oil production.

10

BEFORE OIL, WE WERE POOR. NOW, WE'RE MISERABLE

OIL'S POSITION AT THE MARGINS OF THE STATE

Marginality can only be defined in relation to a centre, as Das and Poole (2004) have famously argued. In this perspective, those who are not part of the centre do not belong: they become external, unimportant or even dangerous (see also Appadurai 2006). The eastern borderlands in Chad are a case in point: although the former president Idriss Déby originated from the northern part of this region and invested heavily in modernising that area, he regarded the remainder of the Chad–Sudan borderlands as hostile to his presidential agenda. There, the government put its citizens' lives in jeopardy by fighting the rebellion at the population's expense. Similarly, the president justified spending oil revenues on weapons by claiming that this would provide stability, but this stability was only for himself and his regime. His rule through force of arms affected the borderlands in both foreseeable and unforeseeable ways. Margins, according to Das and Poole, are 'bristling with life that is certainly managed and controlled, but that also flows outside this control' (2004: 30). My study reinforces this view, especially about the precariousness of those at the margins as well as about how particular lives are relegated to the margins and at times 'also reconfigure the state as a margin to the citizen-body' (ibid.). The images of stabilisation and development that the national centre so eagerly promotes have become a farce for many in the borderlands, where the image of the state is dominated by the impunity of the local representatives of a highly neglectful and exploitative regime.¹

*Fighting for oil?*²

A focus on the beginning of Chadian oil production and exports in 2003 conjures up powerful images of the state and its global entanglements as it pursues economic advancement through business deals that often supersede all prior forms of trade and commerce. It also spotlights negative images of states 'in decay' that are related to what Karl (1997) has called 'the paradox of plenty' or the 'resource curse' (Auty 1994), an extreme rise in gross domestic product through resource extraction that is paradoxically paired with economic stagnation in other sectors. Hopes of development and economic well-being come up against ecological degradation, increasing social inequality and a rise in national conflict in the form of modes of resistance that are likewise globally entangled, through migration, international advocacy, or the small arms trade. In the case of Gabon, Yates (1996) has shown how the concept of the 'rentier state', with its immense and sudden increase in current oil revenues and almost unlimited possibilities for incurring debts secured by future ones, can explain the fundamental changes of all existing relations in a state's economy. In this situation, internal and external political relations and those between the government and populace can lead to an acceleration of existing turbulence, as Remadji Hoinathy and I have shown for the early years of oil production in southern Chad (Behrends and Hoinathy 2017).³

It has become a commonplace that the governmental and international project of developing oil production has changed Chad in a rapid and highly visible way. Most observers agree that it has evoked both fears of war and future hopes about development. Their publications focus on the oil companies themselves, as well as their various impacts on the Chadian government (Cash 2012; Coll 2012, Dittgen and Large 2012; Magrin 2005; Magrin et al. 2011), on those of international involvement on the country's population (Behrends and Hoinathy 2017; Hoinathy 2012; Leonard 2016; Reyna 2007), and on socio-economic changes (Guyer 2002, 2015)—especially the mobilisation of increased international awareness of state and the oil companies' interests (Miankeol 1999; Petry and Bambé 2005; Zint 2001). I take the beginning of oil production as a moment of rupture (Vigh 2008) in order to approach an understanding of the Chadian state's perspective on its population and vice versa. Together with the notions of uncertainty (Calkins 2016; Whyte 1997, 2005) and marginality (Das and Poole 2004), I discuss oil's relevance for the Chad–Sudan borderlands and in the capital. I start with my own perceptions of the country during the period when it went from being a dark spot on the world map—both metaphorically (after decades of war, the country received little attention in Western public and academic discourse) and literally (with almost no electrical infrastructure, the country was almost invisible in night-time satellite photos)—to being a major producer of crude oil, a supplier of troops for regional counterinsurgency operations, and a highly visible player in the African Union.[4]

My first trips to Chad coincided with the visible beginning of the country's oil project, for which planning had started in the 1990s. As a newcomer, I became aware that every international development agency was talking about oil, whether to raise the awareness of affected communities, to estimate the compensation required for trees, houses and fields confiscated to build up the oil infrastructure, or to plan future collaborations and their legal basis with local NGOs. Internationally, a fear prevailed that Chad might become like the Niger Delta, with extreme pollution, conflict and crime. Oil production had not yet begun in Chad but its influence had already appeared in all sorts of ways: rumours, policies and international deliberations, which led to exceptionally high levels of immigration from neighbouring countries—Cameroon, the Central African Republic, and Nigeria—and even further away (see Behrends and Schareika 2011).[5] In the early years, most immigrants were young men seeking work constructing a 1070-kilometre pipeline from Komé in southern Chad to the Cameroonian port of Kribi, on the Atlantic Ocean.

For the people of Chad, oil seemed at this time to mean excitement. It signified the hope that wealth would offer a chance to improve education, public health and access to clean water and food. Something was about to happen that would leave the country in a different position than ever before. People invoked '*le pétrole*' as the answer to almost all infrastructural problems, from bad roads, frequent power outages, and inadequate public schooling to structural poverty, technological backwardness, and a general feeling of low self-esteem after decades of conflict, displacement and one of the highest poverty rates in the world. In 2003, when Chad pumped its first crude oil, Idriss Déby had been president for 13 years and his reign had brought a volatile peace to the war-torn country—at the high cost of repression, patrimonialism, and extreme uncertainty about the future. Education was low on the government's agenda since it was associated with resistance and oppositional politics. Similarly, health care, economic development or public political discourse had not found their way into everyday governance.

President Déby seemed almost invisible to me. No posters featured his image and he made no public appearances or speeches. Nor was there any future orientation visible in the form of construction sites, nor were there signs of public outrage except the regular—and notorious—strikes by university instructors and schoolteachers over their chronically unpaid wages. Unlike the presidents of other African states, who would occasionally dive into a crowd to shake hands with people, President Déby was absent from the public scene. What *were* visible were the city's wounds from the last war at the end of the 1980s, in which Déby had come to power: there were bullet holes in almost every building and street sign and armed guards and security checkpoints at almost every street corner. When I started doing research in Chad, I was always told when passing the presidential complex that 'if your car stops here, the guards will immediately start shooting'. When Déby travelled around the city, his route was marked by red tape,

BEFORE OIL, WE WERE POOR. NOW, WE'RE MISERABLE

which I was told meant, 'if you step beyond the red tape, you will be arrested or shot'. This changed with the arrival of oil, which seemed to give the president the positive visibility he had lacked. New posters appeared in the streets with pictures of Déby waving a little flag in front of an oil refinery, a pipeline, or high-rise buildings. Commercials showcased the country's progress as Chad became an internationally recognised player. Still, people did not feel things had improved. 'They're making fun of us,' said Beral, a well-known blind musician and a rare critical voice in N'Djamena who was to become an opposition politician in 2011. I met him with some of his friends and we started talking about the current situation of oil investments and ecological degradation and he mused that

> the state has created a dream of the state and the people are now expected to live that dream. The oil wealth is there, and the government promotes the idea of developing the country in all the public speeches, in songs, in television and on the radio. But it can't be felt in the population. It's like if you were hungry and someone drew you a picture of a chicken.

When I returned to Chad in 2007, I first travelled to Doba, the area in the south where the first oil wells were, to take a closer look at the situation. When I asked people there what oil had brought them, they unanimously answered *'rien'* (nothing). The Chadian director of a local Catholic NGO that was trying to mitigate the effects of land being taken for oil production told us that 'all the oil money goes to the east. Chad's real problem is not the lack of resources, but their bad management.' Some stadiums and market halls were built as visible displays of investment—or to divert money to certain construction companies—but no one really needed them.[6] The vast majority of the money—this was what he meant by 'the money going east'—was invested in arms and soldiers to counter the rebellion that had begun along the eastern border with Sudan. 'Before oil, we were poor,' he concluded, 'but now we are miserable.'

Hoinathy (2013) maintains that people had a glimpse of hope in 2000 and 2001, during the pipeline's construction but before oil production actually began. He analyses how the arrival of the first oil money raised hopes that it would continue the flow of money and end poverty. These hopes came to a rough end in 2001, when the pipeline was completed and most of the workers left unemployed. The start of production coincided with the beginning of the Darfur War in Sudan and the situation throughout Chad went from bad to worse. It was not just that the president used the first oil money to increase military equipment and personnel to unprecedented levels (Gary and Karl 2003). Disappointment about the interruption in the flow of money and unkept promises of development, along with bad harvests, had brought about a level of frustration, particularly in the southern oil region, that due to disappointment seemed even higher than the pre-oil situation (Hoinathy 2013; Hoinathy and Behrends 2014; Behrends and Hoinathy 2017). The eastern Chadian rebellion and the forceful interventions by the concerned governments of both Chad and Sudan rendered the situation in the country much more uncertain than it had been before, and the international military and humanitarian presence only helped a little. In 2007, I found people on every street corner who blamed oil for triggering new hopes, followed by harsh disappointment when the oil money went to weapons and security measures to protect the government in power.

During the war in Darfur and the Chadian borderlands, modes of belonging and categorisations of the self and the other constantly shifted. I have shown how this shift was related to issues of geographical, economic and social belonging, to the tracing of eligibility in relation to aid and to the making of life worlds during conflict and 'states of emergency'. Now, I will look at how categories of belonging overlap and cross each other in relating to the state and opposing it and trace how oil's position came to be negotiated differently during the war. As Barth (1969) and many others have maintained, social boundaries can become visible during conflicts. I maintain that during such ruptures these boundaries most often come to be situationally undone. This (un) doing of boundaries also shows what is important to the actors involved: for instance, when they consider it worthwhile to fight in an army uniform and when they quickly discard it to get out of the line of fire. Ultimately, this relates back to how people live in an area of war and the highest level of volatility without turning to a state to safeguard or care for them and choose instead to rely on local modes of belonging and surviving war.

The war in Darfur began in February 2003 with a rebel attack on Sudanese army bases there. From mid-2003 into 2004, it was widely covered by the world media, which described it as the 'first genocide of the twenty-first century' and was invoked (particularly by the United States) as a reason to increase efforts to counter the spread of 'terrorism in the Sahel' (Prunier 2005). The rebels' first public demand was for peace negotiations on the sharing of power and wealth between the northern and southern parts of the country in order to represent all the marginalised regions of Sudan. The Sudanese government's reaction was immediate and extremely violent: they unleashed the militia groups, of very diverse origin, known as the Janjaweed. These attacked villagers all over Darfur and, after 2006, across the border in Chad as well.

In December 2005, a different process led to a parallel war across the border, where a united front of Chadian rebel groups attacked Adré. Over the next six months, a number of senior Chadian army officers deserted and formed a fast-changing array of rebel groups which mostly operated from bases in Darfur and were at least initially supported by the Sudanese government. The Chadian rebels operated in the same area as the Darfur insurgents and the Sudanese militias and many also shared their cross-border ethnic affiliations. In contrast to those from Darfur, however, the Chadian rebels did not justify taking up arms based on a deep-rooted and enduring feeling of exclusion and neglect by the state. Their leaders' oft-proclaimed aim of ousting President Déby rather stemmed from their former closeness to the president and the partial breakdown of what might be described as Déby's patrimonial system. Despite their intricate connections, which make it difficult to distinguish different underlying motives or power structures, it thus makes sense to speak of two separate wars. I will now discuss the role of oil in the war on the Chadian side of the border.[7]

LIFEWORLDS IN CRISIS

The president's people: A family feud gains momentum

When oil money started to flow in July 2003, the Darfur crisis was already well under way. In Darfur, many of Déby's Zaghawa kin had been fighting the Sudanese government with the rebels and were under attack. In Chad, they monopolised the higher levels of both the government and the army. Many seem to have been disappointed that Déby would not defend them against the aggressors in Sudan. His reluctance was often connected to a series of failed coups against him beginning in May 2004. After the first coup attempt, Déby stopped trying to mediate between the Sudanese rebels and government, but he did not want to oppose the Sudanese government openly. According to reports, his own interests were divided. On the one hand, he sought a solution for the dangerous situation in the country's east, the region where he himself had once prepared a successful coup with help from Sudan. On the other, he did not want to jeopardise his access to oil revenue as the head of state.

To secure this oil money, in 2006 Déby had the law that barred him from a third term as president changed. This heightened opposition to his regime further. Defections from the army and rebellion had escalated before the 2008 attack on N'Djamena, with coup attempts in 2005, 2006 and early 2007. However, most of these had been even less successful than the 2008 one was to be. Even as he fought the rebel threat from the east, Déby renegotiated the oil consortium's taxes. He also prevailed in a power struggle with the World Bank in which he managed to gain access to oil revenues reserved for future generations that were worth about USD 425 million. This provided him with additional funds for fighting the rebels and starting his development programme. In a second move, the Chadian president began to support the Sudanese Zaghawa faction of the rebels against the Sudanese regime in Darfur. Déby had repeatedly accused the Sudanese regime of supporting the rebellion against him (ICG 2006: 12) and so the Darfurian rebel groups called *Toroboro* started to roam freely in Chad, ready to fight Chadian rebels and the Sudanese army.[8] By the end of 2006, he had begun to interfere more directly in the conflict, arming local militias along the border with Sudan to fight against the Chadian rebels (and their direct neighbours) in a move to weaken armed opposition against him and restrict fighting to the border region.[9]

What arguments linked the war in Chad to the oil resources—and what were the narratives by which the main actors involved made sense of the war, also in relation to oil? Brian Ferguson (2003: 10) argues that many of the internal conflicts in Africa result from access to the government being the only way to secure a share in revenues from primary commodity exports. The disillusionment of Déby's followers in the army and civil service over his failed internal politics—as well as anger over unpaid wages—was probably enhanced by the prospect of participating in profits from Chadian oil revenues after elections for a 'new government of Chad'. Along the same lines, it makes perfect sense that Déby used the oil money intended for future generations to strengthen his military against the insurgents and maintain his power.

This explanation does not account for many other reasons people in the country's east had to join the fighting, although discontent with Déby's alleged embezzlement of oil revenues might have motivated some in the president's inner circle. As I have mentioned repeatedly, Déby's kin group, the Zaghawa, was very unpopular in eastern Chad. In particular, the Tama, whose homeland lies from about 40 to 120 kilometres to the north of Adré, had suffered what they perceived as continuous harassment and injustice from their Zaghawa neighbours. Jánszky's (2014) thorough and enlightening report on the Tama's survival and risk management in the Chad–Sudan borderlands analyses the conflict-laden relations between Tama and Zaghawa. Many Tama people claim to have once had good relations and regular trade with the Zaghawa, but Jánszky clearly shows a marked increase in conflict after Déby violently took power in 1990 (although climatic conditions were already causing Zaghawa to intrude into their southern neighbours' territory). She reports that Tama, like others along the borderlands, were regularly searched for automatic rifles by government troops; meanwhile those who claimed to be Zaghawa not only carried weapons with impunity but seem to have been regularly supplied with arms to guarantee their regional power (2015: 149). When a group of Tama rebelled under the leadership of Mahamat Nour,[10] many young men, particularly in the borderlands, saw a chance to act on their feelings towards a group they had long despised. A German employee of a development agency in Abéché told me about a Chadian colleague who had suddenly disappeared. Worried about his whereabouts, she contacted his family, who said that their son had been ill. Later they said he was travelling. When the organisation suggested announcing his disappearance over a radio station, the family reluctantly admitted that he had joined Nour's rebels in the east. In December 2006, Mahamat Nour signed a peace deal with Déby and was incorporated into the Chadian government as Minister of Defence, only to resume his rebel position the following year after he failed to make peace between the Tama and the Zaghawa along the border with Sudan (Jánszky 2014: 147). However, during his tenure as minister his fighters could move freely and so the missing son came to visit his colleagues at the development agency in Abéché in full uniform and was proudly photographed with the organisation's staff. In this case and many similar ones, oil probably had little to do with his joining the rebel movement: it is more likely that he joined the rebellion as a Tama who was motivated by anger at a hated regime. Still, the movement's leader might have considered oil corruption one reason to fight Déby, as oil money helped equally in fighting the rebels and later arming them when they had joined the government's side. When Mahamat Nour left N'Djamena again, his rebel fighters had new equipment to oppose Déby thanks to oil revenues.

On the other hand, oil has also played a significant part in negotiating territorial claims on both sides of the borderlands. When the EU prepared their military intervention, Albissaty Saleh Allazam, the spokesman of one of the first Chadian rebel groups, was quoted in a report of the UN-funded Integrated Regional Information Network (IRIN) as 'question[ing] the EU's intentions' (IRIN Humanitarian News and Analysis 2007). He suggested that the EU, by sending military to the Chad–Sudan borderlands, was more interested in exploiting the country's oil resources than bringing lasting peace to the country. In this way, the supposed oil interests of international interveners in the Chad–Sudan border area figured in the power play between regional (rebel) claims and national negotiations between the government and international agencies rather than a real fear of foreign exploitation. From the perspective of the Chadian side of the borderlands, state images did not so much centre around a government practice of marginalising the border zones as the fear of despotic exploitation and a loss of livelihoods through theft and arbitrary harassment. From the government's side, meanwhile, the borderlands also certainly posed a threat as the rebels' rear base and as an area of political opposition.

Looking at this situation, I argue that oil has influenced the way the war in the borderlands has come to be perceived in different ways that are mainly expressed as assumptions and rumours. The individual narratives those fighting in Darfur have used to make sense of the war only rarely mention oil, although they do allude to issues such as international interest in the region, the possibility of the inclusion of their region in the global economy, or simply the improvement of the very land on which and about which the fighting took place. Asked whether oil had played a role in launching the Justice and Equality Movement (JEM)—one of the rebel groups that had originally mainly recruited among the Sudanese Zaghawa and later allied with the Chadian president—its UK spokesperson, Abdullahi El-Tom, said that his own rebel group was promoting oil exploration. When the government of Sudan wanted to stop exploration by foreign companies in Darfur, the rebels had tried to convince them to continue. The fighting was connected to oil in different ways on both sides of the border, but I would argue that it was mainly directed against the respective governments of Chad and Sudan, and was to contest continued marginalisation and to state territorial claims, rather than being motivated by a desire for gaining direct access to oil revenues on the ground.

Moving away from the local perspective from the borderlands, I will now look at international intervention in relation to oil revenues, represented mainly by a World Bank-mediated model for fair revenue distribution. This model was first implemented in Chad but never replicated, probably because of the complex tensions it caused. The Chadian state, from this point of view, was to become a laboratory for international intervention where possibilities for producing resources even in countries that were not generally deemed safe enough for large foreign investments could be tried out.

World Bank and Chadian state: No oil model for peace[11]

The World Bank's model for development-oriented oil revenue distribution was made binding law in Chad in 1999 and was intended to ensure infrastructural development and conservation of the environment.[12] Ten years later, on 9 September 2009, the World Bank withdrew from the project, claiming that the Chadian government had disregarded its initial intentions on how to use the oil revenues to alleviate poverty.[13] Looking back at the process, one might wonder how the international actors actually imagined they would influence national governmental decision-making without this constituting outside interference. The other question that had remained open was that the model had anticipated that the Chadian population was to use the oil money, and this implied that it should be channelled to them directly for purposes of development and creating future savings. But how could they guarantee the people's adherence to an ideal model which had been drawn up far away from the country's 'realities'? It seems that all the parties involved considered signing the contracts and passing the laws specified by the model as sufficient proof of commitment on all sides— an effect corresponding to official adherence to 'metacodes', as Rottenburg (2002, 2005, 2009) has called them. The first palpable result of the new oil law ('Law 001') was a sudden infusion of financial support for oil regulation matters from the international development community already present in Chad that promoted the formation of many new national NGOs and civil society organisations. Their *raison d'être* lay in interpreting the World Bank model to the people and helping to regulate the use of the money for development-oriented purposes, so that it was expected to flow into the country's rural areas. In 2000–1, the oil model apparently became the 'new horse' on which the development and human rights community was prepared to bet.

The anticipated ordering—or at least the image of preventing substantial disorder caused by oil—that lay at the basis of the model did not only fail, as Geoffrey Bergen, the World Bank's former representative in Chad, maintained, because the 'Chadian state could not be trusted' (Behrends and Hoinathy 2017: 58). I argue that the model was flawed because it imagined the Chadian state's legal apparatus to have more influence in directing the revenues to the populations' needs than it actually did. It could be argued that the World Bank model has always been more oriented towards facilitating business interests than providing 'justice', as Li (2007) concludes about a large-scale World Bank initiative supporting palm oil production in Indonesia. The notion that the politics of oil were more complicated than setting up a model to anticipate and prevent (or solve) conflicts closely corresponds to Andrew Barry's (2013) study on the specific political relations involved in the Caucasian Baku-Tbilisi-Ceyhan (BTC) pipeline project, in which he postulates that material politics can be found in the particular relations created in each political situation along the pipeline around material and non-material matter. In Chad, this becomes clearer when one considers that the oil companies had originally made the Chadian government's compliance with the bank's model their main condition for a USD 3.7 billion investment in the 1080-kilometre pipeline connecting the oil fields in southern Chad to Port Kribi in southern Cameroon, the largest single-sector investment in sub-Saharan Africa up to that point. Accordingly, the Chadian government diligently enacted the Revenue Management Law, which specified the process for distributing of oil revenue, designated its main actors, and established a committee to oversee the flow of oil revenues. This was taken to guarantee that oil money would actually be invested in social infrastructures.

Much has been written about this model and its major failings: the dual-track development of the oil infrastructure and the institutions intended to control and observe the spending of revenues (Guyer 2002, 2015; Pegg 2005). I interpret them here as images that provoked certain expectations of how the state would go about spending oil money that were based on mistrust of the state's performance and thus secured by legal measures. Here, the main argument is that the international image of the Chadian state did not correspond to its own self-image and, accordingly, to the expectations of practices it induced. The World Bank's inability to prevent the Chadian government from changing the laws regulating oil money and President Déby's ability to unilaterally change the key investment areas designated by the model were the most prominent points of contention among the observing experts. Less attention was paid to how the oil companies had turned out to play a disruptive double role. Steve Coll (2012) describes the reasoning of the major oil companies operating in Chad, Chevron and ExxonMobil, in some detail: at first, when they depended on the World Bank to secure their investments, they complied with the prescribed order of the model but later, when they had recouped their investments and production became profitable, they turned against it and classified it as a superfluous and insubstantial experiment in nation building.

Capitalist interests in oil production not only provided the framework for all further elaborations of the Chadian oil project but, as Li (2007: 262) has also observed, 'shaped what the project became'. Consequently, those who invested the most—the US-based multinationals Chevron and ExxonMobil—ultimately had the upper hand in deciding who would receive the revenues, hindering the World Bank's leverage in Chad. These interests, together with the powerful images conjured up by oil (Apter 1996; Coronil 1997), seem to me to have been among the main drivers of turbulence in the oil-producing region. In contrast to Geoffrey Bergen's analysis of the bank's flawed intervention, a lack of knowledge about the intentions and structures of the other side—the Chadian state—was not the main source of the model's flaw. Instead, the revenue management model was never actually oriented towards securing the livelihoods of the rural population but solely addressed the national government. In turn, the government, in cooperation with the oil consortium, established a zone of oversight that appeared clean only from the outside—a configuration that Barry (2006) has called a 'technological zone'—intended only to improve its own international reputation. This neither alleviated poverty nor prevented the outbreak of civil war in Chad.

However, I would argue that one area of the original oil model, its intention to boost the country's infrastructure, might have influenced some of the construction spree that followed the 2008 attack on N'Djamena. In conjunction with all the other historical developments, the World Bank model thus contributed to a new direction of turbulence following this particular attack and defeat of the rebels, marking the beginning of 'development' according not to the World Bank's but the Chadian president's understanding.

11

THIS MONEY BELONGS TO THE PEOPLE OF CHAD

OIL, DEVELOPMENT, AND IMAGINING THE STATE

The February 2008 attack on N'Djamena turned out to be both a link in a long historical chain of repeating patterns of attack and counterattack and a singular and game-changing event in the country's history. Most people had already recognised this pattern when the rebels were still en route to N'Djamena and knew what to expect: since independence in 1960, they had never experienced a change in government other than through military coups. (The most recent of these was in April 2021, when the rebels entered Chad from Southern Libya and President Idriss Déby Itno died during an attack while visiting his troops in the field.) Rulership that was basically hostile to the population, fast-changing but usually negligent and marginalising forms of government, and raids were the norm, not only after colonial rule but during it and since long before (Alio 2002; Behrends 2007; Buijtenhuijs 1978, 1987; Burr and Collins 1999; de Bruijn and van Dijk 2007; Meier 1995; Reyna 1990; Salih and Harir 1994). Before the N'Djamena attack in February 2008, the city's inhabitants had stockpiled food and found it hard to decide between fleeing across the river to Cameroon or waiting out the attack at home. They knew from experience that those who left might well return and find that none of their belongings remained, so many stayed even though it meant facing other forms of uncertainty. Staying depended on feeling safe near relatives and neighbours who had also decided not to leave, and at least some in N'Djamena knew they lived in the right neighbourhoods and had connections to higher-ups who could help in troubled times. But most people who stayed seem either to have been worried about whether all their relatives were up to life on the run or to have had material reasons: by remaining close to their houses and belongings, they could protect what they would need to resume their previous lives, which many preferred to leaving for a presumed safe haven in a neighbouring country or even just outside the city.

On another level, the attack on N'Djamena—as a singular and game-changing event—caused a 180-degree turn in President Déby's governing strategy, from waging a proxy war with Sudan in which each state supported the other's rebellion, to making peace with the government of the then Sudanese president Omar al-Bashir.[1] At this point, the president started to shift most oil revenues from expanding the military to investing in (his version of) large-scale development. In many ways, this new form of development did not accord with the priority sectors laid out in the World Bank model I discussed in the previous chapter, which prioritised quality investments in infrastructures of education, economic opportunities and health (including access to clean water and food) rather than building roads, soccer stadiums, and high-rise buildings. The government, however, started to invest in its own vision of infrastructure.

From this point on, the city's atmosphere changed perceptibly, and more large-scale displacement took place. The government tore down whole neighbourhoods and turned them into huge construction sites. This form of development was not based on indicators collected by international data institutions, like the poverty index. Instead—as some commented—the high modernist aesthetics of Abu Dhabi, Kuwait or Singapore were its main models. Chadian development after the 2008 attack focused on planning and preconstruction work for shiny office towers, monumental plazas, elaborate roundabouts, new roads and bridges, and mega-structures like soccer stadiums, markets and airports—not to mention rebuilding the presidential palace in the capital with even higher walls and larger buildings and the most modern security technology. In the event, a later collapse of oil prices pushed the economy into a debt cycle and only a few of these buildings were actually completed. For instance, ground has not yet been broken for the new airport that was to be built north of the capital as a new Central African hub.

International agencies started to cut back development aid spending in Chad following the attack on the capital. However, their previous main argument that the government had misspent oil revenues on internal fighting, as Guyer (2002) critically remarked during the early phase of oil production, no longer held. In an unforeseen twist, the large, well-trained and well-equipped Chadian military became 'the West's' strongest ally against the threat that Islamic extremists would regroup in West and Central Africa after the former Libyan leader Muammar al-Gaddafi's downfall in October 2011.[2] Meanwhile, the Chadian government was now spending its oil money mainly on white elephant projects in the capital city. Its rhetoric was about turning Chad into a sub-Saharan hub with the capital as its *vitrine* (showcase): it was anxious to communicate to the world the country's prosperity, peace, power, and most of all its development.

New wealth and an old plan: Rebuilding N'Djamena

The building phase that followed the raids on the quarters of N'Djamena that had allegedly hosted rebels was put into the hands of the mayor's office. To carry out large-scale construction projects, a colonial-era plan was unearthed. This so-called *ancien plan* ('ancien' does not just mean 'very old' but implies a relationship or situation that no longer exists) gave the mayor's office the authority to evict people and demolish their houses. Von Hirschhausen et al. (2015) reflect on the use of such old and half-forgotten plans in justifying or resisting action and show how they were reanimated as a means of resistance. In N'Djamena, however, the *ancien plan* became an instrument of power for the already powerful (Doumbia 2021): after the attack, it was incorporated into governmental discourse and served as a pretext to severely limit people's right to contest evictions.

In 2010, just two years after the attack on N'Djamena, I was very struck by the city's frantic state of rebuilding and reconstruction. 'The *ancien plan* was already there and Déby already wanted to start construction in 2005 and 2006. But back then the population knew how to resist. Every time the military showed up to evict the population, we blew whistles and soon the whole neighbourhood gathered to fight them back.' Baldal Oyamta, the head of the *Ligue Tchadienne des Droits de l'Homme* (Chadian League for Human Rights), told me this story. A friend had introduced us, and I wanted to find out more about how the city was supposed to be rebuilt by evicting people from their homes. Baldal had experienced more than his share of governmental harassment. 'I've been beaten up three times already, I hope that will be enough for a while,' he told me, beaming with confidence despite these severe threats to his life. After the attack on N'Djamena, he had sent photos of the city to international friends, then fled to Yaoundé, in Cameroon, where he had to stay for four months before he felt it was safe to return to N'Djamena. 'After the 2008 attacks, the president saw his chance and declared a state of emergency that changed the legal situation in such a way that he immediately started to demolish houses.' Resistance was extremely dangerous at that time and everyone who spoke up 'was thrown into jail right away', he recalled. According to the *ancien plan*, which had been prepared by French urban planners, certain areas were 'already dedicated to specific purposes in the sixties'. In those days, most people who could afford to build houses preferred to build them close to these designated areas. As these quarters grew and the 'special purpose areas' were not developed, people started to build everywhere. The government had no plan of their own, so they revived the French planners' old designations and seized the land back from the people who had built there decades before. The plan to turn N'Djamena into a Central African showcase became known as Déby's new *projet présidentiel*. To achieve it, not only houses but whole neighbourhoods were torn down. According to Baldal, however, categorisations of the capital's inhabitants generated a very different handling of this reconstruction. 'You can observe two big differences between the *quartiers* of people from the south and from the north. One lies in the fact that Northerners receive compensation and Southerners do not, and the quality of the new buildings is much better in the Northern *quartiers*.' Baldal remarked that there were signs crediting the *projet présidentiel* in front of every construction site to give the impression that Déby 'took the money from his own pocket—which is not the case'. He asserted that this money in fact came from oil production, adding that 'this money belongs to the people of Chad'. He believed that it should not be spent on shiny buildings and plazas, but 'used to fight cholera and other diseases caused by dirty water and food'. Even the new hospital was 'there, but no one works in it. They say that doctors will be recruited from Cuba. But will they come? And how long will they stay?' His conclusion was the same I had heard again and again: '*Ils se moquent de nous*—they're making fun of us.' His criticism sounded bitter, disappointed by the lost chance to improve the country's situation. Instead, the reconstruction of the capital followed a well-trodden path of corruption and clientelism that he had known all his life. Baldal had more to say about how tenders for construction projects were distributed among the government's cronies and worried about important international donors withdrawing from a state that did not seem to intend to take over where aid agencies had been investing for decades. According to his calculations, the government was highly indebted. The construction plans were extremely expensive, and only the contractors became rich. 'The contractor gets 10% of the overall costs of construction. And since the overall costs are extremely inflated to make more profits, they put up to 100 million US dollars into their pockets. Construction is the best way to make money disappear, so they build without any limits of cost or common sense.' This construction boom led to rising prices for cement, whose price doubled from 2006 to 2010. Similarly, the prices for staple foods like millet and meat had soared. The rentier economy that Yates (1996) has described in great detail, particularly for oil rents, disadvantaged the country's population. Meanwhile, taxes had increased from 12% to 16% with no corresponding increase in wages. Baldal concluded that 'even if someone spent 50,000 CFA francs a month, he couldn't build a four-metre-square house.'

Preparing for the construction of the *plan présidentiel* changed the city dramatically. The streets were still cramped with cars and motorcycles, pedestrians, people with handcarts and an occasional bicyclist, but everywhere houses were being torn down and new roads and squares constructed. As we drove through the city, one of my colleagues frequently commented: 'This new road, no one knows where it goes.' The population feverishly tried to adapt to these changes to avoid what was about to happen. In 2010, the eviction phase started, and I saw '*3 jours pavé!*' (to be paved within three days) spraypainted on many houses along the city streets. Small shop owners in the city could add false fronts to their mud brick houses to render them 'modern' according to the government's standards; then the small patches of street in front of their houses would be paved with a mixture of mud and cement. Meanwhile, owners who failed to meet these requirements would have their houses demolished without compensation and the residents or shop owners would be expected to go to relatives in the countryside or move to refugee camps in Cameroon (Amnesty International 2009: 5). Striking aerial photographs in an Amnesty International report (ibid.) confirmed what Baldal told me: whole neighbourhoods had been destroyed. Their inhabitants were left homeless and only a few educated and well-connected people had a chance to fight for the possibility of partial compensation many years later.

One person whose house was destroyed was the late Khalil Alio. A professor at, and the former president of, the University of N'Djamena, Khalil had lived and worked in the capital for more than 30 years. I had met him as a research partner in 2000, and later we became close colleagues: in 2007, we started a research centre together and Khalil became its first director. Just briefly after the N'Djamena attack in 2008, he was told that the land where he had built was part of the *ancien plan* that would now be carried out. All unauthorised buildings would be torn down by mayoral decree. 'The mayor's office gave me three days to vacate the place. It took me three lawyers to at least extend this to two weeks! After that, my new house was reduced to ruins,' he recalled in May 2008, still in shock from this sad event. 'They said the house had been built on government land.' Khalil had built on land which he had registered with the traditional authorities responsible for all land outside the city and added that 'it is the usual practice here'. 'I was *déguerpi* [expelled] twice: in 2008 from Sara Dégaule, that is the name of the quarter. The Hilton Hotel is built on my land. In fact, the *pierre* [foundation stone] was laid by the president just where I had my gate, where you visited us.' The second time was in 2012, only 500 metres away in the neighbouring Sabangali quarter. 'I again managed to get a plot and build a big house.' But he could not stay there either. 'There again, a presidential decree was made to tell us to leave.' What made him and many others particularly angry was that some of the president's kin, who had built their houses in the direct vicinity of the president's palace on what 'certainly must have been government land', were also ordered to leave but had immediately received compensation of 'up to ten billion CFA francs' (about 15 million euros). In 2013, Khalil finally received compensation for the second house. 'But they gave us what they wanted to, not the real value of our houses.' His family had won in the case of the first house, where he had taken lawyers, but had only received part of the compensation due to them. 'We are still waiting for the second part—since 2008!' Khalil lived through many troubles, some of which he published in a fictionalised memoir (Alio 2011, 2017).

Faced with the state of emergency and the thousands of people in the same predicament as Alio, the city instituted a new model of security. Some measures were quite primitive: a 3-metre-deep trench was dug around the city 'to force vehicles through one of a few fortified gateways' as the BBC reported on 4 March 2008,[3] and the century-old trees that lined the main avenue were all cut down so that attackers could not hide behind them. Another more sophisticated measure was to move all ministries to new buildings outside the city centre, dispersing them in various neighbourhoods to prevent them from easily being targeted. The US embassy was also moved outside the city centre, and the area within a 1-kilometre radius of it was to be cleared of its inhabitants and buildings. A new elevated road was originally supposed to be torn down as well since it overlooked the new high-security embassy, but that never happened.[4]

An array of new laws rendered the city cleaner. Everywhere, groups of uniformed street cleaners (mainly women) walked through the dusty streets in small groups picking up trash. Millions of small black plastic bags had once covered every dusty square, bush, tree and puddle and banning them totally changed the city centre's appearance. But while the city looked cleaner, the food vendors who had used them excessively before had to find creative ways to wrap oily food like *beignets*—brown paper or natural leaves. Similarly, the restriction on charcoal fires within the city limits drove many Chadians to desperation. 'The city is no place for the poor', the president was reported to have said, following his aim to make the capital *la vitrine de l'Afrique Centrale*, the showcase of Central Africa. 'After he has beaten the rebels and succeeded in securing his position, he now wants to prepare his departure through the big gate', as Claus Auer, German ambassador in Chad from 2011 to 2013, wrote to me. He meant that Déby was trying to move beyond his image as a desert warrior and that the new policies were intended as his main legacy to Chad: making the previously run-down and dilapidated-seeming city of N'Djamena a cleaner and more impressive place.

One wide new road, which is commonly called 'Rue de Soixante Métres' (Sixty-Metre Road) is flanked by double rows of palm trees and connects to the colonial Rue de Quarante (Forty [-Metre] Road), previously the second widest road in N'Djamena after the Avenue Charles de Gaulle. The new road will lead to the Rond Point de la Grande Armée, a roundabout where ten roads converge on an equestrian statue. When I asked people in N'Djamena what they thought of it, they only mentioned the costs of construction: 10 billion CFA francs or 15 million euros. This roundabout, so far, does not join important streets, only 'streets leading nowhere', as my colleague put it. It is in a quiet part of the city, but very close to the airport. The names of all the buildings and streets pay tribute to the president. *La Grande Armée* is the army that toppled Hissein Habré, *Aéroport Hassan Djamous* is named after an army general and older cousin of Déby who was killed on the orders of then president Hissein Habré while trying to escape to Sudan after a failed coup against Habré's government.[5] Together with the monument statue at the centre of the Rond Point de la Grande Armée, they speak of an intention to develop the nation whose aesthetics do not start with what was lacking—like health, education or nutrition—but aim to display pride and project an aura of grandeur over the city (see Pinther et al. 2010).[6]

At first, the purposes of some of the new buildings were unclear to residents, and rumours circulated and fanned the flames of suspicion about whom they really served. Another whole neighbourhood was demolished to construct a new maternity hospital, but the architects were said to have left out the delivery room. People joked that the babies could be born in the (non-functioning) elevator. There were no doctors to staff the hospital or football teams to play at the stadiums being built all over the country. People said, 'to play football your stomach has to be full', meaning that poor people could not play professional football. Everyone wanted to see the country progress and, since football is one of the great passions of nearly every Chadian, would also love to cheer their national team. Some might even want to send their children to the paradise donated by former president Idriss Déby's wife, Madame Hinda Déby, a hangar-sized building that contained a playground with toys. In 2010, it was absolutely deserted: it was 'too expensive to go in', my friends told me, and the toys they had there were kinds that were unfamiliar to Chadian children. In the end, all these governmental investments seemed oversized and out of place to the population, who did not see the point of them.

The construction spree was far less visible outside the capital, but when it *was* visible it seemed even more absurd. While the new roads seemed at first to connect the larger cities better, many didn't last through even one rainy season. School buildings and water towers sometimes stood two in a row, but many had not yet been put into use and gave the impression of building for the sake of building, with no thought given to renovating existing structures or consulting with the population about what was actually needed. Many new school buildings were thus put to other uses, like the girls' school in Adré that was turned over to the new mixed Chadian–Sudanese military force in 2010. While the Chadian state intended the construction sites as a demonstration of the country's rise from poverty, development agencies took this display as an opportunity to withdraw aid. This was not felt as much in N'Djamena, where less international aid was invested in visible projects. But in areas that received more attention from aid agencies, like the Chad–Sudan borderlands, this withdrawal had visible effects, especially on people's ways of flexibly dealing with uncertainty.

Post-war development and the withdrawal of aid: Getting by in Abéché

When I returned to Abéché in 2011, I particularly looked for signs of the region's possible future in the period after the war. Turning my gaze from the governmental centre in N'Djamena to Abéché in the east of Chad, I wondered how the game-changing rebel attack that had led to the construction boom in the capital had impacted that area of the country, which had mainly relied on international aid to survive since long before the Darfur War. What images of the state and of the region's future emerged after the president's declaration of the state of emergency in February 2008, and which practices followed his novel form of spending oil money on 'developing the nation'?

During this visit, I did not go straight to the borderlands as usual. Instead, I talked with the city's officials: the mayor of Abéché and his secretary, the current governor, and his chief of staff. I also met the Sultan of Wadai in his palace. Despite an atmosphere of post-war malaise, everyone still had specific ideas about the region's future.

Chad's governmental centre and the country's eastern region have always had an ambiguous relationship. The ambiguity lies in Abéché's simultaneous socio-economic marginality and political centrality. As Reyna (1990) shows, the Wadai Sultanate had historically occupied large parts of the current country's territory. This area first became Muslim when pilgrims from West Africa travelled through it to Mecca on the Hajj (Khayar 1984; Seesemann 2005). It is widely considered to have the most devout population of the Muslim regions in the north of the country. The *Lycée Nationale Franco-Arabe* (Franco-Arab National High School), opened in Abéché in 1957, was the first of its kind, and continues to be a centre of Islamic learning combined with Western knowledge. A number of elite individuals were educated there, including both President Déby and my colleague Khalil Alio. This regional image and history hold a special power that has definitely acted as a counterbalance to the current government, as was sadly demonstrated by the disappearance and presumed murder of the opposition politician Ibni Oumar Mahamat Saleh during the 2008 N'Djamena attack.[7] At the same time, the region's marginalisation is undeniable. Until most recently, no paved roads connected it to the rest of the world (unlike the southern regions) and the trade routes were directed east towards Sudan rather than the rest of Chad. The region's ambiguous centrality stems from two main causes: it has been the origin of rebellions for almost forty years (see Buijtenhuijs 1978, 1987) and it is Déby's region of origin. This second aspect, especially, has been the cause of significant unease among the eastern region's population (except for the president's own people). For instance, it is common knowledge that his otherwise completely insignificant hometown, Am Djerress, has been developed far more than the rest of the region.[8] The region has become central due to the extent of government attention devoted to it. Otherwise, it has remained remote from the centres of political decision-making as well as the provision of infrastructure. It is only in the last decade that there has even been a regular bus service to the rest of the country. This double centrality in the margins makes it a peripheral centre in the sense of Das and Poole (2004). How did Déby's development plan affect this region after 2008? And how did the borderlanders perceive the intended withdrawal of international aid?

LIFEWORLDS IN CRISIS

During the several phases of my research, I repeatedly returned to Abéché. There, I was able to see the immense impact of war, international aid, and the government's attempts at organising the situation by, for instance, granting and then withdrawing authorisation for foreign military interventions like the French Opération Épervier and the United Nations Mission in the Central African Republic and Chad (MINURCAT). During the war, the constant presence of hundreds of international aid workers and their foreign and national staff not only caused food prices to rise. In addition, luxury houses were built, with rents reaching USD 5,000 per month. But while these infrastructures developed the city, they were not intended for the local population—even though issues like increased prices affected everyone. I remembered the white four-wheel-drive cars circling the city every time I looked up during my visit in 2007, the barbed wire around the international agencies' headquarters, the UN signs, and the new restaurants for foreigners, mainly run by southern Chadians or Cameroonian migrants who had moved to the city to work in bars and restaurants as well as for the international organisations. In 2011, the same development aid agencies were also still there but had either put their programmes on hold or turned fully towards the humanitarian sector. Thus, the Gesellschaft für Internationale Zusammenarbeit (GIZ) now took care of water provision for a refugee camp near the town Iriba and the educational programmes at Camp Farchana. All these changes were related to aid and its sudden increase or withdrawal. With humanitarian aid during the Darfur War, the city had dramatically transformed from a slow-moving, sleepy and dusty town to a buzzing, globally connected hub with an hourly air service to N'Djamena and beyond. However, this infrastructure was of very little use to the local population and when I talked to people after the war they seemed depressed. A new factor had also appeared: uncertainty about the city's future.

The new phase of the government's development project that had taken hold in N'Djamena also seemed to be making itself felt in Abéché. In line with the presidential development plan, I had heard talk about Abéché becoming the second capital of Chad. As with the *ancien plan* of N'Djamena, Abéché was to be reconstructed;

here, based not on a long-lost colonial document but the argument that supposedly nationally owned land had not been officially registered.[9] But Baldal, the human rights lawyer I quoted above, also highly doubted those announcements, particularly since he saw economic potential and development as being centred in the country's south. As he remarked during our interview in N'Djamena, 'Abéché cannot pride itself on an economy of its own'. He added that there would be nothing there comparable to the economic boom in Moundou. The same uncertainty had taken hold in Abéché as in N'Djamena about what would happen to homes, shops and other structures. 'They want to tear down houses,' my friends Abdoullai Peter and Ekhlas told me. 'Everything that has been built on national land can be torn down.' Abdoullai Peter had come to Chad from Switzerland in the late 1970s and stayed after he married Ekhlas, who had been born and raised in Abéché. He worked in the city's hospital as an anaesthetist's assistant (although sometimes doing the work of a doctor); meanwhile the couple had also started an NGO to fund self-help initiatives, provide vocational training (particularly for women) and build on the international aid structures present in the city since independence (Otto 2011). They felt a little less uncertainty in the Darfur War's aftermath than during it, but it took a different form. They were no longer sure that their own property, a large house with several courtyards as well as smaller outbuildings and offices, was not on national land. Nor could they be sure about the hospital's future: it was mainly international funding that kept the institution alive. Like the greater part of the city's population (at least those who were not members of the president's Zaghawa family), the two had started to seek employment with, or at least occasional funding from, the international aid agencies. And while they had received such support during the heyday of international aid in the city, the agencies, even those present for decades, now were preparing to leave, which once again rendered the couple's future uncertain.

The aid agencies' withdrawal from the city was closely related to the declaration that the rebellion was over, and to the president's redirection of oil money to development, the second major issue of the time immediately following the 2008 attack.

This also marked a turning point in Abéché that had started with the withdrawal of the UNHCR. The organisation's first step was to immediately close its main office in Abéché. What followed did not at first evoke the image of a withdrawal: based on the argument that it had to continue to serve the existing refugee camps while also planning an orderly exit, the agency massively increased its presence in the villages near the twelve remaining camps, as I have shown in the previous part of the book. But as the UNHCR was considered the flagship of Western humanitarian aid in Abéché, this move determined all the other agencies' approaches and areas of activity in the borderlands. When the UNHCR left Abéché, the other agencies also started to withdraw from the city and most ended their interventions altogether. Prices for food went down, which generally pleased urban residents, but many also lost their jobs. The situation was particularly difficult for those who had left other jobs and come as migrants to work for the international organisations.

No one could afford to live in the expat villas anymore, so they were left vacant and have remained more or less unused. No more hostels were needed, nor anyone to guard them. The area around the former aid facilities came to be perceived as dangerous. Drunk men staggered past, and the national military eventually took over most of the places the international agencies had vacated. Abdoullai Peter openly regretted this: 'No one's interested in the hospital anymore. Since we no longer have to treat victims of war, the flow of money has ebbed.' He reported that even Médicins Sans Frontières was now focusing on routine operations like removing cysts, treating victims of car accidents and common illnesses, and delivering babies. 'These are still sapping our energy, but we're back to our very limited staff. It's so frustrating. Sometimes I feel like giving up,' he said, summarising his feelings about the city's atmosphere. Another problem he had observed was that unemployed young people were visible everywhere. 'The young people who came here to find work with the aid agencies now hang out in the streets, unemployed.' He said that they took Tramadol, an opioid that was also used as stimulant for racehorses. 'When they take this drug, they drive like crazy through town on their motorbikes, but sometimes even the rickshaw drivers take it![10] The government's reacted too slowly, they've only now started to check cars here and there.' Government checks on those selling the drugs, however, seemed to proceed even more slowly. Those profiting from the business were said to be those close to the president, but even they suffered: most had been counting on large amounts of income from houses they had built and rented to the international staff of aid agencies and military and had now lost this business.

J-P, a young chef who had moved from Cameroon just after the war, when Abéché's new restaurants were still open, talked with me about the prospects of the city's young people. He considered the international community's withdrawal from Abéché and the resultant unemployment the most obvious effects of war. 'For the young men, there is one option that appeals most to them: going back to rebellion,' he said. He believed that the rebels still surrounded the city and that 'some rich people' were paying for their equipment and training as well as their salaries and food so that there were better- and worse-paid rebel groups. 'They're not gone like everybody claims, but the massive unemployment is calling them back into action,' he explained excitedly. 'They don't fight for anything—it's only a decision of lifestyle, how you want to make money.' 'To many, it's the more attractive style of living,' he sighed. Being a rebel gained young men more prestige than working hard on a piece of land, 'where all you do is fight with herders about their animals entering the field and sweat and haul the crops to market for a very small profit'. Although I cannot say whether his perspective was typical among Abéché's youth, it certainly reflected what young people talked about and how they commented on their prospects for the future. In effect, rebel activities turned out to be one of the few options for the local youth that were still funded by those who could boast of having money after employment had rapidly decreased after the war.

Monsieur Kodjinar Toloum, the chief of staff for the governor of Wadai during my visit, shared this gloomy outlook. He originally came from the country's south, but his response when I asked about the situation of Abéché was very clear and straightforward.

'The current situation and the changes we perceive are results of the war,' he began. 'We still have 200,000 people living in twelve refugee camps, and the city had been flooded by the military mission of MINURCAT, as well as by humanitarian organisations who also hired a lot of people.' He estimated that the presence of humanitarian agencies had created 6,000 new jobs in a city with a population of 200,000. Toloum also remarked on the recently risen drug abuse. 'At the time there was a lot of construction, with jobs and prospects. Now the city is a hangout for the newly unemployed, who take drugs, vandalise and render the city a more dangerous place.' On the other hand, he related that the government had just established security committees that were developing a public safety plan in cooperation with the gendarmerie, the police, the military, and the *Détachement Intégré de Sécurité* (Integrated Security Detachment or DIS). Originally known as *Police Tchadienne pour la Protection Humanitaire*, the DIS had been set up April 2008, shortly before MINURCAT's withdrawal, was made up of UN-trained local police officers, and was assigned to protect 'refugees' and 'internally displaced persons' as well as humanitarian aid workers. Thus, the Chadian government's main contribution to aid in the borderlands and to the response to war and displacement was in the security sector. Similarly, the government had built a high-security prison in an area known as 'Koro-Toro' in the north of Chad. This notorious institution had come up during several of my conversations with people: while some unruly youths were supposedly deterred by the prospect of being thrown into a remote cell with guards who were not subject to any international or even national oversight, that prospect also frightened the general population (Amnesty International 2012). Ironically, both the prison and the funding of rebel activities were local effects of the post-war phase.

Before I left Abéché, I met with both the new governor and the mayor, Mahamat Saleh Ahmat Adam, who would soon be up for re-election. In the morning I visited the governor, who politely welcomed me with a soft drink but had nothing to say about the current situation. He would only refer me to other officials: the mayor was responsible for the city, the minister planned the distribution of governmental funding, and other questions should be directed to the respective prefects and subprefects. He could not tell us anything interesting, he was only there to oversee other institutions. He might be here for a long time or a short one, the president decided where to assign his governors. I finished my soft drink and left, thanking him for the meeting. Abdoullai Peter later told me that the hospital's director had gone to introduce himself to the governor that same day and been told that he was taking a nap after watering the trees in his garden. I could not help but take this as indicating his lack of engagement.

The mayor, in contrast, came from Abéché and seemed to be both far more committed to the city and an energetic and dedicated man. When I arrived at his comfortable but unassuming house, he offered me soft drinks, water and sweets and began to introduce 'his city' to me in a very frank, open and engaged way. He described his perspective on the city's place in the country and its prospects for the future considering the current difficulties. He started by recounting the impressive historical significance of Abéché and how it had become the capital of Wadai: 'This was only in 1850, when the powerful sultanate was still in full sway.' He continued to talk about the former empire's move to Abéché from the historical capital of Ouara, further to the north. The ruins of the sultan's palace there can still be visited, but Mahamat Saleh explained that a long drought during the 1820s and 1830s had impelled the sultan at the time, Mahamat Sherif, to establish a commission for finding a new capital site. According to local history, Imam Al-Djazouli, who led the commission, found the new location by following the nomads south. 'After about fifty kilometres, they reached a small mountain range and found a herder who was giving water to his cattle at the well. The herder's name was Abu Aché and this gave the city its current name.' 'When the place was found,' the mayor continued, 'the sultan sent for Turkish architects to design the city. Back then, the sultanate of Wadai had intensive contacts with Turkey through trade.' The centre of town was the sultan's palace, and separate quarters for the different parts of the population encircled it. 'Originally, the quarters were constructed according to ethnic origin,' he explained, 'but later they got mixed up.' Only the historical names remained, although today some people wanted to rename quarters 'to make them sound more modern. A quarter that was called "some woman's mat" was now to be called "that woman's carpet",' he said. He seemed amused (as I was) about how the carpet served as an indicator of modernity since it was a clear sign of increased wealth compared to a straw mat.

The mayor's secretary, Haoua Abdullai, also explained some of the city's most pressing difficulties, but more in terms of long-term trends than the immediate effects of war. 'Water continues to be our most pressing problem,' she explained, 'and the second is waste. With the city's size tripling, waste disposal has become extremely difficult. We have no waste dump, and the one the German development cooperation built has become too small.' Water had been the city's main problem for a long time, she said: the German-built waterworks had not been renovated since their construction and if they failed, the city would have no water at all. Moreover, very few households were connected to the system and most had to pay to have water delivered at variable prices that were highest at the peak of the dry season, even though the government has built two dams and the UN official in charge of MINURCAT's Abéché office, Dr. Rima Salah,[11] funded two more as a goodwill contribution to the city. Meanwhile, the city's rapid growth had made sanitation more complex and costly, and disposal much more complicated. Haoua Abdullai observed that the city was growing simply because people were leaving their rural homes to look for better opportunities. 'Some also take refuge in the city,' she conceded, 'but those who came to work with the internationals have, by now, left the city again.' She concluded by addressing the problem of youth and unemployment. For instance, if you needed people to work on a construction project, 'you only have to look underneath the next tree for them, *voilà*, there they are.' Then she turned to the future. 'The city has developed enormously,' she continued. 'While we used to live in total darkness, we now have paved roads, lights, and a university, which has attracted a good number of people.' At least seven new schools had joined the old Lycée Franco-Arabe, and with its revenue from taxes, customs, and fines, as well as grants for public works and infrastructure development, the city paid her department well enough. But when it came to the oil money, she said she had 'no idea' at all where it went or who spent it. It seemed to her that the city had done best in wartime: that is, during the phase between 2003 and 2008, when the arrival of so many humanitarian aid agencies had temporarily eliminated the problem of unemployment.

I supposed that running a city with no outside funding must be hard, but the mayor seemed up to the responsibility. He had only taken office in 2008, after the peak of the crisis. On the other hand, he had to manage a city where the apparent benefits of the extremely high international presence were fading and try to develop it with no external funding. 'I'm working with the local revenues,' he sighed, 'fees for market stalls, for mobile phones, for large automobiles like trucks, buses and the like.' In 2010, the city's public budget amounted to 300 million CFA francs, or about 460,000 euros. In 2011 this was supposed to rise to 340 million CFA francs, but only 210 million had been collected as of October. As the cost of living spiked, the mayor had needed to lower the taxes on produce sold on the market to reduce the cost of goods. Like others, he recounted that 'the national government has invested in paved roads and installing lights in the city', citing national investments that might be related to oil money. 'But these facilities are not maintained. We haven't even been given a long sturdy ladder to be able to climb up to reach the solar panels of our new streetlights.' Meanwhile, drainage had been neglected when they paved the roads, so flooding during the rainy season necessitated constant repairs.

The mayor cited construction and land as issues that were currently causing uncertainty and conflict. 'There is good land and bad land,' he explained. According to a plan drawn up in 1958, three arterial streets were supposed to cut through the city. 'Good land' was that not affected by these streets, while houses built on 'bad land' would have to be torn down. But to implement the large-scale reconstruction now planned for Abéché (this time paid for by oil money), some houses on the good land would also have to be demolished—but the owners of these would be compensated. As these street plans were more than fifty years old, the mayor had promised during his re-election campaign that he would fight for the owners of houses on bad land to be compensated with another plot of land to build new houses on. I wondered whether the sultan, who claimed to own all the land in Abéché, might not have a say in the compensation of land. 'You have put your finger on our problem,' the mayor exclaimed. 'The sultan actually contributed to the current problem by selling land worth 4 million CFA francs!' The mayor had put a hold on these sales, which totalled roughly 6,000 euros, and declared them invalid. Then, the sultan had complained to the former governor, who sent a dispatch to the president. As a result, the mayor was removed and had to justify himself in writing. 'I can show you these letters if you want,' he offered. Later, when President Déby came to Abéché during his own re-election campaign, the people asked him to reinstall the mayor, and eventually he did.

The mayor had quite different ideas about the rebels from the young Cameroonian I had previously talked to. 'The rebels are totally disorganised at the moment,' he insisted. 'That doesn't exist at the moment.' While the issue was not high among his current concerns, he considered decision-making about international development aid 'highly political'. The influx of people and the construction boom had led to an extreme rise in prices. His imagery became medical: aid, he claimed, was like an 'injection' with economic consequences. In its wake the economic pulse of the city had 'slowed down', with higher unemployment rates than before. The state 'never thought about' these consequences and there was no programme to help the city in its current distress. He thought the oil had not helped; rather, it had caused a 'price war' between 'the Chinese' (who run the refinery close to N'Djamena) and the state. Prices for gasoline and diesel had risen so much that they were more expensive than in the days when they had to be imported from Sudan. It was noteworthy that the reach of the government was so long that it could stop fuel imports to boost consumption of domestically produced fuel. When the new Chadian refinery in Djermaya, north of N'Djamena, started production, the prices were very low, and people were 'euphoric'. 'In the beginning the population could scent the smell of petrol,' he said, 'but now the situation is worse than before.' Still, the mayor did not despair. He himself had advanced the city's development by financing the construction of a high school for girls. When he led me around the classrooms, the girls beamed with pride. His vision for the city was one of self-reliance. Not counting on national assets, he defined development as 'economic independence', which I understood to be in relation to the national government.

My final visit was to the sultan of Abéché, Didji Mahamat. A man in his forties, he shared the mayor's perspective on the city's self-reliance. He was the old sultan's eldest son and had previously worked as a consultant with Africare, but when his father died, he was called to office according to custom. His palace was a large adobe building in the regional architectural style and occupied a prominent site on a large square where the council of elders met. When I entered, the sultan was sitting on a fine carpet and his attendants announced my visit and then slowly withdrew. I took off my sandals and sat with him on the carpet and we discussed the city's significance on the national level and from his perspective; the changes it has gone through; and his perceptions of and opinions about these changes. He promoted yet another vision of the city's future. To him the city was above all a meeting place of trade routes coming from Libya and Sudan and its economic base should be the trade in cattle and agricultural products. Oil and oil money, the sultan thought, were less significant. 'Maybe the new roads that will be built here, they're paid for by oil money,' he suggested, 'but what's of most interest to the city is the new railway track that will connect Sudan with Abéché and the capital, N'Djamena.' This would enable selling local produce to the national and international markets, which is still very rare due to the risk of spoilage if anything happens to the trucks on the way. Before I said goodbye, he suggested visiting the old palace, an impressive but dilapidated three-storey building where a number of ostriches were kept in pens, perhaps a vestige of the luxury and exotic riches that had surrounded the sultan of Abéché in the days when he was the principal authority in the region.

The sultan obviously dreamed of a transportation network that would prioritise connections to Sudan and Libya over connections to the country's own capital of N'Djamena. The governor's chief of staff, Mr Kodjinar Toloum, confirmed that the sultan saw the city as gaining most from cattle, trade and agriculture, but he himself had yet another vision for the region. He referred to an official announcement in which President Déby had declared his new-found commitment to *le monde rurale* (the rural world). In 2011, the president had earmarked 2 billion CFA francs for each of the country's regions, and they could spend about 3,050,000 CFA francs on the agricultural sectors, 'that existed before there was oil'. I took these sectors to be mainly farming and herding. In Adré, Brahim's uncle Djamal, a knowledgeable observer of the borderland situation particularly in relation to national developments, later commented on the president's rural outreach. From his perspective as someone working for the ONDR, the state's rural development organisation, the money appeared to support 'revenue generating activities' in the rural agricultural sector. The fact that a total of seven tractors had been bought for the three departments of the Wadai region underlined this commitment in his view. And while I doubted that a mere seven tractors would change the fate of an area as big as many European countries, the local perception should count as evidence for this commitment—even a small sign was better than nothing.

In retrospect, my conversations with the city's officials and some of its inhabitants revealed that the war had various indirect impacts that, for better or worse, were seen as temporary by those who had lived their whole lives in this volatile borderland. While development had come to the city in the form of housing, roads and electricity, its problems with employment, drinking water, public health and (as Mme Haoua underlined) waste had not been addressed by long-term financing and development. It remains to be seen if the government's initiative to 'boost sectors that are independent of oil' will have an impact.[12] The rising number of young people who remained in the city after working for the international agencies has not so far advanced the city, but rather increased the number of unemployed people looking for new opportunities. These seem to lie in the city's informal economy or in risky ventures like gold digging—or rebellion. And while

THIS MONEY BELONGS TO THE PEOPLE OF CHAD

the rich seem to have invested mainly in construction, funding armed rebellion remains in the background as an option for future careers in politics. On an individual basis, manufacturing and selling bricks has recently become a popular venture among those who can afford the initial investment. Brahim himself, who has had various business ideas over the years of our collaboration, started manufacturing bricks to sell to newly rich people who had made some money in the gold mines and now wanted to build houses. The state did not seem to play a part in any future plans people told me about.

12

CONCLUSION

SURVIVAL AT THE MARGINS OF THE WORLD

To survive a crisis like the Darfur War, people depend on their lifeworldly knowledge. They have acquired this through experiencing family, regional and institutional histories and through their relationships, workplaces and government—and on adapting this knowledge to new circumstances, sometimes literally on their feet. This was true both for people already living in the borderlands and for those who moved there for various reasons: 'refugees', aid workers, military, government employees, work migrants or even researchers. In this book, I have tried to show how this knowledge and the actions and practices that resulted from it became even more visible as life routines were shaken up by sudden events, rumoured or actual attacks, the installation of aid infrastructure, military deployments and the presence of rebel bases nearby. There will be significant variation in whether something is considered a crisis, and by whom, and this will, in turn, inspire or dictate very different actions.

LIFEWORLDS IN CRISIS

Analytical conclusions

Multiple lifeworlds are in crisis in the Chad–Sudan borderlands, one of the most volatile and marginal regions of the continent. The stories and experiences that people there have told me throughout the last two decades reveal their knowledge of how to survive situations of deprivation and war. Some remained in their villages and towns because they had found possibilities for economic gain during wartime and could make use of existing advantages like schooling or a talent for business. Others, due to poverty or poor health, simply lacked the ability to flee. Almost no one could imagine leaving family members behind. (Some people, of course, did leave. Some I met, mainly young men, had travelled to Sudan, Libya or even Saudi Arabia to earn the capital to return and start a business; others, of course, did not return.) This book has aimed to provide an in-depth, long-term perspective on how people who remain live through hard times, and people's flexibility in anticipating, adapting to and managing rapid change has been its chief concern. It is this understanding of how encounters of different ways of categorising people or categorising a situation or an institution cause contingent changes in the lives of all involved that I hope will also be useful in understanding similar situations.

My original choice to research this region, in hindsight, was partly a matter of chance, especially the specific regional interests of Günther Schlee, my department chair when I was a postdoctoral researcher at the Max Planck Institute for Social Anthropology in Halle/Saale, and also the generous funding that came with that position. In Chad, I became committed to the people and the place and as many of my questions remained unanswered over time, I continued to study the situation that unfolded during the rising turbulence after 2003. However, it took me some time to find my main analytical aim: understanding the ways people maintain their lifeworlds in the situations of rupture caused by violence, war and displacement. I wanted to know how survival works in situations where social and institutional arrangements are shaken and sometimes fail. And I wanted to understand where people find commonalities in times of duress, how they define belonging and

CONCLUSION

difference and how they negotiate different versions of reality. The answers that I found through long-term research and by maintaining many contacts concern practices in flexibly changing modes of belonging.

Here, the concept of emplacement has been very helpful because it enables a simultaneous analysis of all the actors involved in a process of refuge and arrival. Glick Schiller and Çağlar (2015), as well as Bjarnesen and Vigh (2016), have emphasised this process and the lack of studies related to it, since emplacement is not easily observable on a short-term basis. To understand it, I found it was essential to follow individual processes, keep aware of existing differentiations, and recognise situations where established notions of difference between people became unimportant. All these depended on the relationship networks of individuals and families, as well as local, governmental and international institutions and organisations. Hirschauer's (2014) work on the 'contingency of social belonging' guided my analysis. That contingency, as Luhmann (1984) shows, lies in each (accidental) move, each trigger, or each error, which can become productive for new relations and connectivities. Doing or undoing differences and switching between and translating different codings of reality—as Richard Rottenburg (2005) defines it—is derived from the ability of all actors to interpret, adapt to, tinker with, or 'loop' (give their own meaning to)—to use Ian Hacking's (1995) term—human categories. This figurative flexibility requires knowledge about and an awareness of situational codes of belonging. Wenger, McDermott and Snyder's (2002) definition of 'communities of practice' and Stengers's (2005) 'interacting ecologies' symbolise the relational processes of categorising and sorting out—according to Bowker and Star (1999)—and understanding how different knowledges relate and interact and how boundary objects (Star and Griesemer 1989) carry evidence (Rottenburg et al 2015) and are translated into varying or new circumstances and relations of inequality and power (Callon 1986). Following how knowledge is productive in situations of uncertainty and how it constantly changes and relates with practice became my prime motive in writing this book.

I have used processes of flexible categorising in relation to belonging as my lens in this longitudinal study of events and experiences 'before', 'during' and 'after' the Darfur War. In Part I, I focused on the borderland's villages and towns. In Part II, I looked at the refugee camps and the influence of aid agencies on people there and the borderlands' population more generally. Part III analysed images of the Chadian state and how the state was categorised in significant moments, like the beginning of oil production just as war broke out in the borderlands. In all fields and situations, different people make different categorisations. I have taken up the past events and future aspirations that my interlocutors expressed, and analysed them in light of my own perceptions and understandings of the borderlands, as well as various parts of Chad—mainly the country's east and the capital—and their people. Narratives about events and aspirations are, significantly, entrenched in the temporally and spatially bracketed experiences (following Husserl 1954, but also Desjarlais and Throop 2011, and Ram and Houston 2015) of the people I talked to or was told about. Along this phenomenological line of reasoning, I do not claim to provide an integral understanding of the situation. Aware of the pitfalls of presenting other voices than my own, I have tried to position my voice in the relational and individual process of producing and questioning knowledge and within the unequal possibilities of mobility between continents and sites.

The lifeworlds in crisis that I describe in this book continue to be a highly dynamic way of continuing to live in or near war zones. Several factors were of central importance. For the population that defines itself as Masalit, who figure most prominently in Part I of this book, access to land and vital resources like water (for instance) was regulated by local institutional arrangements and these arrangements were more-or-less functional during times of peace. When war spilled over from Sudan to the Chadian side of the borderlands, the people of the borderland villages continued to rely on their ownership of land, even when they moved to Adré, the largest town in the area. Aware that they could still walk to their fields in the villages, they did not move further away, and rejected the offer of humanitarian aid by not moving

CONCLUSION

to the nearby UNHCR camps then being set up. This was because they relied on the arrangement of land ownership instituted by precolonial and colonial land laws (Abdul-Jalil 2006). They also remembered their experiences during the famine that resulted from the installation of camps in the 1980s across the border in Sudan. During the drought and civil war of the early 1980s, many had left Chad to move into the camps, where the situation, as de Waal's critique (1988) describes, ended up even more dire than that of those who had remained close to their land. On the other hand, the neighbouring Arab villagers, who do not hold official title to their land, maintained a permanent presence in their villages throughout the war. Instead of relying on some form of recognised ownership, they emphasised their Chadian citizenship and connections to the governmental administration. I argue that these two systems of 'traditional' land holding and notions of having a right to land through 'citizenship' collided during the war, leading Arab villagers to remain in their villages to demonstrate claims to land and water that they feared losing if they left. Staying on the land was thus even more vital for them than for the Masalit villagers, who felt safer leaving the villages and moving to Adré when the fighting made staying too risky an option. Even from this distance, they felt they could keep what they defined as their ancestral land. However, it turned out that Masalit villagers who had moved to Hachaba from Sudan, like Ashta Ibrahim and her aged parents Daldoum and Hawaye, had a more limited claim to their land so they left their elders in the villages to secure their claim. But villagers with a more secure claim to land—due to kin ties or established neighbourhood relations (their villages in Sudan were only a short distance from the Chadian ones)—still moved to Adré with the others, not to the camps.

Part II of the book looked more closely at the situation within the UNHCR camps and at interactions between the aid organisations and people living in and around the camps. Those who moved to the refugee camps rather than Adré (in my case study, mainly people considered to be 'Masalit' from Sudan) had no claim to land on the Chadian side of the border, and they had also lost their claims on the Sudanese side. Their villages there were further away, they had no previous relationships with neighbours in Chad, and they did not want to rely on the Chadian government or the state. Thus, they turned to the international agencies and NGOs that ran the camps. I have described the cases of Moussa, of the people who had first stayed in the border village of Wandalou, and of the former rebel Abdallah. In order to survive, they found moving to the camps preferable to remaining marginalised in a community that denied them full access to vital resources. In the camps they were offered housing, health, food, schooling and other amenities but were not officially allowed to support themselves or their families independently through farming or herding outside the camp. Despite this, they started moving out of the camps as soon as the UNHCR officially recognised them as 'refugees' and worked the land that the borderland's villagers had abandoned, thus rejecting the institutional logic of the aid providers that no one should leave the camp because of threats to security. These camp residents combined their knowledge of how to survive a crisis with the institutional arrangements of the refugee camp to create domains of commonality (Glick Schiller and Çağlar 2015) with the former borderland village population and beyond the control of the international aid agencies. Eventually, these knowledges merged, particularly when the aid organisations started to prepare their exit from the aid situation—as I showed regarding the *groupements* and the endeavour to recategorise 'refugees' as Chadian 'refugee-citizens'. This recategorisation was undertaken by knowledgeable brokers and translators (Behrends et al. 2014; Behrends 2021; Lewis and Mosse 2006) or 'middlemen' (Merry 2006) like my friend and interpreter Brahim, who started to group the camp residents along a new logic of richer and poorer people and to turn the aid agencies' measures towards a notion of development and allow the poorer ones to become better off.

Looking at the camp residents' everyday practices of survival and the close links between their practices and the aid agencies' policies and practices allowed me to depart from Mary Douglas's (1986) strict definition of institutions as holding the power to decide over life and death and to move to a more flexible understanding closer to Boltanski's (2010) pragmatic sociology of critique and Stengers's

CONCLUSION

(2005) ecology of the practice of representing. Starting with the notion that institutions are maintained by continuous practice in people's interrelations, Boltanski concludes that these institutions are flexible and not fixed. Critique, in this sense, means the capacity to continually provoke institutional change. Rottenburg's (2002, 2005, 2009) idea of a 'metacode' captures this by establishing a bridge that allows switching between different versions of reality. The camp residents' careful balancing of institutional arrangements—UNHCR regulations on 'refugees' and camps as well as regarding Chadian citizenship—with their knowledge of survival practices eventually led to a mutual adaptation of practices. The UNHCR's exit strategy included mixing camp residents with local host populations to undo their status as 'refugees'. But I have also shown that categorisations sometimes endure. The example of the young contractor, Mahamat Khassim, shows how a certain cement trader, by now a rich man, remained *le réfugié* to him: that was how he met him, even though as a successful businessman he no longer displayed the 'typical traits' of a 'refugee'.

Former status influences survival options in times of violent warfare and forced displacement. Ashta Ibrahim first moved from Sudan to Hachaba and then moved to Adré with the villagers. There, she started to transport bricks to support not only her children but also her aged parents, who had remained on their newly acquired land in the village. She worked very hard and gained little for herself. Her son, however, started out working as a porter in the market but eventually established himself with a family and house in Adré's new quarter of Hille Djidíde. Others survived the hard years of war even more successfully. Younous, who had planted his fruit and vegetable garden and invested in water pumps and equipment before the war, managed to protect his property during the war years. He used his networks and invested his gains to secure his land by building walls, hiring guards, and bribing those with the power to capture or destroy his garden and became a successful fruit supplier for hotels in El Geneina and beyond. Similarly, some of the Arab population in Tiléha who did not leave their village despite being harassed and even bombed during the war years emerged as successful traders and businesspeople. I was told that my acquaintance Fatime, who was a small-time sugar smuggler in 2001, now owns several four-wheel-drive vehicles. Everyone I met underwent transformations in their everyday living conditions. But they did so along lines they had established before the war that influenced what they lost or gained during it.

On an institutional level, the same thing happened to the aid agencies: in their relations with the people of the borderlands, but also through competition and collaboration with each other and the Chadian state. Rejecting the perspective of 'states of emergency' that has become the paradigm for critiques of humanitarian and military operations, governing populations and enforcing new forms of citizenship in a state-like manner, I have looked to Feldman's (2012) analysis of how Palestinian 'refugees' challenge the categories imposed on them, Beckett's (2013) careful analysis of emergent and interactive elements in the provision of aid, and Glasman's (2017, 2020) view that the UNHCR's defining power is more its capacity to mould categories than its actual enforcement of them. These authors have come to similar conclusions to this book's: facing the everyday realities of a site of intervention, agencies must comply with changing circumstances, actors and conditions—just like the recipients of aid.

In Part III, I focused on this interaction of different visions of governing and being governed and on how this reciprocity brought about changes in lifeworlds by presenting the different notions of development of the Chadian government, the aid agencies and the people of the borderlands. While the people of the towns and villages—and even the local government as represented by the mayor's office in Abéché—pursue their visions without expecting too much from the Chadian central government, the actions of each were always influenced by those of the others (see Thelen et al. 2017). To demonstrate this relationality, I followed the flow of the oil revenues that began in 2003, just as rebellion and war broke out on both sides of the Chad–Sudan border. I started with Brahim's experience of the battle of N'Djamena in early 2008, which led to the end of rebellion and a peace treaty between Chad and Sudan. However, instead of peace a renewed situation of inter-

CONCLUSION

war (Debos 2016) emerged, and old patterns of impunity and cronyism returned—and worse, some might say, than before. As a central periphery—that is, a marginal region with high impacts on the central government (following Das and Poole 2004)—the Chad–Sudan borderlands remain in a state of high uncertainty in relation to everyday survival. Living there means having to be dynamic and flexible by actively emplacing oneself and adapting to ever new circumstances. This insight follows those of several authors quoted throughout the book: Bjarnesen and Vigh (2016) on displacement and emplacement, Calkins (2016) on processing uncertainty, Glick Schiller and Çağlar (2015) on domains of commonality and sociabilities within multiscalar systems of power, Hammar's (2014) creativity in crisis, and Whyte's pragmatics of uncertainty (1997, see also 2016).

In this book, I have adopted a lifeworldly perspective and focused on the everydayness of situations of crisis and uncertainty. While I do not deny the urgency and trauma of war or ignore the presence of international agencies and military in the Chad–Sudan borderlands, I have shown how everyday lifeworlds continued during such emergencies and indeed were themselves ways to process the highest uncertainty and survive in the face of forced mobility and displacement. This required knowledge of possibilities to access vital resources including land, housing, food, work and healthcare. Displaced populations, host populations, international agencies and others who intervened all relied on this kind of knowledge, which is connected to categorising and to laws of who is eligible (von Benda Beckmann et al. 2009) for which form of access to the needed resources to survive.

People escaping from immediate or looming violence and threats constantly recategorise and reorder their immediate surroundings. They ask basic questions about whether it is time to move, where to go, who will support it, and who could come along, but others abound. How and with what will one live? Whom and what should one risk leaving behind? These are urgent questions. Moving in search of some form of safety also carries risks (including the possibility of never returning) and creates new formations that could lead to new ways of defining, arranging and shifting understandings and, thereby, categorisations of the social and of social processes. In such situations, aid providers—whether they are host villages or international aid agencies—similarly order situations but ask different questions. Who is eligible to receive aid? On what basis should we decide who is most in need? How can we guarantee protection? Where do we find the means to provide aid? In situations like those I have addressed in this book, many people, technologies, procedures and devices come together with very different understandings of reality and how to survive in it.

Personal conclusions

Above all, this book is made up of stories of how individuals coped with war. But of course, I have had to become involved as well. Since 2000, changing events and, consequently, also changing interests—from displacement to oil extraction to rebellion and humanitarian aid to expulsion and notions of development—have guided my research. My aim throughout has been to tell the stories of the people around the country who I met and came to know—and who have come to know me as well. Their modes of surviving crises have fascinated me throughout the years that I have remained in contact with them through my return visits to Chad and the borderlands. I have retained this commitment as I have come to know them better and continue to visit the region and speak regularly with people who still live there. We exchange news, and sometimes I send money or other goods if the situation seems to call for it.

Brahim now has seven sons. The eldest is in secondary school in N'Djamena, but he and his wife Sureiya still live in Hadjer Hadid, where he used to work for an NGO and in the refugee camps. He no longer does: the NGO has left the country, although the 'refugees' are still there. Several years ago, I helped him find money to start a brick-making business through crowdfunding (and the help of many friends). This went quite well at first: he built more kilns every year and sold the bricks to young men who had made money as gold miners in the north and returned to build

CONCLUSION

houses in Adré or in their native villages. However, the business collapsed in 2022: the war in Ukraine caused prices to increase, the young men spent their money on food rather than bricks, and Brahim's only option was returning to farming peanuts, millet and okra. Meanwhile, his sister needed an operation and could no longer pay for their mother's diabetes medication. He was again back to square one: after all this time, his life had not become much more secure. With time and more capital, he might be able to revive his brick business and make enough to live on again, as well as pay his sons' school fees and any unexpected expenses. On the other hand, and particularly with the new outbreak of war in Sudan, and in Darfur, in 2023, a more severe crisis might strike the Chadian side of the borderlands again. The kind of lasting security where one does not have to choose between losing an arm or a leg (as Ashta's relative put it) is not easy, and most people in the borderlands do not achieve it.

Even today, people ask me what I can offer to better their lives. 'Can't you start a project for us?' 'How can you help?' 'What's the good of all this knowledge you've put together?' I have no really good answers to these questions, but I hope that insights into everyday lifeworlds amidst prolonged states of emergency or crisis can provide insights into people's possible needs. Among those in the borderlands, my place was uncertain. First, I was addressed as daughter, then as sister, and now I am even respectfully called *maman* by some who have known me since their childhood. People knew that I was not an aid worker but still might be able to help them get access to aid. I was not a doctor but could certainly provide essential supplies or first aid. In some situations, my presence helped to resolve or prevent conflict. For months at a time, I shared a simple hut in Ashta's compound in Hachaba with chickens that nested behind the hut's wall hangings and insects that lived in the thatch. I walked back and forth between the Masalit and their alleged foe, the so-called Arabs. Sometimes, I stayed with better-off households in towns and regularly went to the UNHCR camps to visit those who were officially registered as 'refugees'. Brahim has remained my collaborator in everything but the actual writing. He is also a source of first-hand information: he grew up in the borderlands, has experienced several phases of war and inter-war including the 2008 rebel attack on N'Djamena.

When I returned to the borderlands in 2007, I found the people and many of their stories sad and desperate. However, that experience spurred me to return again and again, to follow the individuals I had come to know at the beginning of my work. Completing this book has become an emotional project and has ended up taking a very long time for many reasons. Some of these lie in the twists and turns of (academic) life, but some are also connected to how this field site has constantly changed: what I started before the Darfur War has turned into something very different. There was no sense in publishing an analysis of a relatively minor displacement situation after it had developed into a major one that involved camps the size of small cities, hundreds of aid organisations, and international military operations. Events came thick and fast, and I struggled to keep up. Over time, my relationships intensified. I saw the borderlanders remain calm despite frantic emergency measures on the part of the international aid workers and officials and I emulated their calm. We talked on the phone using codes we had arranged to communicate difficult situations in case the lines were tapped. When I visited, we shared information on what had happened to everyone I knew. The war had shaken all their lives, but in very different ways. Some had initially lost almost everything, but by now most also had partly recovered. Some had found a new life, changing their status from stereotypically poor villagers to upwardly mobile town residents. Some people living in the refugee camps had become wealthy traders or successful gardeners or herders. Others remained extremely poor: these tended to be older, less mobile and less open to contact with strangers, but I gradually came to know some of them as well. I felt that the war had made ways of belonging and of difference more visible even as it simultaneously contributed to undoing them, or at least putting them into question.

EPILOGUE

WAR, AGAIN

While this book was being published, war again started to tear the Chad–Sudan Borderlands apart. Some say what is happening now is worse than the war of 20 years ago, the violence more brutal, the days of possible collaboration and friendly neighbourliness more forgotten, the chances of reconciliation further out of reach. All agree that this war is connected to the events that started to severely escalate in February 2003, which this book is about. Although over the last two decades, those who had fled from Sudan to Chad had begun to move back to their homes across the border, many people never gave up their Chadian status as refugee citizens. Darfur had not returned to peace. Tensions have not been resolved and conflict has simmered in Darfur, also affecting the Chadian side of the border region. In December 2018, a popular uprising in Khartoum and Omdurman led to the ousting of long-term President Omar al-Bashir in April 2019 and to the drafting of a new constitution in August 2019, followed by a second coup d'état in October 2021, ousting the interim Prime Minister Abdalla Hamdok. After that, the interim government's chairman of the Sovereignty Council, General Fattah al-Burhan, shared power with the leader of the so-called Rapid Support Forces (RSF), Mohamed Hamdan Dagalo, a former herder and Janjaweed leader from Darfur whom everyone calls Hemedti. On 15 April 2023 the Sudanese Armed Forces (SAF) under al-Burhan and the RSF under

Hemedti clashed in Khartoum, allegedly over the integration of the RSF forces into the Sudanese army. Their conflict led to a war that caused massive destruction not only in the capital, but also throughout the country and particularly in Hemedti's home region Darfur, threatening, again, to cross into Chadian territory, according to Hoinathy and Bétinbaye (2023) and Tubiana (2023).

In the borderlands, it seems that people were ready to take to arms much faster than they were 20 years ago, and since April 2023, many mourn the death of their youth who followed the calls to arms of the opposing leaders in Sudan. In Khartoum and Omdurman, those who could, fled the country. Those who had to stay see their houses taken by soldiers, looted and destroyed, and people killed every day. On the Chadian side of the border, people arrive in large numbers on a daily basis, trying to find safety from fighting. The Chadian military distributes them to the still existing camps, to Farchana and others. Their numbers are again in the hundreds of thousands. But while international media covered the Darfur War in 2003 (for a while), the current conflict was fast out of the news, although, unlike in 2003, all of Sudan is at risk of falling into prolonged instability in regard to all aspects of social life: governance, security, infrastructures, economy, and religious, cultural and academic life (Nur 2022).

When refugees started to move across the border, Brahim left his current home in Hadjer Hadid and moved to his mother's family house in Adré. There he started to work as a *journalier* for international agencies, hired for a day at a time, to register incoming people from Sudan, to measure arms as a classificatory technology for malnutrition (Glasman 2020), and to help build shelters. As 20 years before, the makeshift shelters do not hold against the rains, leaving people without protection, often with nothing to eat. The villagers and townspeople cater for the newcomers, while waiting for the aid agencies to come in. Once, the new Chadian president, Mahamat Idriss Déby Itno, came to the borderlands in late June 2023 and provided food on the Eid al-Fitr celebration, the Muslim holiday at the end of the month of Ramadan. Brahim kept sending me short films and pictures of people arriving, some malnourished and terrified as members of their families had died in the conflict.

EPILOGUE

He travelled to the Arab village of Tiléha, where he did not find any of the men, but women grieving the loss of their sons who had left to fight and have not returned since. In one of his voicemails, he asks a mother whose son had been killed in El Geneina what had led him to fight. She doesn't know, she said. 'Whatever they have been promised I do not understand, I only know that they fight and kill each other.'

NOTES

1. TOMORROW, THERE WILL BE WAR!

1. An area named after the most numerous population that is grouped under an ethnic label is not necessarily considered its 'original' homeland or registered officially or institutionally. Other places in various parts of Sudan are also called Dar Masalit, especially in agricultural areas that were developed and received many migrants during the colonial era.
2. In Behrends (2007, 2015), I review some of the historical literature on the Chad–Sudan borderlands.
3. Like all categories, 'refugee' is constructed along the rules and regulations set in place by various actors like international agencies, local authorities and the people themselves. As this construct's differing and changing meanings and implications are central to this book, I will always place it in single quotation marks.
4. I plan to examine this family history and its implications on Barth's assumptions about today's Chad–Sudan borderlands in more detail in a future publication.
5. A more detailed account of the Chadian rebellion follows in Chapters 10, particularly pp. 219ff.
6. The two missions were the MINURCAT (United Nations Mission in the Central African Republic and Chad) and its predecessor EUFOR (European Union Force Chad/Central African Republic).

2. WE HAVE TO MAKE A LIST

1. Toyota Hiluxes and Land Cruisers are associated with war because President Hissein Habré's forces successfully used these vehicles as mobile fighting platforms during the 1987 Libyan occupation of northern Chad. This conflict later became known as *Harb Tuyuta*, the Great Toyota War.
2. I address the specific situation of this community in Chapter 4.

3. Wenger, McDermott and Snyder (2002: 4) define 'communities of practice' generally as 'groups of people who share a concern, a set of problems, or a passion about a topic, and who deepen their knowledge and expertise in this area by interacting on an ongoing basis.'
4. As my former host Ashta's daughter Djiti told me in 2010, brick carrying was a communal task. A group of women contracted with an owner, who specified a price for a set number of bricks to be carried to and from the wadi. This money would be divided among the women and the faster they worked the more they would earn. Djiti explained that the standard rate for a thousand bricks was 500 CFA francs. She explained that they 'make a contract with an owner. For instance, if he wants to bake the bricks, you might tell him, "we will make 10,000 bricks for you". Then the tradesman will suggest an advance for the 10,000 bricks. And then, according to your capacity, if you are fast or slow, you gain this sum in two, three or four days. They will give you the advance sum, you share it, you deliver the bricks and finally he will pay the rest of the money.'

3. SO, WE WENT WITH THEM

1. I have elaborated on this issue in Behrends (2007) and Behrends (2015).
2. In the villages, the people harvested both around their houses and on more remote fields. Planting millet around the house made the harvest more convenient and also ensured that curious neighbours could not see into the private areas of the house.
3. See the work of Marielle Debos about impunity as a form of governance and accumulation during what she calls the period of 'inter-war', when people close to the country's president become 'untouchable' in the sense of impunity and no institution can stop them from profiting massively while the rest of the population conspicuously lacks regulatory authority (2016: 147ff; see also Dickow 2014).
4. Concerning the history of Arab supremacy in Sudan, see Aguda (1973), Cunnison (1972), de Waal (2005), El-Battahani (2004), El-Tom (2006), Harir (1994), Johnson (2003), Mans (2004), Prah (2001), Rottenburg (2008), Wai (1981), Wax (2004).
5. One Zaghawa-led Darfurian rebel group in 2003, the Justice and Equality Movement (JEM), later enjoyed the former Chadian president's protection (although not at first). As mentioned, Déby's reluctance to assist his kin in Sudan against Khartoum's aggression was one reason why high-ranking Zaghawa officials in N'Djamena rebelled against him (see also Behrends 2008).
6. Amnesty International stated in early 2017 that the Sudanese regime had used chemical weapons to force non-Arab residents from Darfur. https://www.amnesty.org/en/latest/news/2016/09/chemical-weapons-attacks-darfur/ (last accessed 31 December 2022).

7. On the paradox of crisis and creativity, particularly in relation to displacement economies, see Hammar (2014).
8. While Younous had certainly found inspiration for his orchard in Libya, Barth's (1967) treatment of 'economic spheres in Darfur' extensively discusses the use of orchards as a means to generate a surplus. He maintains, however, that 'only the quite successful and prosperous have embarked on this production beyond the occasional planting of single trees' (1967: 169) due to the additional investment in communal labour required to establish them. According to Barth, the first orchards appeared in the Jebel Marra foothills around 1956, so they should have been a well-established means of generating an income by the time Younous started planting his. However, this did not seem to be the case, at least not in the parts of the borderlands I knew best. Later, around 2019, orchards did become a preferred pastime among better-off town dwellers who could employ relatives at low wages to produce fruit and vegetables, provide themselves with an income, and have a place for picnics with friends on the weekends.
9. In many ways, he *was* an 'elder statesman' in the area: he had been a *chef de canton* from 1991 to 1996 and later returned to office in 2010.
10. From Hassan, I also heard about a conflict in 1958 in a village northwest of Adré that had caused a previous war between Masalit and Arabs in colonial Chad that ended with the French military expelling Arab communities from the territory along the border.
11. The 'Children of Zed' designates one branch of a notional Arab family, some of whose members live in the village of Tiléha.
12. Simply buying food was not an option, as there was no market in Hachaba. I either ate what Ashta prepared with the millet she had stored, or the chicken she had bought from passing traders, or some cookies that I stored in my house. I gave her money to buy food for all of us, but sometimes it was simply difficult to get access to food. Ashta never complained, but I could see that feeding me was a constant worry for her. Sometimes she called me and asked me if I would eat a specific bird or turtle that was for sale alive, and I had to decline because I felt sorry for the animal.
13. From my previous stays in Hachaba I knew that *groupements* were one of the prerequisites to receiving development aid in the villages. It meant forming an official group with a leader and a treasurer who define a target—making a surplus by working a field together, for instance—and investing this surplus money into developing their village. The measure was supposed to combine individual with collective interests and thus motivate people to work together peacefully. Some agencies would only fund the *groupements* if it proved to be successful. As I will show in Chapter 5, competition turned out to be a major factor in this form of development cooperation.
14. Differences in dress are so subtle that an uninformed outsider would not notice them: a certain kind of shoe available only in Sudan or a particular way

of tying one's turban. These minor differences are legible to locals but quite invisible to outsiders.

15. The French policy was similar to the British, although France did not rule its colonies through indirect rule, but through an assimilationist policy. Land was, however, also given to 'native tribes', but the system of rule did not give as much agency to local power holders as in the British colonies.

4. IN GENERAL, THEY ARE COMFORTABLE

1. Zenaba cited security issues as grounds to keep the market in the town's centre. In 2010, only livestock was still sold at the lake. Zenaba and Khassim, like others in town, invested in shops which could be locked and where goods could be kept overnight.
2. Later, I was told that hiding behind such walls offered little protection from bullets, which could easily penetrate them. I suspect that it was mainly a way to stay out of the sight of those sitting on top of passing vehicles.
3. Issa Hassan Khayar (1984) also interviewed the father of Mahamat Ali, the old *marabout* Abdalhak Sanoussi. He dedicates an entire chapter in his book about exchange with Wadaian elites to the memories of the man he calls Abd el-Haqq (1984: 93–114) and his portrait of a 'traditional Muslim elite'. In a poignant analysis, Khayar maintains that, although the French administration aimed at 'hierarchising' local political structures and serving their own political ends by destabilising the power of the sultans, the *chefs de canton*, installed and co-opted by the French administration, remained loyal to the sultans, which not only undermined the local power of the French but was also the only way that the *chefs de canton* could have any authority over their subjects (1984: 71). They thus played an intermediary role by knowing both the colonial and the local sides and referred to those registers that were most effective for maintaining good relations as well as power.
4. Brahim once told me that they also had a clan connection, 'Kolek-Tandjak' (according to Khayar 1984: 106f., this refers to the 'chieftaincy over the blacksmiths' which was given to certain members of the Wadaian elite) which the Barka family has inherited from the time of the Wadai Sultanate.
5. The sequence of kinship is Mahamad Saleh (Barka's maternal uncle), Ahmat (same generation as Barka), Youssouf (same generation as Senoussi), Ali, Assed (Khassim's grandfather), Mahamat, Khassim.
6. GTZ's greatest achievement in the region—and a continuing success story— is the construction of subsoil river dams (Otto 2011: 29ff). Water only flows on the surface of the wadis during the rainy season, when they briefly turn into fierce rivers. Building a subsoil dam in a wadi reduces the flow rate of groundwater during the dry season, widening the area of rain-fed cultivation and providing the population with a richer soil to plant vegetables and cereals needed for their subsistence.

7. When looking at opportunities for economic growth among the Fur, Barth (1967: 163) mentions that young cattle are very hard to come by: 'There are no markets to facilitate trade in such animals, and the supply depends entirely on the whim of the Arab nomads, who offer the beasts for sale individually through random contacts and only in response to unforeseen and urgent cash needs.' Owning a young cow can therefore be regarded as a cornerstone of wealth accumulation that is usually not available to individuals outside the 'Arab' community.
8. Construction contracts were usually considered a way to earn and spend a lot of money, so the most lucrative private houses and hotels for senior international employees were not part of Khassim's portfolio but channelled to members of the president's family.
9. This story was later confirmed by an 'Arab' man I knew in N'Djamena, who said that his family had changed their transhumant routes to avoid the Zaghawa areas and no longer went as far north as they usually did. Other herding groups avoided the area of Abéché altogether to try to keep their animals from being stolen.

5. CLEARLY, THEY ARE 'INTERNALLY DISPLACED PERSONS'

1. This convention was amended by the 1967 Protocol Relating to the Status of Refugees, which extended the category of the 1951 Convention to apply outside of Europe and to people who fled events that took place after 1951.
2. I use the term 'group' only for those constellations of people who have been categorised as such from outside—by international aid providers, for example—or clearly express togetherness or differentiation. Individuals may be more or less attached to such groups. While modes of undoing the group boundary persist, some constellations are referred to here as bounded entities owing to particular challenges, like rebel groups or, in particular, the institutionalised *groupements* discussed in this chapter.
3. Here I follow Lund's (2008) definition of politics, which is oriented towards both history and processes of reproduction and change. It considers people's agendas and the conditions of local politics within a broader field. Although Lund considers the effects of national governments, his approach does not privilege 'the state' as the primary site of politics. In a similar way, Bierschenk and Olivier de Sardan (1997) grant privilege to the *practice* of actors in their everyday state-making within bureaucracies (Bierschenk 2014), but also regarding international development aid and intervention (Bierschenk 2000).
4. Hadjerai communities live in the central mountainous region around the Chadian city of Mongo. During the rebellions of the 1970s and 1980s, they were among the first to fight against the first independent government of Ngarta Tombalbaye and formed the core of the Front de Libération Nationale

NOTES

du Tchad (FROLINAT) (see Alio 2002, Buijtenhuijs 1978, 1987, de Bruijn and van Dijk 2007, and Fuchs 1996).

5. A year later, Jànszky and Pawlitzky (2008) carried out such a study, in close cooperation with Stephen P. Reyna. The UNCHR funding was no longer available (or perhaps they did not need it) as the European Commission funded this well-done analysis of 'Sources of violence, conflict mediation and reconciliation: A socio-anthropological study on Dar Sila.'

6. See Jerome Tubiana (2008: 5, 2017) and Jánszky (2014: 412) for excellent and detailed overviews of the events of the Chadian rebellion, the various rebel movements, and their factions and leaders. The unsuccessful April 2006 attack on Abéché and N'Djamena was conducted by a union of rebel movements of which the RDL was the 'main component' (Tubiana 2008: 5). The movement was officially led by the United Front for Democratic Change (FUC) under the leadership of President Déby's close Zaghawa kin, the twin brothers Tom and Timan Erdimi.

7. While I am not sure why Médecins Sans Frontières and the International Committee of the Red Cross objected to the 'cluster approach' at that particular meeting, both agencies claim a form of sovereignty beyond national and international agreements. Redfield's (2010, 2013) account of MSF's complex global arrangements attributes their differences to the ICRC's unconditional neutrality and non-interference in the politics of any state and MSF placing its morality beyond national governments and international conventions, adhering purely to its ethic of aid.

8. This explanation corresponds to what Nguyen (2010) would later call a Republic of Therapy (in relation to AIDS programmes in West Africa). Regulations of who gets to be treated and who does not influence people's day-to-day visions of reality as if part of a new form of citizenship. Rottenburg (2009) makes the same point more directly, charging that the use of African communities as laboratories and experiments of Western products leads to a 'benevolent dictatorship' (McFalls 2010), caused by technologies and practices of humanitarian aid.

9. This event will be described in more detail in Part III of this book.

10. Back in Berlin, I called several German religious charities who told me that either they had already intervened in the Chad–Sudan borderlands but faced the same restrictions I had learned about there or that they had already allocated their funds.

6. THOSE ARE THE ONLY REAL REFUGEES

1. Dahab was not just the *firché* (village representative of the area's Masalit *chef de canton*). An *ancien combattant* (Debos 2016), he spoke a telegraphic military style of French and his short sentences conveyed the essence of the topic and the wisdom of someone who had seen and experienced many things. Dahab's ex-wife was Ashta, my host in Hachaba. Together, they had lived at army bases

throughout Chad and had raised four daughters. I was told that their marriage had been tumultuous—filled with both love and rage—and had only ended when Dahab decided to marry a younger second wife.
2. See Chapter 3.
3. It was also in character when Mahamat Ismael asked me if I could 'provide more than just some photos and sugar' when I returned to the village during the war, which led to making the list (see Chapter 2).
4. Mobile telephones were actually a side effect of the Darfur War. Soldiers brought their devices starting 2003 and within a few months the area was connected to the networks now operated by Airtel and Tigo.
5. In fact, I had seen a similar document before in N'Djamena, when one evening a group of men knocked on my hotel door. After I let them in, they sat on the floor and showed me handwritten documents with the same content: the government of Sudan was trying to 'clear all land' of 'blacks' to give it to the 'Arab population' (Ibrahim 2000).
6. Although I will not discuss it at length, people did sometimes mention slavery to me. People with enslaved ancestors, or who were seen as dangerous to the host community—like potters or blacksmiths—were denied the possibility of changing their mode of belonging to affiliate to a new place. As de Waal puts it, they are 'outside the scope of kinship, and are indefinitely displaced' (1988: 134).
7. At a minimum, the question of land is one of several factors leading to conflict. In particular, the northern Darfurian 'Arab' groups called 'Rizeigat', in contrast to their southern Darfurian kin, were not accorded their own *dar* during the British colonial epoch, and this later led to their supporting the government's attacks on the Darfur rebels and their villages (Behrends 2007; Behrends and Schlee 2008; de Waal 2005; El-Tom 2006; Flint and de Waal 2005, 2008; see also Mamdani 1996, 2009).

7. THE CAMPS ARE VERY DIFFERENT

1. I will return to this attack in Part III, Chapter 9 of the book.
2. During one of my visits to Camp Farchana, the very friendly head of UNHCR operations told me that she was most concerned with 'making the housing of internationals more attractive' with flowers and more spacious dwellings. Otherwise, her response confirmed my impression that she did not want to commit to the place: 'I have a contract for two years here, but I only have to stay for six months before I'm free to apply for other positions.'
3. I take this and the following quotations from a recorded interview with the delegate on 21 September 2010 in Adré. The translations from French to English are mine.
4. This agency was later renamed Comité National d'Accueil et Enregistrement des Réfugiés et Rapatriés (CNARR) to include people who had returned from

other countries to Chad as refugees, like Chadian citizens who had fled Libya or the Central African Republic.

5. Brahim translated Moussa as having said *que nous devions nous débrouiller*—'that we have to make do'. Berk and Galvan (2009) have analysed the notion of *se débrouiller* that Moussa mentioned. Making do or finding your own way, in their analysis, is not related to Moussa's understanding of being thrown outside aid structures. Instead, the notion corresponds to their concept of creative syncretism, in which institutions are challenged on an everyday and pragmatic basis (Boltanski 2010).

6. Although Stengers makes her point in relation to how she regards the understanding that physicists have of science, a variation in practices or, as is the case here, a variation in how a particular situation is defined as real is well adapted to her analysis.

7. Thévenot developed his approach to practice and engagement by looking at French bureaucrats and thus considered how institutions change through practice in a rather stable environment. In a volatile situation with less stable institutions, his insights might have to be reconsidered on a theoretical level. However, in my view this model also fits in an environment of fluid institutions that are more often newly negotiated through changing relations and changing personnel.

8. THEY ARE OUR RELATIVES NOW

1. The Chadian national army and rebel factions continued to fight, but less intensely and frequently than before the 2008 attack on N'Djamena. In May 2008, the Sudanese rebels, who had a strong presence in Chad, also staged an attack on the Sudanese government in Omdurman, just across the Nile from the capital of Khartoum. When this failed, they too dissolved and dispersed among the displaced populations in Darfur and Wadai—many in the refugee camps as mentioned in the previous chapter—or joined rebellions elsewhere, as had their Chadian counterparts only a few months before.

2. One of my main reasons for regularly visiting N'Djamena was to participate in the anthropological community of the country. In 2007, we inaugurated a Chadian anthropological research centre, the Centre de Recherche en Anthropologie et Sciences Humaines (CRASH). With an international advisory board and Chadian leadership, the centre has now developed into a mature organisation. Its members teach at N'Djamena University, where several students have successfully completed their studies in anthropology. While the country's oil production and the effects of mobile telephony were the centre's first thematic focus, its members and students have sought to explore several other issues that contribute to an analysis of the current socio-economic and political situation in Chad and its effects on a number of localities, particularly in border regions.

3. 'Dabanga' means granary, a metaphor that represents information as a kind of seed for future development. They sent their reports directly to the station, which broadcasts in various languages, including Arabic and Masalit. They focused on Darfur in Sudan and had antennas in various refugee camps.
4. This increase in prices caused by aid money paralleled the situation in southern Chad, where oil money also caused a very localised and temporary rise in prices, including dowries. See Hoinathy (2012), Hoinathy and Behrends (2014), Behrends and Hoinathy (2017).
5. An earlier version of this part of the chapter in German was previously published in an edited volume on *Humandifferenzierung* (Behrends 2021). I thank Stefan Hirschauer for his generous comments on the draft paper.
6. That it still took over two weeks to count the votes suggests that efficiency was not the main motivation for the measure.
7. In contrast to UNICEF, which is run as if it were a ministry of the Chadian government, UNHCR operations maintain more independence from national governmental decision-making processes (private communication by a Chadian UNICEF employee in March 2016).
8. To verify the consistency of refugees' stories, UNHCR staff with special legal training ask questions about war events that have been documented in detail elsewhere. For example, they know the exact timing of a particular attack, which villages were affected, the extent of destruction, etc. For people claiming refugee status who say they witnessed or fled because of a particular event, but whose statements do not match the documented facts, refugee status may be withdrawn. In N'Djamena, I witnessed such interviews and observed how much the outcome depends on the goodwill of the interviewer or what rapport with the applicant develops during the interview. To my knowledge, these interviews and the subsequent categorisations were never conducted by people like Brahim who were familiar with the local situation, but always by outsiders who relied on documentation of the events in question.

9. THIS IS NEITHER MY FIRST NOR SECOND TIME SEEING WAR

1. The following is based on my fieldnotes and on a handwritten report in French that Brahim sent me about his experiences during the failed rebel attack on N'Djamena in 2008. This attack has been credited with ending the war on the Chadian side.
2. Although all neighbourhoods of N'Djamena have mixed populations, some are inhabited mainly by people from the south of Chad and are predominantly Christian and others are inhabited by more people originating in the north and are thus characterised as Muslim.
3. In Behrends (2007), I show that 'siding with the stronger ally' had already formed a pattern of rapidly changing political and social alliances in the borderlands in the era of the two powerful historically powerful empires, Dar

Fur and Wadai. In the quoted text, I also relate this pattern to the Darfur War and the fast-changing alliances and fissions between rebel groups. For the historical political context in this regard see also Kapteijns (1985) and O'Fahey and Spaulding (1974).

4. See Bouju and de Bruijn (2014) for an attempt to categorise everyday forms of violence in African contexts while reflecting the positionality of the observer of and the one affected by violence.

10. BEFORE OIL, WE WERE POOR. NOW, WE'RE MISERABLE

1. See also see Asad 2004; Bayard, Ellis and Hibou 1999; Beck 2003; Behrends 2007; Risse 2008; and Roitman 2006.
2. This chapter includes parts of a reworked article I published in *Focaal* 2008, 52: 39–56, 'Fighting for oil when there is no oil, yet. The case of the Chad–Sudan border', and from an article co-authored with Remadji Hoinathy and published in *Social Analysis* 2017, 61/3 entitled 'The devil's money: A multi-level approach to acceleration and turbulence in oil-producing southern Chad.'
3. The topic of oil and social change has been a significant focus of my previous research. I have written on the anthropological perspective on the study of oil and its socio-cultural, political and economic impact, particularly on countries of the Global South (Behrends 2008; Behrends 2016; Behrends, Reyna and Schlee 2011; Behrends and Schareika 2010; Behrends and Hoinathy 2017; Hoinathy and Behrends 2014; Schritt and Behrends 2014). Here, I restrict my focus on state images and practices to relating them to displacement and emplacement and to the crossing of category boundaries during ruptures such as war and their connections to oil production.
4. In 2016, the Chadian president Idriss Déby Itno succeeded Zimbabwean Robert Mugabe as Chairperson of the African Union, and in 2017 the Chadian foreign minister Moussa Faki Mahamat was elected Chair of the African Union Commission.
5. Gisa Weszkalnys (2016) has written about the administrative and socio-economic effects of false hopes for oil development in São Tomé and Príncipe.
6. Appel (2012) speaks about 'white elephants', construction projects in oil-producing Guinea Bissau where the country's government made oil companies invest in constructions that often remain empty.
7. For a comparison of the war in Chad with the simultaneous war taking place on the Sudanese side and their different relation to oil and oil money, see Behrends (2008).
8. As the rebels and their families often stay in Chadian refugee camps, one could argue that they are in a sense also being supported by international aid organisations.

9. A Human Rights Watch report (2007: 9ff) shows how Déby's army provided local groups with weapons to weaken the rebellion and to turn attention away from the original intention of the rebels to oust Déby. Accordingly, Marchal (2007) suggested that Chad was 'turning into a militia state'.
10. Mahamat Nour, from Dar Tama, is not to be confused with the previously mentioned Goran rebel Mahamat Nouri, who attacked N'Djamena in 2008.
11. The following is a slightly altered excerpt from a 2017 publication in *Social Analysis* 61/3 on 'The Devil's Money. A multi-level approach to turbulences in oil producing southern Chad'. I wrote this article with Remadji Hoinathy based on our separate research on oil in Chad. The parts reworked for this chapter are based on my own findings and do not represent his work.
12. See Miankeol (1999, 2010), Petry and Bambé (2005) and Zint (2001) for further details of this model.
13. Hoinathy (2012: 42) holds that non-governmental actors foresaw this move long before. Relations between the oil consortium and the Chadian government had not been without tensions either, and—in contrast to the World Bank—the partnership between oil producers and government survived these tensions.

11. THIS MONEY BELONGS TO THE PEOPLE OF CHAD

1. Before making peace, however, the Chadian government supported a coup attempt in Omdurman, the twin city of Sudan's capital Khartoum, on 10 May 2008. This coup failed but lingers in people's memory as the first time during the decades of civil war in South Sudan that rebels were able to reach the capital (personal communication with Musa Adam Abdul-Jalil on 26 January 2016). This was, of course, before al-Bashir was ousted by popular and military pressure on 11 April 2019.
2. In particular, the 2012 rebellion in Mali has been connected to the death of Gaddafi, who had recruited large numbers of soldiers from sub-Saharan countries. When they fled Libya with their guns, they found new 'occupations' (as Debos 2011 would argue) and joined a rebel alliance in Northern Mali that aimed to secede from the rest of the country. France was one of the major players in countering this rebellion, with a UN Security Council mandate. Chadian troops were celebrated at the time for their experience as 'desert fighters' and the French operated from an air base in Chad. In 2021 the French government continued to support the country's transitional military government after the recent death of former president Idriss Déby, despite heavy protest from oppositional groups and its violation of the constitutional process for presidential succession.
3. http://news.bbc.co.uk/2/hi/africa/7277830.stm (last accessed on 1 January 2023).
4. The architects' rendering of the building, at http://www.moorerubleyudell.com/projects/new-embassy-campus-ndjamena, does not show any of the features that (at the time of writing) still existed around it. A contractor

working on this building, whom I met in passing at the airport, confirmed that all the people living around the embassy would be expelled. However, he doubted that the road would ever be removed (personal communication, 19 February 2017, N'Djamena).

5. I thank one anonymous reviewer of the book's manuscript for pointing this out.
6. This style of city planning—and even some of the names—also evokes the urban planning of the former colonial power: in Paris, the Avenue de la Grande Armée joins eleven other avenues in the roundabout surrounding the Arc de Triomphe. I thank Daniel Flaumenhaft for pointing this out.
7. Even if Wadaian politicians regularly appear in the (high-turnover) cabinet, no single opposition leader could challenge the former autocrat's position.
8. https://www.google.de/maps/place/Am+Djeress/@16.0435552, 22.7687975,20211m/data=!3m1!1e3!4m5!3m4!1s0x16b4da2ed 1d3fea5:0x9ef3cfb472f4d103!8m2!3d16.1!4d22.85?hl=de (last accessed on 11 May 2021). The objects visible in the lower left-hand side of the satellite image are an airstrip and a paved road that leads directly to a small hamlet clearly visible to the north. By some accounts, the Chadian president uses this mode of travelling to visit his home—which, on Wikipedia, is indicated as being the town of Fada, further to the northwest of Am Djeress, https://en.wikipedia.org/wiki/Idriss_D%C3%A9by (last accessed on 11 May 2021).
9. See Behrends and Hoinathy (2017) and Behrends (2016) for a description of a similar situation in the country's south, where unregistered land reverted to the government to guarantee access for oil drilling.
10. An import from India, auto rickshaws powered by motorbikes found their way via Sudan into the Chadian borderlands after the war. They were highly appreciated for their low transport fares and the fast availability. A problem, however, were the few restrictions and regulations concerning their usage. Particularly in connection with drugs, rickshaws became a cause of accidents daily, thus increasing the insecurity of the city's traffic system.
11. During my 2011 visit to Abéché I heard many stories about Madame Salah, as people always referred to her. An elegant and outspoken Jordanian woman, she was an atypical leader for an international military mission. She lived in the most expensive house in Abéché's now empty quarter of luxury buildings, paying a monthly rent of USD 5,000. She freely conversed with the city's officials in not only French and English but also Arabic. She garnered most praise for her advancement of the city's women and invited many of them to her house on International Women's Day. Of all the characters the war had brought to Abéché, she seemed to be the one who impressed the city's inhabitants the most.
12. According to Yates (1996) all investment of oil-generated revenues is related to the rentier effect, and has adverse effects and cannot easily boost agriculture or other forms of industrial production.

REFERENCES

Abdul-Jalil, Musa Adam. 1984. 'The Dynamics of Ethnic Identification in Northern Darfur, Sudan: A Situational Approach.' *The Sudan: Ethnicity and National Cohesion*, 55–85. Bayreuth: Bayreuth African Studies Series no. 1.

Abdul-Jalil, Musa Adam. 2006. 'The Dynamics of Customary Land Tenure and Natural Resource Management in Darfur.' *FAO Bulletin on Land Reform*, 8–23.

Abdul-Jalil, Musa Adam. 2008. 'Nomad-Sedentary Relations and the Question of Land Rights in Darfur: From Complementarity to Conflict.' *Orientwissenschaftliche Hefte* 26: 1–24.

Abdul-Jalil, Musa Adam. 2016. 'Coping with Uncertainties: The Predicament of Nomadic Pastoralists in Southern White Nile State, Sudan.' *Kujenga Amani*. http://forums.ssrc.org/kujenga-amani/2016/09/15/coping-with-uncertainties-the-predicament-of-nomadic-pastoralists-in-southern-white-nile-state-sudan/#.WY7Mw4ppxE4 (last accessed on 12 August 2017).

Agamben, Giorgio. 2005. *State of Exception*. Chicago, IL: University of Chicago Press.

Agier, Michel. 2011. *Managing the Undesirables: Refugee Camps and Humanitarian Governance*. Cambridge: Polity Press.

Agier, Michel. 2016. *Borderlands:Towards an Anthropology of the Cosmopolitan Condition*. Cambridge: Polity Press.

Aguda, Oluwadare. 1973. 'Arabism and Pan-Arabism in Sudanese Politics.' *Journal of Modern African Studies* 11 (2): 177–200.

Alio, Khalil. 2002. 'The Movements of Population in the Guera Region in the Republic of Chad and Their Consequences.' Unpublished manuscript. Leiden: ASC Leiden.

REFERENCES

Alio, Khalil. 2011. 'Histoire de vie: autopsie d'un témoin de l'histoire du Tchad.' Unpublished Manuscript. N'Djamena: CRASH.

Alio, Khalil. 2017. *Pour qui file la comète*. Cameroon: Langaa Research and Publishing Common Initiative Group.

Allen, Tim. 1996. *In Search of Cool Ground. War, Flight and Homecoming in Northeast Africa*. London: James Currey Ltd.

Allen, Tim, and Hubert Morsink. 1994. 'Introduction: When Refugees Go Home.' In *When Refugees Go Home*, edited by Tim Allen and Hubert Morsink, 1–13. Trenton, New Jersey: Africa World Press, Inc.

Amnesty International. 2009. *Broken Homes, Broken Lives and Forced Evictions in Chad*. London: Amnesty International Publications.

Amnesty International. 2010. *Chad: 'We Too Deserve Protection.' Human Rights Challenges as UN Mission Withdraws*. London: Amnesty International Publications.

Amnesty International. 2012. *Chad: 'We Are All Dying Here.' Human Rights Violations in Prisons*. London: Amnesty International Publications.

Amnesty International. 2017. *Scorched Earth, Poisoned Air*. https://www.amnesty.org/en/latest/news/2016/09/chemical-weapons-attacks-darfur/

Appadurai, Arjun. 2006. *Fear of Small Numbers. An Essay on the Geography of Anger*. Durham, NC and London: Duke University Press.

Appel, Hannah. 2012. 'Walls and White Elephants: Oil Extraction, Responsibility, and Infrastructural Violence in Equatorial Guinea.' *Ethnography* 13 (4): 439–65.

Argenti, Nicolas, and Katharina Schramm. 2010. *Remembering Violence: Anthropological Perspectives on Intergenerational Transmission*. New York: Berghahn Books.

Asad, Talad. 2004. 'Where are the Margins of the State.' In *Anthropology in the Margins of the State*, edited by Veena Das and Deborah, 279–89. Santa Fe, NM: School of American Research Press; Oxford: James Currey.

Autesserre, Séverine. 2009. 'Hobbes and the Congo: Frames, Local Violence, and International Intervention.' *International Organization* 63: 249–80.

Autesserre, Séverine. 2014. *Peaceland: Conflict Resolution and the Everyday Politics of International Intervention*. Cambridge: Cambridge University Press.

Auty, Richard M. 1993. *Sustaining Development in Mineral Economies: The Resource Curse Thesis*. London; New York: Routledge.

REFERENCES

Barry, Andrew. 2006. 'Technological Zones.' *European Journal of Social Theory* 9 (2): 239–53.

Barry, Andrew. 2013. *Material Politics: Disputes Along The Pipeline.* Chichester: Wiley Blackwell.

Barth, Fredrik. 1969. *Ethnic Groups and Boundaries. The Social Organization of Culture Difference.* Bergen; London: Allen & Unwin.

Barth, Fredrik. 1975 (1967). 'Economic Spheres in Darfur.' In *Themes in Economic Anthropology*, edited by Raymond Firth, 149–74. London: Tavistock.

Beck, Kurt. 2003. 'Das vorläufige Ende der Razzien. Nomadisches Grenzkriegertum und staatliche Ordnung im Sudan.' *Orientwissenschaftliche Hefte* 12: 127–50.

Beck, Kurt. 2004. 'Die Massaker in Darfur.' *Zeitschrift für Genozidforschung* 5 (2): 52–80.

Beckett, Greg. 2013. 'The Politics of Emergency.' *Review of Anthropology* 42: 85–101.

Beckett, Greg. 2019. *There is No More Haiti. Between Life and Death in Port-au-Prince.* Oakland, CA: University of California Press.

Behrends, Andrea. 2007. 'The Darfur Conflict and the Chad/Sudan border – Regional Context and Local Re-configurations.' *Sociologus* 57 (1): 99–131.

Behrends, Andrea. 2008. 'Fighting for Oil when There Is No Oil Yet. The Case of The Chad–Sudan Border.' *Focaal* 52: 39–56.

Behrends, Andrea. 2014. 'Securing Livelihoods. Economic Practice in the Darfur–Chad Displacement Arena.' In *Displacement Economies. Paradoxes of Crisis and Creativity in African Contexts*, edited by Amanda Hammar, 35–56. London; New York: Zed Books.

Behrends, Andrea. 2015. 'The Long History of Conflict, Integration and Changing Alliances on the Darfur/Chad Border.' In *Emerging Orders in the Sudans*, edited by Sandra Calkins et al., 39–58. Bamenda: Langaa.

Behrends, Andrea. 2016. 'No Boon At All.' *German Research. Magazine of the Deutsche Forschungsgemeinschaft* 3: 16–20.

Behrends, Andrea. 2020. 'Renegotiating Humanitarian Governance: Challenging Invisibility in the Chad–Sudan Borderlands.' In *Invisibility in African Displacements: From Structural Marginalization to Strategies of Avoidance*, edited by Jesper Bjarnesen and Simon Turner, 19–35. New York: Zed Books.

Behrends, Andrea. 2021. 'Die Verwandlung von sudanesischen Geflüchteten in tschadische Flüchtlingsbürger:innen. Eine

REFERENCES

bürokratische Statuspassage.' In *Humandifferenzierung. Disziplinäre Perspektiven und empirische Sondierungen*, edited by Dilek Dizdar et al., 106–32. Weilerswist: Velbrück Wissenschaft.

Behrends, Andrea, and Remadji Hoinathy. 2017. 'The Devil's Money: A Multi-Level Approach to Acceleration and Turbulence in Oil-Producing Southern Chad.' *Social Analysis. The International Journal of Social and Cultural Practice*, 61 (3): 57–73.

Behrends, Andrea, and Nikolaus Schareika. 2010. 'Significations of Oil in Africa or What (More) Can Anthropologists Contribute to the Study of Oil?' *Suomen Antropologi: Journal of the Finnish Anthropological Society* 35 (1): 83–6.

Behrends, Andrea, and Nikolaus Schareika. 2011. 'Öl, Staat, Ressourcenfluch.' In *Auf dem Boden der Tatsachen. Festschrift für Thomas Bierschenk*, edited by Nikolaus Schareika et al., 465–75. Cologne: Rüdiger Köppe Verlag.

Behrends, Andrea, and Günther Schlee. 2008. 'Lokale Konfliktstrukturen in Darfur und im Osten des Tschad oder: Was ist ethnisch an ethnischen Konflikten?' In *Krisenmanagement in Afrika*, edited by Walter Feichtinger, 159–77. Vienna: Böhlau Verlag.

Behrends, Andrea et al. 2011. *Crude Domination. An Anthropology of Oil*. London; New York: Berghahn.

Behrends, Andrea et al. 2014. 'Travelling Models. Introducing an Analytical Concept to Globalisation Studies.' In *Travelling Models in African Conflict Management. Translating Technologies of Social Ordering*, edited by Andrea Behrends et al., 1–40. Leiden: Brill.

Berk, Gerald, and Dennis Galvan. 2009. 'How People Experience and Change Institutions: A Field Guide to Creative Syncretism.' *Theory and Society* 38: 543–80.

Bierschenk, Thomas. 2000. *Courtiers en développement: les villages africains en quête de projets*. Paris: Karthala.

Bierschenk, Thomas. 2014. 'Sedimentation, Fragmentation and Normative Double-Binds in (West) African Public Services.' In *States at Work. Dynamics of African Bureaucracies*, edited by Thomas Bierschenk and Jean-Pierre Olivier de Sardan, 221–45. Leiden: Brill.

Bierschenk, Thomas, and Jean-Pierre Olivier de Sardan. 1997. 'Local Powers and a Distant State in Rural Central African Republic.' *Journal of Modern African Studies* 35 (3): 441–68.

Bierschenk, Thomas, and Jean-Pierre Olivier de Sardan. 2014. *States at Work: Dynamics of African Bureaucracies*. Leiden: Brill.

REFERENCES

Bjarnesen, Jesper, and Henrik Vigh. 2016. 'The Dialectics of Displacement and Emplacement.' *Conflict and Society. Advances in Research* 2: 9–15.

Blumenberg, Hans. 2018. *Phänomenologische Schriften. 1981–1988*. Herausgegeben von Nicola Zambon. Berlin: Suhrkamp.

Boltanski, Luc. 2010. 'Kritische Soziologie und pragmatische Soziologie der Kritik.' In *Soziologie und Sozialkritik: Frankfurter Adorno-Vorlesungen 2008*, 19–38. Berlin: Suhrkamp.

Bornstein, Erica, and Peter Redfield. 2011. *Forces of Compassion: Humanitarianism between Ethics and Politics*. Santa Fe, NM: School for Advanced Research Press.

Bowker, Geoffrey, and Susan Leigh Star. 1999. *Sorting Things Out. Classification and Its Consequences*. Cambridge, MA; London: The MIT Press.

Braukämper, Ulrich. 1993. 'Notes on the Origin of Baggara Arab Culture with Special Reference to the Shuwa.' *Sprache und Geschichte in Afrika* 14: 13–46.

Breckenridge, Keith. 2014. *Biometric State: The Global Politics of Identification and Surveillance in South Africa, 1850 to the Present*. Cambridge: Cambridge University Press.

Buijtenhuijs, Robert. 1978. *Le Frolinat et les révoltes populaires du Tchad, 1965–1976, Change and Continuity in Africa 12*. The Hague; New York: Mouton Publishers.

Buijtenhuijs, Robert. 1987. *Le Frolinat et les guerres civiles du Tchad (1977–1984): la révolution introuvable, Hommes et sociétés*. Paris; Leiden: Karthala; Afrika-Studiecentrum.

Burr, J. Millard, and Robert O. Collins. 1999. *Africa's Thirty Years War. Libya, Chad, and the Sudan 1963–1993*. Boulder, CO: Westview Press.

Calkins, Sandra 2016. *Who Knows Tomorrow? Uncertainty in North-Eastern Sudan*. New York; Oxford: Berghahn.

Callon, Michel. 1986. 'Some Elements of a Sociology of Translation: Domestication of the Scallops and the Fishermen of St. Brieuc Bay.' In *Power, Action and Belief. A New Sociology of Knowledge?*, edited by John Law, 196–233. London; Boston, MA: Routledge & Kegan Paul.

Cash, Audrey C. 2012. 'Corporate Social Responsibility and Petroleum Development in Sub-Saharan Africa: The Case of Chad.' *Resources Policy* 37: 144–51.

Chatty, Dawn, and N. Mansour. 2011. 'Unlocking Protracted Displacement: An Iraqi Case Study.' Oxford: Refugees Studies Centre, *Working Paper* No. 78.

REFERENCES

Coll, Steve. 2012. *Private Empire. ExxonMobil and American Power.* London: Penguin.

Coronil, Fernando. 1997. *The Magical State: Nature, Money, and Modernity in Venezuela.* Chicago, IL: University of Chicago Press.

Cunnison, Ian. 1972. 'Blood Money, Vengeance and Joint Responsibility: The Baggara Case.' In *Sudan Ethnography Presented to Sir Edward Evans-Pritchard,* edited by Ian Cunnison and Wendy James, 105–25. London: C. Hurst & Company.

Das, Veena, and Deborah Poole. 2004. *Anthropology in the Margins of the State.* Santa Fe, NM; Oxford: School of American Research Press; James Currey.

Debos, Marielle. 2011. 'Living by the Gun in Chad: Armed Violence as a Practical Occupation.' *Journal of Modern African Studies* 49 (3): 409–28.

Debos, Marielle. 2016. *Living by the Gun in Chad. Combatants, Impunity and State Formation.* London: Zed Books.

Debos, Marielle. 2017. 'Biométrie au Tchad : nouvelles technologies et vieilles recettes électorales.' *The Conversation.* https://theconversation.com/biometrie-au-tchad-nouvelles-technologies-et-vieilles-recettes-electorales-58394

De Bruijn, Mirjam. 2008. 'The Impossibility of Civil Organisations in Post-war Chad.' In *Beside the State, Emergent Powers in Contemporary Africa,* edited by Alice Bellagamba and Georg Klute. Cologne: Rüdiger Köppe Verlag.

De Bruijn, Mirjam, and Han van Dijk. 2007. 'The Multiple Experiences of Civil War in the Guéra Region of Chad, 1965–1990.' *Sociologus* 57 (1): 61–98.

De Waal, Alex. 1988. 'Refugees and the Creation of Famine: The Case of Dar Masalit, Sudan.' *Journal of Refugee Studies* 1 (2): 127–40.

De Waal, Alex. 1989. *Famine that Kills.* New York: Oxford University Press.

De Waal, Alex. 2004. 'Counter-Insurgency on the Cheap.' *London Review of Books* 26 (15): 1–8.

De Waal, Alex. 2005. 'Who are the Darfurians? Arab and African Identities, Violence and External Engagement.' *African Affairs* 104 (415): 181–205.

Desjarlais, Robert, and Jason C. Throop. 2011. 'Phenomenological Approaches in Anthropology.' *Annual Review of Anthropology* 40: 87–102.

Desrosières, Alain. 1998. *The Politics of Large Numbers: A History of Statistical Reasoning.* Cambridge MA; London: Harvard University Press.

REFERENCES

Dickow, Helga 2014. 'Autoritäre Strukturen im Tschad: Macht aus Sicht derer, die sie nicht haben.' *Sociologus* 64 (1): 53–78.

Dittgen, Romain and Daniel Large. 2012. 'China's Growing Involvement in Chad: Escaping Enclosure?' *South African Institute for International Affairs Occasional Paper* 116: 1–26.

Dizdar, Dilek et al. 2021. *Humandifferenzierung. Disziplinäre Perspektiven und empirische Sondierungen.* Weilerswist: Velbrück Wissenschaft.

Douglas, Mary. 1986. *How Institutions Think.* New York: Syracuse University Press.

Doumbia, Lamine. 2021. 'Eviction and Relocation in West Africa. A Socio-Anthropological Essay on Bureaucratized Processes.' In *Francia. Forschungen zur westeuropäischen Geschichte* 48: 469–79.

Eckert, Julia M. 2003. *The Charisma of Direct Action: Power, Politics, and the Shiv Sena.* New Delhi; New York: Oxford University Press.

Eckert, Julia, Andrea Behrends and Andreas Dafinger. 2012. 'Governance—and the State: An Anthropological Approach.' *Ethnoscripts* 14 (1): 14–34.

El-Battahani, Atta. 2004. 'Ideologische, expansionistische Bewegungen und historische indigene Rechte in der Region Darfur, Sudan. Vom Massenmord zum Genozid.' *Zeitschrift für Genozidforschung* 5 (2): 8–51.

El-Tom, Abdullahi Osman. 2006. 'Darfur People: Too Black for the Arab-Islamic Project of Sudan.' *Irish Journal of Anthropology* 9 (1): 5–11.

Falge, Christiane. 1999. 'The Change in Continuity: Nuer Refugees and Substituted Cattle.' *Sociologus* 49 (1): 27–56.

Fassin, Didier, and Mariella Pandolfi. 2010. *Contemporary States of Emergency: The Politics of Military and Humanitarian Interventions.* New York; Cambridge, MA: Zone Books.

Feldman, Ilana. 2012. 'The Challenge of Categories: UNWRA and the Definition of a "Palestine Refugee".' *Journal of Refugee Studies* 25 (3): 387–406.

Ferguson, James. 1990. *The Anti-Politics Machine: 'Development', Depoliticization, and Bureaucratic Power in Lesotho.* Minneapolis, MN: University of Minnesota Press.

Ferguson, James, and Akhil Gupta. 2002. 'Spatializing States: Toward an Ethnography of Neoliberal Governmentality.' *American Ethnologist* 29 (4): 981–1002.

Ferguson, R. Brian. 2003. 'Introduction: Violent Conflict and Control of the State.' In *The State, Identity and Violence: Political Disintegration in the Post-Cold War World*, edited by R. Brian Ferguson, 1–58. London; New York: Routledge.

REFERENCES

Finnstrøm, Sverker. 2008. *Living with Bad Surroundings: War, History, and Everyday Moments in Northern Uganda*. Durham, NC: Duke University Press.

Fischer, Anja. 2017. 'From Tent to Hut: Mutual Adaption of Shelter in Tuareg Refugee Camps of Burkina Faso.' Presentation at the DGV conference on 'Zugehörigkeiten: Affektive, moralische und politische Praxen in einer vernetzten Welt,' 4–7.10.2017, Freie Universität Berlin.

Flint, Julie, and Alex de Waal. 2005. *Darfur: A Short History of a Long War*. London; New York: Zed Books.

Flint, Julie, and Alex de Waal. 2008. *Darfur: A New History of a Long War*. London; New York: Zed Books.

Foucault, Michel. 2007. *Security, Territory, Population. Lectures at the College de France, 1977–78*. Edited by Michel Senellart. Hampshire; New York: Palgrave Macmillan.

Garfinkel, Harold. 1967. *Studies in Ethnomethodology*. Englewood Cliffs, NJ: Prentice Hall, Inc.

Gary, Ian, and Terry Lynn Karl. 2003. *Bottom of the Barrel. Africa's Oil Boom and the Poor*. Baltimore, MD: Catholic Relief Services.

Glasman, Joël. 2017. 'Seeing like a Refugee Agency: A Short History of UNHCR Classifications in Central Africa (1961–2015).' *Journal of Refugee Studies* 30 (2): 1–26.

Glasman, Joël. 2020. *Humanitarianism and the Quantification of Human Needs. Minimal Humanity*. New York: Routledge.

Glick Schiller, Nina, and Ayse Çağlar. 2015. 'Displacement, Emplacement, and Migrant Newcomers: Rethinking Urban Sociabilities within Multiscalar Power.' *Identities Global Studies in Culture and Power* 23 (1): 17–34.

Glick Schiller, Nina, and Ayse Çağlar. 2018. Multi-scalar City-Making and Emplacement. Processes, Concepts, and Methods. In *Migrants and City-Making. Dispossession, Displacement, and Urban Regeneration*. Durham, NC: Duke University Press.

Gupta, Akhil, and Aradhana Sharma. 2006. 'Globalization and Postcolonial States.' *Current Anthropology* 47 (2): 277–93.

Guyer, Jane I. 2002. 'Briefing: The Chad–Cameroon Petroleum and Pipeline Development Project.' *African Affairs* (101): 109–15.

Guyer, Jane I. 2015. 'Oil Assemblages and the Production of Confusion. Price Fluctuations in Two West-African Oil-Producing Economies.' In *Subterranean Estates. Life Worlds of Oil and Gas*, edited by Hannah Appel et al., 237–52. Ithaca, NY: Cornell University Press.

REFERENCES

Haaland, Gunnar. 1968. *Nomadization as an Economic Career among Sedentaries in the Sudanic Savannah Belt.* Department of Social Anthropology, University of Bergen. Mimeo.

Hacking, Ian. 1995. 'The Looping Effects of Human Kinds.' In *Causal Cognition: A Multi-Disciplinary Debate*, edited by Dan Sperber et al., 351–83. Oxford: Oxford University Press.

Hacking, Ian. 1999. 'Making Up People.' In *The Science Studies Reader*, edited by Mario Biagioli, 161–71. New York: Routledge.

Hammar, Amanda. 2014. *Displacement Economies in Africa. Paradoxes of Crisis and Creativity.* London; New York: Zed Books.

Hansen, Ketil F. 2011. 'Conflicts in Chad: The Porous Boundaries between Politicians and Rebels.' In *Pluralité des langues, pluralité des cultures: regards sur l'Afrique et au-delà. Mélanges offerts à Ingse Skattum à l'occasion de son 70ième anniversaire*, edited by Kristin Vold Lexander et al., 55–64. Oslo: Novus: Institutt for sammenlignende kulturforskning.

Hansen, Thomas Blom, and Finn Stepputat. 2001. *States of Imagination*: Durham, NC: Duke University Press.

Harir, Sharif. 1994. '"Arab Belt" versus "African Belt". Ethno-Political Conflict in Dar Fur and the Regional Cultural Factors.' In *Short-Cut to Decay. The Case of the Sudan*, edited by Sharif Harir and Terje Tvedt, 144–85. Uppsala, Sweden: Nordiska Afrikainstitutet.

Harir, Sharif, and Terje Tvedt. 1994. *Short-Cut to Decay. The Case of the Sudan.* Uppsala, Sweden: Nordiska Afrikainstitutet.

Harrell-Bond, Barbara E., Anthony Richmond, Gertrud Neuwirth, and Robert E. Mazur. 1988. 'The Sociology of Involuntary Migration.' *Current Sociology* 36 (2): 1–60.

Hassan, Salah M., and Carina E. Ray (eds.). 2009. *Darfur and the Crisis of Governance in Sudan. A Critical Reader.* Ithaca, NY: Cornell University Press.

Hirschauer, Stefan. 2014. 'Un/doing Differences. Die Kontingenz sozialer Zugehörigkeiten.' *Zeitschrift für Soziologie* 43 (3): 170–91.

Hoinathy, Remadji. 2012. *Pétrole et changement sociale. Rente pétrolière et monétisation des relations économiques et sociales dans la zone pétrolière de Doba.* PhD Thesis, Martin Luther University of Halle-Wittenberg.

Hoinathy, Remadji. 2013. *Pétrole et changement sociale. Rente pétrolière et monétisation des relations économiques et sociales dans la zone pétrolière de Doba.* Paris: Karthala.

Hoinathy, Remadji, and Andrea Behrends. 2014. 'Does Rationality Travel? Translating a World Bank Model for Fair Revenue Distribution

REFERENCES

in Chad.' In *Travelling Models in African Conflict Management. Translating Technologies of Social Ordering*, edited by Andrea Behrends et al., 76–91. Leiden: Brill.

Hoinathy, Remadji, and Yamingué Bétinbaye. 2023. La guerre au Soudan fait peser de graves risques sur le Tchad et la RCA. *ISS Today*, 8 May. https://issafrica.org/fr/iss-today/la-guerre-au-soudan-fait-peser-de-graves-risques-sur-le-tchad-et-la-rca (last accessed 30 July 2023).

Horst, Cindy, and Katarzyna Grabska. 2015. 'Flight and Exile—Uncertainty in the Context of Conflict-Induced Displacement.' *Social Analysis* 59 (1): 1–18.

Human Rights Watch. 2007. '"They Came Here to Kill Us": Militia Attacks and Ethnic Targeting of Civilians in Eastern Chad.' *Human Rights Watch* 19 (1).

Husserl, Edmund. 1913. *Ideen zu einer reinen Phänomenologie und phänomenologischen Philosophie*. Halle a.d. Saale: Verlag von Max Niemeyer.

Husserl, Edmund. 1954. *Die Krisis der europäischen Wissenschaften und die transzendentale Phänomenologie*, The Hague: Nijhoff.

Hyndman, Jennifer. 1997. 'Refugee Self-management and the Question of Governance.' *Refuge* 16 (2): 16–22.

Hyndman, Jennifer. 2000. *Managing Displacement. Refugees and the Politics of Humanitarianism*. Minneapolis, MN: University of Minnesota Press.

Ibrahim, Adam Ahmed. 2000. 'Masalit Documents.' Handwritten report, N'Djamena.

Jánszky, Babett. 2014. *Überleben an Grenzen: Ressourcenkonflikte und Risikomanagement im Sahel*. Universität Köln: Philosophische Fakultät der Universität Köln.

Johnson, Douglas H. 2003. *The Root Causes of Sudan's Civil Wars*. Oxford: James Currey.

Kalfelis, Melina C., 2020. *NGOs als Lebenswelt. Transnationale Verflechtungen im Arbeitsalltag von Entwicklungsakteuren*. Frankfurt am Main: Campus.

Kalfelis, Melina C. and Kathrin Knodel (eds.). 2021. *NGOs and Lifeworlds. Historical and Contemporary Perspectives*. New York: Berghahn.

Kapteijns, Lidwien. 1985. *Mahdist Faith and Sudanic Tradition. The History of the Masalit Sultanate 1870–1930*. London: Routledge and Kegan Paul.

Kapteijns, Lidwien, and J. L. Spaulding. 1988. *After the Millennium: Diplomatic Correspondence from Wadai and Dar Fur on the Eve of Colonial Conquest 1885–1916*. East Lansing, MI: Michigan State University, African Studies Center.

REFERENCES

Karl, Terry Lynn. 1997. *The Paradox of Plenty: Oil Booms and Petro-States*. Berkeley, CA: University of California Press.

Kopytoff, Igor. 1987. *The African Frontier. The Reproduction of Traditional African Societies*. Bloomington, IN: Indiana University Press.

Krause, Kristine, and Katharina Schramm. 2011. 'Thinking through Political Subjectivity.' *African Diaspora* 4 (2): 115–34.

Kurimoto, Eisei. 2001. 'Changing Identifications among the Pari Refugees in Kakuma.' Paper read at the conference on 'Changing Identifications and Alliances in North-Eastern Africa,' 5–9 June, Halle/Saale.

Lakoff, George. 1987. *Women, Fire, and Dangerous Things. What Categories Reveal about the Mind*. Chicago, IL: University of Chicago Press.

Lentz, Carola. 2000. 'Contested Identities: The History of Ethnicity in Northwestern Ghana.' In *Ethnicity in Ghana. The Limits of Invention*, edited by Carola Lentz and Paul Nugent, 137–59. London: Macmillan.

Lentz, Carola. 2003. '"This Is Ghanaian Territory!": Land Conflicts on a West African Border.' *American Ethnologist* 30 (2): 273–89.

Lentz, Carola. 2006. 'Decentralization, the State and Conflicts over Local Boundaries in Northern Ghana.' *Development and Change* 37 (4): 901–19.

Lentz, Carola. 2013. *Land, Mobility, and Belonging in West Africa*. Bloomington, IN: Indiana University Press.

Lentz, Carola. 2016. 'Culture: The Making, Unmaking and Remaking of an Anthropological Concept.' *Working Papers of the Department of Anthropology and African Studies* 166, Mainz: Johannes Gutenberg University.

Leonard, Lori. 2016. *Life in the Time of Oil: A Pipeline and Poverty in Chad*. Bloomington, IN: Indiana University Press

Leutloff, Carolin. 1998. *'Du gehörst weder hierher noch dahin. Du bist im Niemandsland'. Zum Wandel des Selbstverständnisses von Krajina-Serben nach dem Exodus im August 1995*. Master's Thesis, Institut für Ethnologie, Freie Universität Berlin, Berlin.

Lewis, David, and David Mosse. 2005. *The Aid Effect: Giving and Governing in International Development*. London; Ann Arbor, MI: Pluto.

Lewis, David, and David Mosse. 2006. *Development Brokers and Translators: The Ethnography of Aid and Agencies*. Bloomfield, CT: Kumarian Press.

Li, Tania. 2007. *The Will To Improve: Governmentality, Development, and Practice of Politics*. Durham, NC: Duke University Press.

REFERENCES

Long, Katy. 2010. 'Home Alone? A Review of the Relationship between Repatriation, Mobility and Durable Solutions for Refugees.' United Nations High Commissioner for Refugees Policy Development and Evaluation Service (PDES).

Long, Katy. 2011. 'Permanent Crises? Unlocking the Protracted Displacement of Refugees and Internally Displaced Persons.' Refugee Studies Centre, Oxford Department of International Development, University of Oxford.

Lucht, Hans. 2011. *Darkness Before Daybreak. African Migrants Living on the Margins in Southern Italy Today*. Stanford, CA: University of California Press.

Luhmann, Niklas. 1984. *Soziale Systeme. Grundriß einer allgemeinen Theorie*. Frankfurt a.M.: Suhrkamp.

Lund, Christian. 2008. *Local Politics and the Dynamics of Property in Africa*. Cambridge: Cambridge University Press.

Magrin, Géraud. 2005. 'Greffe pétrolière et dynamiques territoriales: l'exemple de l'on-shore tchadien.' *Afrique contemporaine* 216: 87–105.

Magrin, Géraud et al. 2011. *Chinese and American Oil Companies and Their Environmental Practices in Chad: A Quiet Confluence of Streams or Silence Before the Battle?* Vol. 2, Rising Power and Global Standards: Working Paper 2. Manchester: Rising Powers.

Malkki, Liisa H. 1995. *Purity and Exile. Violence, Memory, and National Cosmology among Hutu Refugees in Tanzania*. Chicago, IL: University of Chicago Press.

Mamdani, Mahmood. 1996. 'Customary Law: The Theory of Decentralized Despotism.' In *Citizen and Subject. Contemporary Africa and the Legacy of Late Colonialism*, 109–37. Princeton, NJ: Princeton University Press.

Mamdani, Mahmood. 2009. *Saviors and Survivors: Darfur, Politics, and the War on Terror*. 1st ed. New York: Pantheon Books.

Mamdani, Mahmood. 2012. *Define and Rule: Native as Political Identity*. Cambridge, MA; London: Harvard University Press.

Mans, Ulrich. 2004. 'Briefing: Sudan: The New War in Darfur.' *African Affairs* 103 (411): 291–94.

Marchal, Roland. 2004. 'Le Soudan d'un conflit à l'autre.' *Les Études du CERI. Centre d'études et de recherches internationales Sciences Po* 107–8.

Marchal, Roland. 2006. 'Chad/Darfur: How Two Crises Merge.' *Review of African Political Economy* 109: 467–82.

REFERENCES

Marchal, Roland. 2007. 'Chad. Towards a Militia State?' Unpublished manuscript. Centre d'études et de recherches international CERI/ Centre national de la recherche scientifique CNRS.

Massey, Doreen. 1993. 'Power-Geometry and a Progressive Sense of Place.' In *Mapping the Futures: Local Cultures, Global Change*, edited by John Bird, 56–69. London: Routledge.

Massumi, Brian. 2010. 'The Future Birth of the Affective Fact: The Political Ontology of Threat.' In *The Affect Theory Reader*, edited by Gregory J. Seigworth and Melissa Gregg, 52–70. Durham, NC; London: Duke University Press.

Maxwell, Audrey. 1986. *The Tribes at the Chadian Refugee Camp at Angi Koti, South Darfur Sudan*. A Working Report. Association of Christian Resource Organizations Serving Sudan (ACROSS).

McFalls, Laurence. 2010. 'Benevolent Dictatorship: The Formal Logic of Humanitarian Government.' In *Contemporary States of Emergency: The Politics of Military and Humanitarian Interventions*, edited by Didier and Mariella Pandolfi Fassin, 317–34. Cambridge, MA: Zone Books.

M'charek, Amade, Katharina Schramm, and David Skinner. 2013. 'Topologies of Race: Doing Territory, Population and Identity in Europe.' *Science, Technology and Human Values* 39 (4): 468–87.

Meier, Astrid. 1995. *Hunger und Herrschaft: vorkoloniale und frühe koloniale Hungerkrisen im Nordtschad*. Stuttgart: Steiner.

Merry, Sally Engle. 2006. 'Transnational Human Rights and Local Activism: Mapping the Middle.' *American Anthropologist* 108 (1): 38–51.

Miankeol, Djéralar. 2010. 'Vivre avec le pétrole, étude sur les conditions de vie des villages en zone pétrolière de Doba auTchad.' Chad Group. http://peaceresources.net/files/docs/publications/Rapport_Etude_villages_final_101123.pdf.

Miankeol, Djéralar, and Jean Ngamine. 1999. *Etude sur les mesures de compensation et d'indemnisation: évaluation des montants des arbres—constats—suggestions*. N'Djamena: CILONG/COLONG and Commission Permanente Pétrole.

Migdal, Joel, and Klaus Schlichte. 2005. 'Rethinking the State.' In *The Dynamics of States. The Formation and Crises of State Domination*, edited by Klaus Schlichte, 1–38. Aldershot: Ashgate.

Mitchell, Timothy. 1999. 'Society, Economy and the State Effect.' In *State/Culture: State Formation After the Cultural Turn*, edited by Georg Steinmetz, 76–97. Ithaca, NY: Cornell University Press.

REFERENCES

Nguyen, Vinh-Kim. 2010. *The Republic of Therapy. Triage and Sovereignty in West Africa's time of AIDS*. Durham, NC; London: Duke University Press.

Nordstrom, Carolyn. 2004. *Shadows of War: Violence, Power, and International Profiteering in the Twenty-First Century*, Berkeley, CA: University of California Press.

Nur, Bakheit Mohammed. 2022. 'Politics of Epistemology in Postcolonial Africa: The Islamisation of Knowledge in the Sudan.' *Politics, Religion and Ideology* 23 (4): 475–96.

O'Fahey, Rex S. 1980. *State and Society in Dar Fur*. London: C. Hurst & Company.

O'Fahey, Rex S. 2007. 'Umm Kwakdiyya or the Damnation of Darfur. Review Article.' *African Affairs* 106 (425): 709–17.

O'Fahey, Rex S., and Jay L. Spaulding. 1974. *Kingdoms of the Sudan*. London: Methuen & Co. Ltd.

Otto, Ralf et al. 2011. *Die deutsche humanitäre Hilfe im Ausland. Länderstudie Tschad*. Unveröffentlichter Evaluierungsbericht. Bonn/Berlin: Bundesministerium für wirtschaftliche Zusammenarbeit und Entwicklung/Auswärtiges Amt.

Palmberger, Monika. 2016. *How Generations Remember: Conflicting Histories and Shared Memories in Post-War Bosnia and Herzegovina*. London: Palgrave Macmillan.

Pegg, Scott. 2005. 'Can Policy Intervention Beat the Resource Curse? Evidence from the Chad–Cameroon Pipeline Project.' *African Affairs* 105 (418): 1–25.

Petry, Martin, and Naygotimti Bambé. 2005. *Le pétrole du Tchad: rêve ou cauchemar pour les populations?* Paris: Khartala.

Pinther, Kerstin et al. *Afropolis. Stadt, Medien, Kunst*. Cologne: Walther Koenig.

Prah, Kwesi Kwaa. 2001. 'Race, Discrimination, Slavery, Nationalism and Citizenship in the Afro-Arab Borderlands.' In *Racism and Public Policy*. Durban: UNRISD.

Prunier, Gérard. 2005. *Darfur: The Ambiguous Genocide*. Ithaca, NY: Cornell University Press.

Ram, Kalpana, and Christopher Houston. 2015. *Phenomenology in Anthropology: A Sense of Perspective*. Bloomington, IN: Indiana University Press.

Redfield, Peter. 2010. 'The Verge of Crisis. Doctors without Borders in Uganda.' In *Contemporary States of Emergency. The Politics of Military and Humanitarian Interventions*, edited by Didier and Mariella Pandolfi Fassin, 173–95. New York: Zone Books.

REFERENCES

Redfield, Peter. 2012. 'Bioexpectations: Life Technologies as Humanitarian Goods.' *Public Culture* 24 (1).

Redfield, Peter. 2013. *Life in Crisis: The Ethical Journey of Doctors without Borders*. Berkeley, CA: University of California Press.

Reyna, Stephen. 1990. *Wars Without End: The Political Economy of a Precolonial African State*. Hanover, NH: University Press of New England.

Reyna, Stephen P. 2007. 'The Traveling Model That Would Not Travel: Oil, Empire, and Patrimonialism in Contemporary Chad.' *Social Analysis* 51 (3): 78–102.

Reyna, Stephen P. 2010. 'The Disasters of War in Darfur, 1950–2004.' *Third World Quarterly* 31 (8): 24.

Risse, Thomas. 2008. 'Governance in Areas of Limited Statehood: How Far Do Concepts Travel?' In *the Annual Convention of the International Studies Association, San Francisco CA, USA, March 26–30, 2008*. San Francisco, CA: Research Center.

Roitman, Janet. 2006. 'The Ethics of Illegality in the Chad Basin.' In *Law and Disorder in the Postcolony*, edited by Jean and John L. Comaroff, 247–72. Chicago, IL: University of Chicago Press.

Roitman, Janet. 2014. *Anti-crisis*. Durham, NC: Duke University Press.

Rottenburg, Richard. 2002. *Weit hergeholte Fakten: eine Parabel der Entwicklungshilfe*. Stuttgart: Lucius & Lucius.

Rottenburg, Richard. 2005. 'Code Switching, or Why a Metacode Is Good to Have.' In *Global Ideas: How Ideas, Objects and Practices Travel in the Global Economy*, edited by Barbara Czarniawska and Guje Sevón, 259–74. Copenhagen: Copenhagen Business School Press.

Rottenburg, Richard. 2009. 'Social and Public Experiments and New Figurations of Science and Politics in Postcolonial Africa.' *Postcolonial Studies* 12 (4): 423–40.

Rottenburg, Richard. 2013. 'Ethnologie und Kritik.' In *Ethnologie im 21. Jahrhundert*, edited by Thomas Bierschenk et al., 55–76. Berlin: Reimer.

Rottenburg, Richard et al. 2008. 'Nomadic-sedentary Relations and Failing State Institutions in Darfur and Kordofan (Sudan).' *Orientwissenschaftliche Hefte* 26.

Rottenburg, Richard et al. 2015. *The World of Indicators: The Making of Governmental Knowledge through Quantification*. Cambridge: Cambridge University Press.

Ruiz, Hiram. 1987. 'When Refugees Won't Go Home. The Dilemma of Chadians in Sudan.' In *Refugees Studies Programme*, Documentation Centre, Oxford.

REFERENCES

Salih, Mohamed M. A., and Sharif Harir. 1994. 'Tribal Militias.' In *Short-Cut to Decay. The Case of the Sudan*, edited by Sharif Harir and Terje Tvedt, 186–203. Uppsala: Nordiska Afrikainstitutet.

Sassen, Saskia. 2013. 'When Territory Deborders Territoriality.' *Territory, Politics, Governance* 1 (1): 21–45.

Scheper-Hughes, Nancy. 1992. 'Introduction.' In *Death Without Weeping. The Violence of Everyday Life in Brazil*, 1–30. Berkeley, CA and Los Angeles, CA: Berkeley University Press.

Schmitz, Alexander, and Bernd Stiegler (eds.). 2015. *Hans Blumenberg, Schriften zur Technik*. Berlin: Suhrkamp Verlag.

Schnegg, Michael. 2019. 'The Life of Winds: Knowing the Namibian Weather from Someplace and from Noplace.' *American Anthropologist* 121 (4): 830–44.

Schnegg, Michael. 2021. 'Ontologies of Climate Change. Reconciling Indigenous and Scientific Explanations for the Lack of Rain in Namibia.' *American Ethnologist* 48 (3): 260–73.

Schramm, Katharina, and Claire Beaudevin. 2019. 'Sorting, Typing, Classifying: The Elephants in Our Ethnographic Rooms.' *Medicine Anthropology Theory* 6 (4): 276–90.

Schritt, Jannik, and Andrea Behrends. 2014. '"Western" and "Chinese" Oil Zones. Petro-Infrastructures and the Emergence of New Transterritorial Spaces of Order in Niger and Chad.' In *Spatial Practices: Territory, Border and Infrastructure in Africa*, edited by Ulf Engel et al., 211–30. Leiden: Brill.

Seesemann, Rüdiger. 2005. 'The Quotidian Dimension of Islamic reformism in Wahadi (Chad).' In *L'islam politique au sud du Sahara—Identités, discours et enjeux*, edited by Muriel Gomez-Perez, 327–47. Paris: Karthala.

Simmel, Georg. [1910] 1949. 'The Sociology of Sociability.' *American Journal of Sociology* 55 (3): 254–61.

Spittler, Gerd. 1989. *Handeln in einer Hungerkrise: Tuaregnomaden und die grosse Dürre von 1984*. Opladen: Westdeutscher Verlag.

Star, Susan Leigh. 1999. 'The Ethnography of Infrastructure.' *American Behavioral Scientist* 43 (3): 377–91.

Star, Susan Leigh, and James R. Griesemer. 1989. 'Institutional Ecology, "Translations" and Boundary Objects: Amateurs and Professionals in Berkeley's Museum of Vertebrate Zoology, 1907–39.' *Social Studies of Science* 19: 387–420.

Stengers, Isabelle. 2005. 'Introductory Notes on an Ecology of Practices.' *Cultural Studies Review* 11 (1): 183–96.

REFERENCES

Stepputat, Finn. 1994. 'Repatriation and the Politics of Space: the Case of the Mayan Diaspora and Return Movement.' *Journal of Refugee Studies* 7 (2/3): 175–85.

Stepputat, Finn, and Ninna Nyberg Sørensen. 2014. 'Sociology and Forced Migration.' In *The Oxford Handbook of Refugee and Forced Migration Studies*, edited by Elena Fiddian-Qasmiyeh, 86–98. Oxford: Oxford University Press.

Thelen, Tatjana et al. 2017. *Stategraphy. Toward A Relational Anthropology of the State*. London; New York: Berghahn.

Thévenot, Laurent. 2001. 'Pragmatic Regimes Governing the Engagement with the World.' In *The Practice Turn in Contemporary Theory*, edited by Theodore R. Schatzki et al. 56–73. New York: Routledge.

Tubiana, Jerome. 2008. 'The Chad–Sudan Proxy War and the 'Darfurization' of Chad: Myths and Reality.' *Small Arms Survey. HSBA for Sudan and South Sudan.Working Paper* 12: 1–79.

Tubiana, Jérôme. 2023. 'Darfur: Between Two Wars. Twenty Years of Conflict in Sudan, From Darfur to Khartoum and Back.' Al Jazeera, 30 June. https://www.aljazeera.com/features/longform/2023/6/30/between-two-wars-20-years-of-conflict-in-sudans-darfur (last accessed 30 July 2023).

Tubiana, Jérôme et al. 2012. 'Traditional Authorities' Peacemaking Role in Darfur.' Working Paper with *Peaceworks*, edited by United States Institute of Peace.

Turner, Simon. 2006. 'Biopolitics and Bare Life in a Refugee Camp: Some Conceptual Reflections.' In *Flucht als Politik: Berichte von fünf Kontinenten*, edited by Katharina Inhetveen, 39–62. Cologne: Rüdiger Köppe Verlag.

UNHCR. 2013. UNHCR Chad. Strategic Re-orientation: Exploring and Realizing Alternatives in 2014 and Beyond. N'Djamena: UNHCR.

UNHCR. 2015a. *Seeds for Solutions. Promotion de l'Autosuffisance et des Moyens d'Existence des Réfugiés et des Population Hôtes du Tchad*. N'Djamena: UNHCR.

UNHCR. 2015b. *Opération de vérification et enrôlement biométrique des réfugies et demandeurs d'asile vivant au Tchad*. N'Djamena: UNHCR.

Vigh, Henrik. 2008. 'Crisis and Chronicity: Anthropological Perspectives on Continuous Conflict and Decline.' *Ethnos* 73 (1): 5–24.

von Hirschhausen, Béatrice et al. 2015. *Phantomgrenzen. Räume und Akteure in der Zeit neu denken*. Göttingen: Wallstein Verlag.

REFERENCES

Wai, Dunston. 1981. *The Africa-Arab Conflict in the Sudan*. New York: Africana.

Wax, Emily. 2004. 'In Sudan, "a Big Sheik" Roams Free.' Washington Post Foreign Service. http://www.washingtonpost.com/ac2/wp-dyn/A58171-2004Jul17?language=printer

Wenger, Etienne et al. 'Communities of Practice and their Value to Organizations.' In *A Guide to Managing Knowledge. Cultivating Communities of Practice*, edited by Etienne Wenger et al., 1–22, 261–74. Boston, MA: Harvard Business School Press.

Weszkalnys, Gisa. 2016. 'A Doubtful Hope: Resource Affect in a Future Oil Economy.' *Journal of the Royal Anthropological Institute* 22 (S1): 127–46.

Whyte, Susan Reynolds. 1997. *Questioning Misfortune: The Pragmatics of Uncertainty in Eastern Uganda*. Cambridge; New York: Cambridge University Press.

Whyte, Susan Reynolds. 2005. 'Uncertain Undertakings: Practicing Health Care in the Subjunctive Mood.' In *Managing Uncertainty: Ethnographic Studies of Illness, Risk and the Struggle for Control*, edited by Vibeke Steffen et al., 245–64. Copenhagen: Museum Tusculanum Press.

Yates, Douglas A. 1996. *The Rentier State in Africa: Oil Rent Dependency and Neocolonialism in the Republic of Gabon*. Trenton, NJ: Africa World Press.

Zint, Martin. 2001. 'Mobilisierung ohne Beispiel.' *Der Überblick* 3/2001: 45–9.

Zolberg, Aristide R. et al. 1989. *Escape from Violence. Conflict and the Refugee Crisis in the Developing World*. Oxford: Oxford University Press.

INDEX

Note: Page numbers followed by 'n' refer to notes.

Abdallah (a rebel-turned-refugee), 142, 143–4, 155–9, 173–4, 176, 258
Abdullai, Haoua, 127, 246–8
Abéché, 21, 86, 90, 93, 104–5, 106, 131, 160, 209, 211, 222, 260
  post-war development, 238–51
  rebellion in, 207–8
Abu Dhabi, 230
Aché, Abu, 245
Adjidey, Idriss Saley, 142–3, 144, 145–8, 153–4, 155, 158, 164
Adré, 18, 20, 30, 31, 43, 54, 60, 64, 68, 77, 79–80, 90, 94, 160, 162, 183, 184, 205, 211, 219, 221, 238, 250, 256–9, 263
  borders, 209–10
  geography, 81–2
  lands, 41
  Maba of, 85–6, 87, 95
  quarters of, 81–5
Aéroport Hassan Djamous, 237

'affective threats', 97
African Union: Chadian oil production, 214–19
Africare, 124–5, 127, 128, 130, 140, 147
Ahmat Adam, Mahamat Saleh, 244–5
aid agencies, 41, 42, 65, 84, 91, 92, 95
  anthropologists on approaches, 121–2
  categories, 43–4, 76, 101–2, 115–16, 127, 130, 140
  controlling aid, 110–16
  structure of aid, 103
  See also list-making; UNHCR refugee camps, aid and competition
al-Bashir, Omar, 21, 49, 60, 154–5, 230, 265
Ali, Brahim Mahamat, 1, 14, 60, 82, 147, 168, 202
Alio, Khalil, 234–6
Allazam, Albissaty Saleh, 222
Am Djerress, 239

INDEX

Amkharouba, 82–3
ancien plan, 231–2, 234–5, 240–1
Annan, Kofi, 153, 154
Arab settlements, 50–1, 52, 75, 82–3
Arab–Masalit conflict, 54, 61, 63, 64
Arabs, 30, 44, 59–60, 63, 69–70, 78, 123, 136
  opportunities, 77
  ownership claims, 67
  Sudanese, 61
  supremacy, 137
  women, 76
Ardébé, 128
Ashta, 3, 27, 51, 263
Asoungha, 162–3
Assed, Khassim Mahamat 36, 80, 89
Auer, Claus, 236

banking system, 92
Barka family, 87–9, 94, 95–6
Barry, Andrew, 225, 226–7
Barth, Fredrik, 14, 218–19

Beckett, Greg, 8, 260
Beral, 217
Bergen, Geoffrey, 225
Bierschenk, Thomas, 201–2, 273n3
biometric identity management system (BIMS), 186
'biometric state', 187
biometric verification, 185–96
  registration process, 189–93
biopolitics, 194
Bjarnesen, Jesper, 17, 255, 261
Blumenberg, Hans, 8–9
Boltanski, Luc, 38, 42, 43, 258–9

borderlands attacks, 2–3
Borno, 83
Bowker, Geoffrey, 37, 38, 255
Brahim, 1, 14, 60, 82, 147, 168, 202
al-Burhan, Fattah, 265–6
Burkina Faso refugee camp, 122
Bush, George W., 134

Çağlar, Ayse, 16, 255, 261
Calkins, Sandra, 53, 261
Cameroon, 203–5, 215, 229–30, 232, 234, 243
Cameroonian migrants, 240
'capacity building', 109
cattle and field damaging, 54–5
Caucasian Baku-Tbilisi-Ceyhan (BTC) pipeline project, 225
Central Africa, 231, 232–3, 236
Central African hub, 231
Central African Republic, 205, 215, 275–6n4
Centre de Recherche en Anthropologie et Sciences Humaines (CRASH), 276n2
Chad
  Abéché, post-war development, 238–51
  Chadian oil production, 214–19
  N'Djamena, rebellion in, 202–7
  rebel groups vs. army, 220–4
  UNHCR and, 199–200
  World Bank, 224–7, 230
Chadian army, 69
Chadian bank, 203
Chadian citizenship, 194–5
Chadian city, 273–4n4
Chadian civil war, 117

300

INDEX

Chadian oil project, 226
Chadian rebellion, 203, 218
Chad–Sudan peace agreement, 71–2, 108, 165, 166, 169
Chari river, 205
Chevron, 226
class, 86–7, 89–92
Coll, Steve, 226
Comité National d'Accueil et Enregistrement des Réfugiés (CNAR), 146
Comité National d'Accueil et Enregistrement des Réfugiés et Rapatriés (CNARR), 275–6n4
Commission Nationale d'Accueil et de Réinsertion des Réfugiés et des Rapatriés (CNARR), 185, 186, 195
crisis
   categorising people during, 11–13
   implications of, 42–5
   individual adaptations, 62–3
   observing crisis as an outsider, 69–71
   term, 8, 9
Cuba, 233

Daldoum, 1–2, 28, 36, 50, 67–8, 97, 257
Dar Masalit, 3, 4, 85, 136
Darfur Liberation Army/Movement (DLA/M), 20
Darfur War, 6–7, 18, 20, 29, 63–4, 67, 86, 95, 117, 151, 165, 200, 202, 208, 238, 240, 241, 253, 256, 264, 266
   aid agencies, influx of, 102, 103–4
   Chadian oil production, 214–19
   everyday life, 104
   as a genocide, 141
   impacts, 29–30
   internal competition and social differentiation after crisis, 71–8
   origins of, 49
   'post-war' phase, 165–8
   rebel groups vs. army, 220–4
   war zone survival, 67–9
   World Bank and Chadian state, 224–7
Darfur, 2, 5, 138, 149–50, 160, 220, 263, 265
   ethnicisation of government positions, 49
Das, Veena, 202, 213, 239
de Bruijn, Mirjam, 201
de Waal, Alex, 65, 67, 68, 114, 135, 136–7, 138, 139, 140, 257
Déby, Hinda, 237
Déby Itno, Mahamat Idriss, 266
Déby, Idriss, 20, 21, 29, 58–9, 63, 157, 161, 164, 166, 199, 204, 207, 213, 226, 230, 232, 239, 248, 250, 279n2, 279n9
   Chadian oil production, 214–19
   N'Djamena, rebuilding, 231–8
   rebel groups vs. army, 220–4
   World Bank and Chadian state, 224–7
'define and rule' system, 78
Détachement Intégré de Sécurité (Integrated Security Detachment) (DIS), 244

301

INDEX

difference and belonging, 82–5, 97–8
  See also kinship
'diplomacy', 13
displacement, 16–17, 103, 104
Djamal, 31, 40, 71, 250
Al-Djazouli, Imam, 245
Djermaya, 248
Djiti, 3, 54
Doba, 217
Dor village, 135–6
Douglas, Mary, 258
drought, 34, 42, 65, 84

'ecologies of practice', 159
Ekhlas, 241
El Geneina, 4, 61, 62, 68, 75, 169, 210, 259, 267
El-Tom, Abdullahi, 223
'emplacement', 16–17, 175–7
endogamy, 94
ethnic belonging, 13–16, 19, 118
Europe, 273n1
European Union (EU), 222–3
European Union Force (EUFOR), 141, 162
ExxonMobil, 226

Farchana market, 169
Farchana refugee camp, 95, 96, 140, 142–4, 172, 240, 266
  international agencies and, 148–55
  local alliances, making, 155–9
  making, 145–8
  need for emplacement, 155–7
  negotiating 'realities', 159–64
  population, 142, 176, 177
  process of integration, 169–75
  regulations, 150

resistance in, 151–3
security practices, 160–1
Feldman, Ilana, 260
Ferguson, Brian, 139, 221
Food and Agriculture Organization (FAO), 28, 40, 41, 42, 73, 107
food crisis, 65
France, 272n15, 279n2
French Opération Épervier, 240
French, 82–3
Front de Libération Nationale du Tchad (FROLINAT), 273–4n4
Fur, 30, 49, 95, 137

Gabon, 214
al-Gaddafi, Muammar, 231, 279n2
Gedarif, 136
generosity, 93, 98
Gesellschaft für Technische Zusammenarbeit (GTZ), 146, 272n6
GIZ (Gesellschaft für Internationale Zusammenarbeit), 91, 96, 105, 106, 115, 166, 240
Glasman, Joël, 260
Glick Schiller, Nina, 16, 255, 261
Goran, 59, 207
groupe mobile, 170
groupements, 73–4, 123, 124–31, 132, 133, 145, 148–9, 153, 159, 180
Guilane village, 32, 35, 36, 42, 127, 128, 130, 135, 139, 140
Guyer, Jane I., 231

Haaland, Gunnar, 14
Habré, Hissein, 86, 117, 237

INDEX

Hachaba village, 1, 3, 19, 27, 42, 43, 64, 75, 127, 128–9, 135, 139, 140, 257, 259, 263, 271n13
  hierarchies, 65–6
  list of people in, 31–7
  minor conflicts, 54
  modes of hosting, 139
  refused to go refugee camps, 65, 67
  villagers to Adré, 77
  See also list-making
Hacking, Ian, 255
Hadjer Hadid, 262
Hafadine, Abdoulaye, 3, 59, 64
Hajj, 136, 239
Halle/Saale, 254
Hamdok, Abdalla, 265
Hammar, Amanda, 261
Harir, Sharif, 49
Hawaye, 257
Hemedti, 266
Hille Borno ('Borno Town'), 82, 83
Hille Djidíde, 28, 29, 34, 34, 67, 71, 72, 73–4, 76, 105, 259
  UNHCR on people of, 107, 176
  See also list-making
Hilton Hotel, 235
Hirschauer, Stefan, 12–13, 255
Hoinathy, Remadji, 214, 217–18, 266, 279n13
'host population', 11
hosting strangers, 135–9
  Islamic mode, 136–8
Human Rights Watch report, 279n9
Husserl, Edmund, 8

Ibrahim, Ashta, 257, 259
identity cards, issuing, 185
impunity, 58, 59, 60, 96–7
Indonesia, 225
'integrated refugees', 11–12, 188–9
Interagency Committee (IAC), 113
inter-communal rivalries, 7
'internally displaced people (IDPs)', 11, 101, 105, 106, 107, 108, 199—201
International Committee of the Red Cross (ICRC), 109, 110, 111, 112, 114, 147, 160
Iriba, 240
Islamic hospitality, 136–8
Ismael, Mahamat, 27, 31, 32, 33, 129

Janjaweed, 30, 69, 86, 219
Jánszky, Babett, 221
Jebel Marra foothills, 271n8
J-P, 243
Justice and Equality Movement (JEM), 223

Khartoum, 7, 49, 265, 279n1
Khassim, 36, 80, 89
Khayar, Issa Hassan, 272n3
kinship, 81, 86–92, 95–6
Kreditanstalt für Wiederaufbau (KfW), 105
Kuwait, 230

la vitrine de l'Afrique Centrale, 236
land ownership, 77–8
Li, Tania, 225, 226
Libya, 249–50, 275–6n4, 279n2
lifeworld, defined, 8–9

303

INDEX

Ligné Disang, 59
Ligue Tchadienne des Droits de l'Homme (Chadian League for Human Rights), 232
list-making, 31–7
delivering the list, 104–5
list as 'boundary objects', 37–40
list, translating, 40–2, 105–10
Lund, Christian, 273n3
Lycée Franco-Arabe, 246–7

'Maba', 20, 31, 59, 77, 81, 82–3, 94, 137
kin relations, 88–9, 95–6
Mahamat, Didji, 249
Mahamat, Ibrahim Bakhit (Daldoum), 1–2, 28, 36, 50, 67–8, 97
experience of displacement, 47–8
'Mahariye', 136
Mali, 279n2
Mamdani, Mahmood, 77, 201
Marcel, Henri, 131, 132
marginalisation, 21, 60
marginality, 202, 213–14
'Masalit', 18, 44, 49, 50, 69, 87, 96, 148, 256–7, 263, 271n10
governmental support, lack of, 61
sense of insecurity, 59
stories about Masalit villager, 51–2
term, 3
in UN camps, 30
Massaguet, 203–4
Max Planck Institute for Social Anthropology, 254

McDermott, Richard A., 255
Mecca, 136, 239
Médecins Sans Frontières (MSF), 111, 112, 121, 146, 242
Migdal, Joel, 200–1
MINURCAT (United Nations Mission in the Central African Republic and Chad), 142, 161–3, 166, 167, 171
Mongo, 85, 273–4n4
Moundou, 241
Moussa, 132, 133, 140, 142, 143, 148–55, 156, 159, 171–3, 175, 258
Muslims, 239

Nanyalta, 106, 125, 130, 148, 207
N'Djamena, 22, 110–16, 133, 186, 199, 201, 210–11, 217, 222, 227, 264, 274n6, 277n8
Abéché, post-war development, 238–51
aid agencies in, 104–5
attack, 220, 229–30
biometric registration, 187
Chadian oil production, 214–19
February 2008 attack, 21, 155, 165
rebellion in, 202–7
rebuilding, 231–8
National Office of Rural Development (ONDR), 31, 95, 250
'nationalist' ideology, 137, 139
Niger Delta, 215
Nigeria, 215
Nimeiry, Jaafar, 49
'nomads', 136

INDEX

non-governmental organisations (NGOs), 8, 9, 20, 84, 110, 112, 125, 133, 147, 150, 167
Northern Mali, 279n2
Nour, Mahamat, 207, 222

Office for the Coordination of Humanitarian Affairs (OCHA), 106–7, 108, 109, 111
Oil Revenue Management Law, 255
Olivier de Sardan, Jean-Pierre, 201–2, 273n3
Omdurman, 266, 279n1
'Operation of Verification and Biometric Enrolment of Refugees and Asylum Seekers Living in Chad—2015', 177, 185–6
Ouara, 245
Oyamta, Baldal, 232–4, 241

PADL (Programme d'Appui au Développement Local/ Local Development Support Programme), 73
Parti pour les Libertés et le Développement (Party for Freedom and Development) (PLD), 206–7
peace agreement (2010), 199, 202
Peter, Abdoullai, 241–3, 245
placenames, changing, 83
Police Tchadienne pour la Protection Humanitaire, 244
Poole, Deborah, 202, 213, 239
Port Kribi, 225

'pragmatic engagement', 159–60
pre-war humanitarian aid programme, 118
projet présidentiel (Déby), 232–4
proxy war, 65

Quartier Zombo, 82, 83, 85, 86–9, 94

Radio Dabanga, 174
raids, 4, 5, 52, 229, 231
Rally for Democracy and Freedom (RDL), 108
Rapid Support Forces (RSF), 265–6
Rashaida, 53
rebel recruitment, 29, 166
'refugee citizenship', 138
redefining, 185–96
'refugeehood', 135–6, 138
refugees
  Abéché, 105–10
  categorisations, 199–201
  category, undoing, 175–84
  controlling aid, 110–16
  'integrated refugees', 11–12, 188–9
  making of, 101–2
  'spontaneously settled refugees', 118
  vs. 'villagers', 32
  See also Farchana refugee camp; list-making; UNHCR refugee camps, aid and competition
Revenue Management Law, 225
Reyna, Stephen P., 239
Rottenburg, Richard, 37, 38–9, 224–5, 255, 259, 274n8

305

INDEX

Salah, Rima, 246, 280n11
Saleh, Ibni Oumar Mahamat, 206–7, 239
Sanoussi, Abdalhak, 272n3
Schlee, Günther, 254
Schlichte, Klaus, 200–1
Secours Catholique du Développement (SECADEV), 114, 118–19, 124, 125–7, 129, 130, 133, 134, 140, 145–7
seed distribution, 40, 41–2
'Seeds for Solutions' programme, 179–80
self-reliance, 179
self-sufficiency, 150
September 11 attacks, 134
Sherif, Mahamat, 245
Singapore, 230
Snyder, William, 255
southern Cameroon, 225
'spontaneously settled refugees', 118
Star, Susan Leigh, 255
'state of emergency', 202
Stengers, Isabelle, 255, 258–9
Sudan
    Abéché, post-war development, 238–51
    Chadian oil production, 214–19
    rebel groups vs. army, 220–4
Sudanese Armed Forces (SAF), 265–6
Sudanese rebels, 18, 20, 49, 69, 167, 205
Sureiya, 262
survival, practices of everyday, 53–7
Switzerland, 241

Tama, 221–2
tax collection, 66
Terry Lynn, Karl, 214
Thévenot, Laurent, 276n7
Tiléha, 50, 54, 55, 61, 62, 65, 68, 69–71, 75, 76, 77, 78, 95, 259, 267
Toloum, Monsieur Kodjinar, 243–4, 250
Tombalbaye, Ngarta, 273–4n4
Toroboro, 68–9, 157, 164, 220–1
Touboudja, Ashta, 3, 27, 51
townspeople, 92
Toyota trucks, 160, 209
    N'Djamena, rebellion in, 202–7
tree-planting programme, 151–2
Turkey, 245

Uganda, 121
Ukraine, 263
UN Convention on the Status of Refugees (1951), 101
UN Security Council, 279n2
uncertainty, 53–7
UN-funded Integrated Regional Information Network (IRIN), 222
UNHCR refugee camps, 20, 21, 30, 31, 34, 65, 67, 104, 107, 113, 179
    arrival of former rebels in, 155
    famine in, 35
UNHCR refugee camps, aid and competition, 117–40
    competition between villages, 126–31
    ideologies of hosting strangers, 135–9